SAGE was founded in 1965 by Sara Miller McCune to support the dissemination of usable knowledge by publishing innovative and high-quality research and teaching content. Today, we publish more than 750 journals, including those of more than 300 learned societies, more than 800 new books per year, and a growing range of library products including archives, data, case studies, reports, conference highlights, and video. SAGE remains majority-owned by our founder, and on her passing will become owned by a charitable trust that secures our continued independence.

Los Angeles | London | Washington DC | New Delhi | Singapore

A Moving Faith

Thank you for choosing a SAGE product! If you have any comment, observation or feedback, I would like to personally hear from you. Please write to me at contactceo@sagepub.in

—Vivek Mehra, Managing Director and CEO,
SAGE Publications India Pvt Ltd, New Delhi

Bulk Sales

SAGE India offers special discounts for purchase of books in bulk. We also make available special imprints and excerpts from our books on demand.

For orders and enquiries, write to us at

Marketing Department
SAGE Publications India Pvt Ltd
B1/I-1, Mohan Cooperative Industrial Area
Mathura Road, Post Bag 7
New Delhi 110044, India
E-mail us at marketing@sagepub.in

Get to know more about SAGE, be invited to SAGE events, get on our mailing list. Write today to marketing@sagepub.in

This book is also available as an e-book.

A Moving Faith
Mega Churches Go South

**Edited By
Jonathan D. James**

www.sagepublications.com
Los Angeles • London • New Delhi • Singapore • Washington DC

Copyright © Jonathan D. James, 2015

All rights reserved. No part of this book may be reproduced or utilized in any form or by any means, electronic or mechanical, including photocopying, recording, or by any information storage or retrieval system, without permission in writing from the publisher.

First published in 2015 by

SAGE Publications India Pvt Ltd
B1/I-1 Mohan Cooperative Industrial Area
Mathura Road, New Delhi 110 044, India
www.sagepub.in

SAGE Publications Inc
2455 Teller Road
Thousand Oaks, California 91320, USA

SAGE Publications Ltd
1 Oliver's Yard, 55 City Road
London EC1Y 1SP, United Kingdom

SAGE Publications Asia-Pacific Pte Ltd
3 Church Street
#10-04 Samsung Hub
Singapore 049483

Published by Vivek Mehra for SAGE Publications India Pvt. Ltd, typeset in 10/13 pt Bembo by Diligent Typesetter, Delhi and printed at Saurabh Printers Pvt Ltd, New Delhi.

Library of Congress Cataloging-in-Publication Data Available

ISBN: 978-93-515-0058-2 (HB)

The SAGE Team: N. Unni Nair, Sanghamitra Patowary, Anju Saxena, and Anupama Krishnan

Contents

List of Abbreviations	vii
Foreword by Virginia Garrard-Burnett	ix
Acknowledgments	xv

A Moving Faith: An Introduction   1
Jonathan D. James

SECTION I
Understanding Southern Christianity   19

CHAPTER 1
Southern Christianity: Key Considerations and Characteristics   21
Jesudas M. Athyal

SECTION II
Mega Churches in Africa   41

CHAPTER 2
Doing Greater Things: Mega Church as an African Phenomenon   43
J. Kwabena Asamoah-Gyadu

CHAPTER 3
Mega Churches and Megaphones: Nigerian Church Leaders
and Their Media Ministries   62
Walter C. Ihejirika and Godwin B. Okon

SECTION III
Mega Churches in Asia and the Pacific   83

CHAPTER 4
Mega Churches in South Korea: Their Impact and Prospect
in the Public Sphere   85
Sebastian C.H. Kim

vi   *A Moving Faith*

CHAPTER 5
Marketing the Sacred: The Case of Hillsong Church, Australia   106
Jeaney Yip

CHAPTER 6
Populist Movement to Mega Church: El Shaddai in
Manila, Philippines   127
Katharine L. Wiegele

CHAPTER 7
Nurturing Globalized Faith Seekers: Mega Churches
in Andhra Pradesh, India   143
Y.A. Sudhakar Reddy

SECTION IV
Mega Churches in Latin America   **167**

CHAPTER 8
Concentrations of Faith: Mega Churches in Brazil   169
Dennis A. Smith and Leonildo S. Campos

CHAPTER 9
Evangelical Representations in the Public Sphere:
The Peruvian Case   191
Rolando Pérez

The Southern Factor: Prospects and Challenges   215
Jonathan D. James

About the Editor and Contributors   232
Index   236

List of Abbreviations

ABN	African Broadcasting Network
ACI	Action Chapel International
ABCFM	American Board of Commissioners of Foreign Missions
AICs	African Independent Churches
AMEN	Adoration Ministries Enugu Nigeria
AoG	Assemblies of God
BCs	Backward Classes
CBCP	Catholic Bishops Conference of the Philippines
CHAI	Church History Association of India
CMS	Church Missionary Society
CONEP	National Evangelical Council of Peru
CoP	Church of Pentecost
CSI	Church of South India
EATWOT	Ecumenical Association of Third World Theologians
HMA	Hillsong Music Australia
IBGE	Instituto Brasileiro de Geografia e Estadística
ICGC	International Central Gospel Church
IMC	International Missionary Conference
IPC	Indian Pentecostal Church of God
KICC	Kingsway International Christian Center
LCI	Lighthouse Chapel International
LCWE	Lausanne Committee for World Evangelization
MDCC	Musama Disco Christo Church
MFM	Mountain of Fire and Miracle Ministries
NGO	Nongovernmental Organization
PICC	Philippine International Cultural Center
RCCG	Redeemed Christian Church of God
SC	Scheduled Caste
STBC	Samavesham of Telugu Baptist Churches

US	United States
WEA	World Evangelical Alliance
WMSCG	World Mission Society Church of God
YFGC	Yoido Full Gospel Church

Foreword

The *Time* magazine pronounced, in its October 1965 issue, God is dead. "We must recognize that the death of God is a historical event: God has died in our time, in our history, in our existence." *Time*, a popular news magazine that was widely read and respected by the middle-century, middle-class Americans, went on to explain:

> The words would seem shocking enough coming from someone like Jean-Paul Sartre. As it happens, they were written not by a moody French existentialist but by Thomas J. J. Altizer, an associate professor of religion at Atlanta's Emory University, a Methodist school. Moreover, Altizer is not alone in proclaiming his 'atheism.' Today, [it is] one of the most hotly debated trends in U.S. Protestant seminaries.[1]

Despite *Time*'s cautious use of quotation marks to defang the word *atheism* and setting aside the cheap shot at the *moody French existentialist*, the article, correctly, spoke to an unprecedented rise of atheism in the United States (US). In a nation that had (and continues to) pride itself on its Christian, Protestant core values and culture (a pride that is perhaps based more on a national ethnogenesis myth than in reality), the article provoked a flurry of public declamation and breast beating. Was the US on the road to becoming, of all things, as Godless and secular as Europe?

Since 1965, the US has indeed witnessed a substantial rise in professed atheism, though this has been partly compensated by the rise of the kinds of mega churches described in this book, as well as by large-scale immigration from places, such as Mexico, where immigrants have not only offset, but in fact far surpassed the significant demographic loss of native-born Americans in the Catholic Church. Europe, too, has experienced religious growth through immigration, but here Christianity has been far less the

---

[1] Elson, John T. October 22, 1965, "Theology: The God is Dead Movement," *Time*. Retrieved from http://content.time.com/time/magazine/article/0,9171,941410,00. html#ixzz2vJTFrluC on March 10, 2014.

beneficiary. By 2002, so removed was Europe from its Christian roots—that debates broke out as to whether it was appropriate for the new constitution of the European Union to include a reference to a *Christian heritage* as a source of traditional European identity—this in a region of the world that was once so profoundly Christian that it was known as *Christendom*.[2] Yet *Time's* prognostication of a half-century ago clearly missed its mark: To paraphrase Mark Twain's famous quotation, the rumors of God's death were greatly exaggerated.[3] Europe and the US—the Global North, as the current literature would have it—have continued to secularize pockets of Christianity even in the North, which not only survive, but also thrive, inspired in part by the robust expansion of Christianity—most especially of the Pentecostal and Charismatic variety—in the Global South. In this way, the Global South, the post-colonial worlds of Africa, Asia, Australia, and Latin America have helped make way for a new movement in Northern Christianity—known as the *emerging church*—a *new* take on Christianity that is less liturgical, less denominational, less formal, and less theology-driven, more communitarian, and more postmodern than traditional Protestant forms of the faith.[4] The emerging church movement in the North is a response to and, in some sense, inspired by Southern Christianity, but it is not a direct product of it. Instead, it is indicative of the fact that transcultural flows that characterize modern Christianity, and especially Pentecostalism, have managed to appeal to postmodern (and postcolonial) seekers in a way that traditional Christianity apparently no longer does.

In her 1994 work, *Charismatic Christianity as Global Culture*, Poewe has written of *global Charismatic streams* that link nodes and networks of Pentecostalism across national borders and class, and ethnic boundaries.[5] Poewe and others do not promote the notion that there is a one single shared habitus of Pentecostal belief and lifestyle that carries from one context to

---

[2] Schlesinger, P. and F. Foret. 2006. "Political Roof and Sacred Canopy? Religion and the EU Constitution," *European Journal of Social Theory*, 9(1): 59–81.

[3] This is the popular, but incorrect, form of Twain's actual words to the *New York Journal* of June 2, 1897: "The report of my death was an exaggeration." Retrieved from http://oupacademic.tumblr.com/post/48310773463/misquotation-reports-of-my-death-have-been-greatly#sthash.PYP2BMGc.dpuf on March 1, 2014.

[4] Tickle, P. 2008. *The Great Emergence: How Christianity is Changing and Why.* Grand Rapids, MI: Baker Books.

[5] Poewe, K. 1994. "Introduction." In Karla Poewe (ed), *Charismatic Christianity as a Global Culture* (p. 5). Columbia, South Carolina: University of South Carolina Press.

another, but rather they promote the notion that the common ideas, persons, and religious identities do transcend borders, and affect and alter the epistemologies of Pentecostal believers across time and place. She argues, for example, that Pentecostal migrants might maintain transnational links between *home* and *host* countries where continuous flows of cultural goods move back and forth, illustrating the construction of new ways of being Pentecostal, including hybrid forms.[6] By way of example, Korean televangelism itself—initially modeled after US television ministries—today heavily influence the performance of Pentecostal worship in many parts of the world.

As we will see, in the pages that follow, the emergence of the mega church (typically, a congregation of 2,000 members or more, often much more) is the example par excellence of a Pentecostal trope that crosses all national, ethnic, and cultural boundaries. As these chapters demonstrate, size matters in modern global Pentecostal and Evangelical Christianity. Nearly worldwide, church size, along with the prosperity gospel and delivery of the *abundant life* as expressed through good health, deliverance from evil, and an unapologetic embrace of God's supernatural power are the hallmarks of a dramatically expanding faith.

The idea of the mega church has its origins in the 20th century US, where Evangelists, such as Kenneth Copeland, developed new terms, such as the *word-faith* movement to explicate a material and here-and-now–based theology that appealed to marginalized and aspirational people. Over time, this translated into a reification of church size: within contemporary global Pentecostalism, and to a lesser extent, within Catholic Charismatic Renewal, the sheer size of a church is thought to be a strong indicator of its spiritual legitimacy and authority. (This is one reason, perhaps, why so much of the literature on Christianity in the Global South is dense with church-growth statistics and demographic information.) The rush-to-growth emphasis accelerated during the 1990s, when pastors were enthusiastic early adapters of new technologies, such as the Internet, which they quickly recognized as an unparalleled tool to expand the presence of their ministries and to reach a much broader audience than ever before. Even in very poor countries, the presence of Internet cafes and inexpensive cell phones has allowed for digital ministries to thrive and prosper.

[6] Wilkinson, M. 2013. "Global Pentecostal Studies: Cultural Globalization and Pentecostal Responses to the World." Retrieved from http://globalpentecostal.blogspot.com/2013/04/cultural-globalization-and-pentecostal.html on April 3, 2013.

Today, North American pastors, such as Joel Osteen and Rick Warren, are internationally known, their influential books translated into multiple languages, and their social media presence vibrant. But their churches are tiny compared to the massive church empires run by Nigeria's Enoch Adejare Adeboye, Brazil's Edir Macedo, or South Korea's David (Paul) Yonggi Cho. Osteen's Lakewood Church in Houston, Texas, a former sports arena, seats 16,800, while Warren's Saddleback Church in Lake Forest, California, claims an average church attendance of 20,000.[7] No one would question that Osteen and Warren enjoy successful international ministries, but their congregational membership numbers are pale when compared to even mid-sized African or Korean churches; and in the calculus of church-growth metrics, these things matter. More importantly, at least to our purposes, the reification of church size is indicative of the way in which a single trope can become universalized and normative within a common Pentecostal global culture.

On the other hand, each of the chapters of this book illustrates the flip side of Poewe's thesis, which is that global Charismatic religion is also profoundly local. It is *glocal* in the way that transforms religious ideas and habitus, and its theological plasticity allows for considerable innovation and cultural adaptation from one place to another. While some of these adaptations remain close to home—Charismatics in the Philippines or Brazil, for example, have none of the concerns about the caste system that vexes Indian Christians, while Australian members of the Hillsong Ministry care nothing about the witchcraft and ancestor vengeance that preoccupies Nigerian Pentecostals—yet pertinent local religious innovations can, and do, easily enter the Charismatic mainstream, traveling from the center to the periphery (wherever these may be) and back again. These ongoing transnational flows are made all the more simple, both by technology and by the relatively easy movement of people from one part of the world to another.

In this book, we see for the first time, in a single coherent volume, not only that global Christianity in the mega church is on the rise, but in a concrete way, we are able to observe in detail what this looks like, across a wide variety of locations, cultures, and habitus. Christianity in the

---

[7] For more on Osteen, see Sinitiere, P.L. Forthcoming. *Salvation with a Smile: Joel Osteen, Lakewood Church, and American Evangelicalism*. New York University Press.

Global South is, without a doubt, dynamic and vibrant. It also faces serious challenges, especially from itself, for example, as when a prominent mega church pastor's extreme wealth might seem to distance him both from his followers and from the faith's own founder. It is possible that the plasticity and flows of global Charismatic culture may help these challenges to either self-correct, or, by contrast, to replicate and become more pathological across time and space. But whichever the case is, the giant mega churches of the Global South are, without doubt, home to modern Christianity's boldest expression.

Virginia Garrard-Burnett
Professor of History and Religious Studies,
Associate Chair, Department of History,
University of Texas, Austin, TX, USA

Acknowledgments

This book represents a two-year project in terms of research, writing, and production. I am reminded of a saying: "A book in your head helps no one ... it takes a writer inspiration as well as perspiration to bring an idea into fruition." It would be equally true to say that writing a book is by no means a solitary achievement. Therefore, I am deeply grateful to a host of institutions and individuals for their significant involvement in bringing out this volume.

This project builds on the pioneering efforts of formidable scholars, such as Andrew Walls, Philip Jenkins, and Lamin Sanneh, and so I am indeed humbled to be, in a sense, walking in the shadow of giants.

I am honored by Professor Virginia-Garrard Burnett, University of Texas in Austin, USA, an acclaimed author on Christianity in Latin America for her willingness to pen the foreword which forms a rather compelling prologue to the book.

I am most appreciative of the Faculty of Education and Arts at Edith Cowan University for encouraging me to pursue this project, and also making available to me the services of Dr John Hall, who provided excellent editorial support. My appreciation is also extended to Avrille Wasserman for her invaluable help in proofreading and putting the whole manuscript together.

I thank Ashgate, the publishing company, for their kind permission to reproduce a chapter which I adapted from their book *Mediating Faiths* (eds Michael Bailey and Guy Redden, 2010) in Chapter 6 of my book.

I say a big *thank you* to all the contributors for their insightful and rigorous research, as well as the timely submission of their respective chapters. I really owe an intellectual debt to each one of them.

To the hard working team at SAGE Publications, which includes N. Unni Nair, I salute you for your professionalism, consistency, and, above all, your belief in my project from day one itself.

Last and by no means, least, I thank my family: my wife Elizabeth, children—Ben and Mel—and my siblings and their families for helping me in more ways than they can ever imagine.

Whilst every effort has been made to give proper attribution to the numerous sources quoted in the book, if we have omitted anyone, the publishers and I would be more than happy to make the necessary amendments.

A Moving Faith: An Introduction
Jonathan D. James

The epicenter of Christianity is shifting. Sixty percent of today's two billion Christians are from the Global South (Africa, Asia, and Latin America)—a figure that will rise to 75 percent of three billion Christians by 2050 (Reynalds, 2012).[1]

North America and Europe lost their position as the nexus of world Christianity in the late 1980s. Now, the church in the Southern Hemisphere (Africa, Asia, and Latin America) has been positioned to take that place. Missiologists (scholars who study Christian missions) use the terms *North* and the *Northern Hemisphere* to mean the countries that represented the heartland of Christianity for the last 500 years (the *West*, USA, and Europe) in contrast to the *South* and the *Southern Hemisphere*.

One hundred years ago, the average Christian was a Western male in his mid 40s. Today, the average Christian could be an African female in her 20s (ibid.). If Christianity is flourishing in the South, it would make sense to learn more about its growth there. Fortunately, a few studies have addressed this phenomenon (Jenkins, 2002, 2006; Sanneh, 2008; Walls, 1996), and a brief review of two primary studies follows.

Andrew Walls' Contribution

Walls was one of the pioneering scholars to challenge the view that Christianity is a European religion, pointing out that during the first millennium itself Christianity had key representatives in Africa, Middle East, and India (Walls, 1996). He is well known for his startling theory that Christianity expansion, unlike the spread of Islam, is not linear but serial. It is based on a series of movements, involving both advancement and recession. This continual shifting explains the current recession of Christianity in the

European heartlands and the corresponding expansion of Christianity to new centers, which were previously considered to be in the margins:

> The Christian story is serial; its center moves from place to place. No one church or place or culture owns it. At different times, different peoples ... have become its heartlands ... Christian history reveals the faith often withering in its heartlands, in its centers of seeming strength and importance, to establish itself...beyond its margins. It has a vulnerability, a certain fragility at its heart—the vulnerability of the cross, the fragility of the earthen vessel. (Walls, 2005: 66–67)

Furthermore, Walls contends that Christianity, unlike Islam, is based on an act of translation (referring to the incarnation; the act of Christ becoming man). Christ's incarnation is about cultural specificity, and the expansion of Christianity is the diffusion of the gospel across cultures. This, according to Walls, is what Christianity is in essence:

> At the heart of Jewish faith, as at the heart of Islamic faith, is the Prophetic Word—God speaks to humanity. At the heart of the Christian faith is the Incarnate Word—God becomes human. The divine Word was expressed under the conditions of a particular human society; the divine Word was, as it were, translated. And since the divine Word is for all humanity, he is translated again in terms of every culture where he finds acceptance among its people. (Walls, 1996: 47)

Conversion is understood by Walls not in the sense of cultures adopting something new to the old ways (that is proselytization), but in the sense of a fresh appropriation or *translation* into the particular context. Taking the New Testament account of the Jerusalem Council, in Acts 15, as a foundational passage of the early church's cross-cultural activity, Walls concludes that Peter and James, who "though circumcised, Torah-keeping Jews themselves ... recognized that Gentile believers in the Messiah could enter Israel without becoming Jews" (Walls, 1997: 147). Walls sees Christian conversion as a profound and enriching reality:

> ... the application of the mind of Christ to these points of reference will mean that the master's word is constantly penetrating new realms of human reality. In consequence, the Christian expression in that 'nation' will take on a distinctive shape, have a distinctive set of priorities and concerns; because the word of Christ has to be applied to its distinctive. The word

... is accordingly for ever meeting new situations, going into conditions that Christians have never experienced before. (Walls, 1996: 47)

Philip Jenkins' Contribution

Jenkins, a historian, studies the social impact of the growth and spread of Christianity as a world religion. He agrees with Walls that Christianity's center of gravity is shifting to the South, making mention of the explosive growth of the faith, particularly in Africa and Latin America, calling this "one of the transforming moments in the history of religion worldwide" (Jenkins, 2002: 1–2). Jenkins continues: "Amazing as it may appear to a blasé West, Christianity exercises an overwhelming global appeal, which shows not the slightest sign of waning" (ibid., 39). Jenkins identifies the Pentecostal brand of Christianity as the most successful social movement of the past century, which is responsible for much of the current rapid spread of Christianity (ibid.).

Jenkins asserts that while Westerners see missionary Christianity with prejudiced eyes as *a kind of cultural leprosy*, Southerners are espousing Christianity for many remarkable reasons, the most common one being the belief system: "[They] believe the message offered and found this the best means of explaining the world around them" (ibid., 44). Jenkins is aware that the spread of Christianity is in the context of socio-political struggles and postulates that "issues of faith will increasingly shape politics, domestic and international" (ibid., 185). In between the explanation of Christianity's spread, Jenkins also alludes to Christianity's contestation with other world religions:

> Whether Muslim or Christian, religious zeal can easily turn into fanaticism. Such struggles might well provoke civil wars, which could in turn become international conflicts ... A worst case scenario would include a wave of religious conflicts reminiscent of the Middle Ages, a new age of Christian crusades and Muslim Jihads. (ibid., 13)

Even then, Jenkins takes into consideration the whole narrative of this global faith and concludes on a rather balanced and positive note: "Christianity is never as weak as it appears, nor as strong as it appears.

And whether we look backward or forward in history, we can see that time and again Christianity demonstrates a breathtaking ability to transform weakness into strength" (ibid., 220).

Mega Churches in the South

One phenomenon about the Southern churches that has not been sufficiently studied is the rapid rise of *mega churches* in Africa, Asia, and Latin America. Size-based definitions of mega churches vary in most parts of the world; a mega church is a church with a congregation of 2,000 people or more.[2] Thumma and Travis (2007: xix–xxi) argue that "the key distinction in mega churches ... is attendance ... the two thousand average attendance is primarily a baseline indicator of the relative size, character, and complexity of the church." However, this American perspective does not fit in the South, as we will see in Chapter 4, especially in South Korea where a mega church consists of 10,000 people or more. It is a fact that Charismatic Christianity (a brand of Christianity that emphasizes the gift of tongues, miracles, prosperity, and spiritual experiences) celebrates the physicality of built-up environments and places of worship (James, Unpublished).

Thumma and Travis' study (2007) looks mainly at the Protestant mega churches, while this study attempts to take a more inclusive approach by including a few Catholic groups as well (see Chapters 6 and 8).

The concept of mega churches may have originated in the West, but today there are many more mega churches in the Southern Hemisphere than in the North. Nine out of ten of the world's largest Christian churches are located in the continents of Africa, Asia, and Latin America. The largest church in the world is in Seoul, South Korea, and it boasts of a record weekly attendance of 700,000 people compared to the USA's largest mega church (Joel Osteen's *Lakewood Church*) with 47,000 attendees (Anderson, 2004). Africa's mega church, *Deeper Life Ministry*, in Lagos, Nigeria, has a weekly attendance of 75,000 people, whereas India's mega church, *New Life*, attracts 70,000 attendees in Mumbai (Bird, n.d.).

Are mega churches in the Southern Hemisphere simply imitating the Western mega churches? Or are they *rebranding* the global Charismatic faith in ways that suit their local situation—incorporating local issues, animism, superstition, hybridities, and the like? This book takes the reader into the major cities of the South to observe firsthand work of the gospel by the mega churches. It shows the reader the unique qualities of the mega church in the Southern Hemisphere.

Mega churches in the Philippines seem to be in a continuum: On the *left* is what is generally considered to be the cultic groups, not really sanctioned by mainline Christianity; on the right are the Evangelical, conservative ministries, and then there are groups in the middle (M. Castillo, personal interview, Singapore, 2013). The group that clearly fits the label of *left* is the *Iglesia Ni Christo*, a Seventh-Day Adventist-cum-Catholic-cum-Methodist group which works on a standardized *fixed* sermon that originates from their headquarters every Sunday. In the middle of the spectrum is the Catholic Charismatic *El Shaddai* group (see Chapter 6), and on the right is the Evangelical, conservative group. The Evangelical group is represented by the *Jesus Miracle Crusade* led by Quiboloy, who calls himself *the anointed one* and even *the Son of God* (ibid.). He has developed the headquarters in Davao, Mindanao (he calls Davao City *the new Jerusalem*), where he is building a huge theme park patterned after the Garden of Eden. He has an extensive TV program, a state-of-the-art Bible school, and amasses international support for his programs. In the course of his ministry, Quiboloy has also established strong political links. He conducts rallies and open air meetings catering thousands, which is what led him to his present-day fame.

In reality, it is difficult to distinguish whether these mega churches are on the right, left, or center of the theological spectrum because they all share some strong, common elements. These common elements make up the major research standpoints for this volume.

Research Standpoints

There are nine major research standpoints:

1. *The global–local continuum*: The global Charismatic movement, with its emphasis on the *second blessing* of being filled with the Spirit, signs, wonders, deliverance, and speaking in tongues, has its roots in the Azusa Street Pentecostal Revival of 1906 (James, 2010). This global faith when amalgamated with the Southern emphasis of spirit worship and animism, especially in the African context, creates a

new and more intense spirituality of power and deliverance. The local worldview in many African countries is that there is a strong link between the spiritual and the material worlds. Those who can skillfully mediate the material world and the spiritual world are given a revered status as spiritual leaders. Charismatic leaders of mega churches are given that status because of their gifts of prophecy, deliverance from evil spirits, answered prayers, and the obvious blessings of wealth they have received. Therefore, Charismatic theology "... has found a fertile soil in the African religious imagination partly because like primal religiosity, Pentecostalism is a religion that advocates immediate experiences of the supernatural and an interventionist theology" (Asamoah-Gyadu, 2009a: 3).

The mega churches in the South, while being to some extent replicas of Western prototypes, marvelously integrate local variations in language, dialect, aesthetics, culture, and social outreach. For example, Yoido Full Gospel Church (YFGC) in Seoul has successfully broadened its church membership from the working-class poor to include middle-class elements of the population. This is a clear example of the church's impact on the wider community.

In interesting ways, the Christianity practiced in Africa, Asia, and Latin America is more conservative and traditional than that in the North, guided by a strong belief in the power of the supernatural to directly shape their lives. Whereas Americans think of the ideal church as the one free from wasteful hierarchy, superstition, and dogma, Southerners look with expectation to a church filled with revival crusades, "spiritual power ... and the ability to exorcise the demonic forces that cause sickness and poverty" (Jenkins, 2006).

2. *The political and spiritual economy of Charismatic (neo-Pentecostal) entities[3]:* The doctrines of prosperity, wealth, and healing, seen as objectifying the body and materialism, are part and parcel of this framework that link Charismatic entities worldwide. The project of the worldwide mega church is indeed a material one—the merchandizing of Charismatic goods, be they products, resources, or messages of spiritual support, encouragement, and motivation for people. Furthermore, many networks and alliances link the Southern and Northern churches. Success in local church ministries seems to make local church leaders susceptible to imitation,

commercialization, and strategic linkages with global ministries in the North (James, 2012b). There is interconnectedness with the larger fraternity of global Charismatic and neo-Pentecostal organizations. At the annual Hillsong Conferences in Sydney, Australia, which attract more than 25,000 delegates, the lineup of mega church pastors, worship leaders, and workshop speakers shows pastors from the South, such as Joseph Prince of Singapore. An announcement in the Hillsong website (blog page) expresses the sheer excitement and sense of oneness within the Charismatic Church from the South:

> Ps Brian Houston was giving the closing speech for Hillsong Conference 2011 and he said, 'I just got off the phone earlier this afternoon with a very dear friend of mine and he's confirmed that he will be coming for Hillsong Conference 2012.' Everyone in the crowd was just silent waiting for what he would share next. 'He isn't from down under... he isn't from the US.' Then the crowd started to chant, 'Joseph Prince ... Joseph Prince ... Joseph Prince ...' which was finally confirmed by Ps Brian to be a yes~![14]

3. *The apparent paradox related to the sacred, and the profane consumerism and spirituality:* The growing consumption of religious products and experiences in mega churches begs the question: Have the boundaries between consumption (self-indulgence) and spirituality been changed? How do postmodern Christians in these churches explain the sacred and the profane? While the messages may have an aura of righteousness, the commercialization of the ministries emits an aroma of seduction.

Ms Ho Yeow Sun, the controversial wife of Pastor Kong Hee of City Harvest Church in Singapore, with 23,000 members, is pursuing a pop music career in the USA, which involves her appearance in *racy* video clips. She lived for a period of time in a Los Angeles property that costs US$20,000 a month (Zengkun, 2014).[5]

Mega church preachers, such as Duncan Williams of Africa boldly proclaim that Jesus wore *designer robes,* since the Bible says that the solders at the cross gambled for Christ's robes at his crucifixion (Asamoah-Gyadu, 2009b).

And in this example from Latin America, faith itself is packaged and sold in exchange for money:

> The great innovation of the Neo-Pentecostal media preachers has been to simplify the message even further, eliminating doctrine and reducing the message to a commercial transaction of symbolic goods. They have deepened and more effectively individualized the emotive content of religious television. 'Do you want hope? Do you long for forgiveness and liberation? Do you need healing, wealth, power? Demonstrate your faith by entrusting your offering to me, the intermediary with Mystery, the channel of Transcendence. In exchange, I grant your desire in God's name! Furthermore I give you the symbol of the sacred: a rose, a vial of holy water, a few drops of healing oil. Use the sacred substance .... resolve your problems. (Smith & Campos, 2005: 61)

4. *The marketing and branding of the faith:* Dr Jeaney Yip, of the University of Sydney, contends that mega churches are basically *faith brands:* [T]hey exhibit continuous growth albeit the decline in other traditional churches and adopt a model that appears to reconcile theology, business and marketplace ideologies successfully" (see Chapter 5). Furthermore, she adds that mega churches "do not resist but reify and reproduce ideologies related to the market and business which, in turn, transform [their] own [identities]."[6]

The Economist reports that mega churches in Africa have borrowed the techniques of the prosperity Gospel from American Evangelists and are "re-exporting them in exaggerated form," adding that African churches "manifest bull market versions of competitive 'market religion'" (*The Economist*, 2012).

At YFGC in Seoul, the senior pastor has family business interests ranging from private universities to newspapers. Members of his church are routinely asked to pray at church services for higher sales and good profits for his business ventures. Many of the mega churches own multiple businesses that are named *ministries* and are led by *celebrity-type* leaders, who brand themselves as the ultimate *product* of Christianity.

5. *The mediatization of the faith:* These churches warmly embrace the latest in technology, state-of-the-art sound and projection systems,

television, radio, and social media for their services and other media productions. Mega churches have turned to social networks to spread their message and increase their audience share. Buzzplant, a Christian-based digital advertising agency, surveyed churches in the USA and found that more than 67 percent of churches use social media blogs and update them at least once or twice a week.[7] This media-savvy orientation is seen in the Southern churches as well. The church services of Rev Sam Chelladurai (senior pastor of one of the fast growing Indian churches) of Chennai, besides being broadcast on radio and television are also offered as live webcasts on the Internet and are available to download on iPhone, iPad, and Android. There is also a live chat facility on their website.[8]

The *anointing* of the preacher flows even through technology and onto the TV screen as evidenced in Pastor Duncan-Williams' TV program in Africa:

> On one occasion when he preached at the Potter's House, Duncan-Williams directed the members and by extension viewers in Ghana, to place their hands on wherever they were ailing on the body. He subsequently, through prayer, went on to 'bind' sicknesses and by the power of the word, rebuked infirmities to depart .... (Asamoah-Gyadu, 2005: 17)

6. *A niche for postmodern faith seekers:* Whereas mainline churches are often critical of mega churches, some of their leaders secretly admire the abilities of these new churches to connect with today's generation (James, 2012). Mega churches in the South attract scores of young people to the main services which are orchestrated like rock concerts.

What is the appeal of mega churches in the South? Is it the fact that they deliberately avoid anything that make their meeting place look like a church, portraying their churches as pew-less, cross-less convention centers? Is it generation X's familiarity with huge crowds at the services similar to what is seen in shopping malls, commercial spaces, movie theaters, and rock concerts? Based on a model of worship known as *seeker sensitivity*, mega churches have reformatted their weekly services, making worship more *relevant* and attractive to the world by using marketing ploys and high-tech entertainment gimmicks. Pastor Lawrence Khong, the senior pastor of Faith Community Baptist Church, a Baptist-cum-Charismatic mega church in Singapore, discovered the effectiveness of magic shows in his worship services. He later joined Project Smile (Sharing Magic in Love Everywhere), started in 2002, "and picked up more than just the secrets behind illusionists' tricks.... He rediscovered his confidence and the love of performing for an audience."[9]

Strauss (n.d.) asserts that the worship style in mega churches worldwide is based on television:

> ... its format [is] from media, MTV, from audibility to visibility ... Now in some mega churches there is a one hundred member choir, a full orchestra and several soloists, who seek to express today's media and concert stars. Many mega churches have services for the 'seeker' perhaps an Olympic sized swimming pool and adjoining saunas and a full schedule of athletic and social services for all age groups. Church gurus have cloned postmodern preachers to respond to our 'consumer culture' in which people are going to make choices. This phenomenon [turns the church into]...a 'theological cafeteria' and 'Christian shoppers' mall. (para 6)

Professor James Wellman found that mega churches are *powerful purveyors of emotional religious experience*. Wellman's research team has found that in addition to incorporating state-of-the-art video technology into sermons, "these churches have mastered the art of creating a welcoming, non-intimidating ethos and aesthetic." (cited in Hamilton, 2012).

7. *An anointed leadership with a loose accountability structure:* In mega churches, typically, the senior pastor (the chief executive officer) is the ultimate authority in the church's organizational structure, which is independent of any external system of accountability. Not surprisingly, in a few of these churches there have been some serious moral and/or ethical failures on the part of the senior pastor. Recently, the high profile leader of City Harvest Church in Singapore, Pastor Kong Hee, was investigated by the government for fraudulent business dealings when he allegedly comingled church donations and business funds (*The Straits Times*, 2012). When in 2012, Senior Pastor Rev Chris Okotie of the Household of God Church in

Nigeria announced to his congregation that his marriage with his wife Stephanie had ended due to irreconcilable differences, most of the church members were devastated.[10]

As a consequence of these leadership failures, there is the phenomenon of many disillusioned and hurting church members "who transfer their allegiance from one church to another (like swinging voters in a general election) in a hopeful effort to find a safe church home free from spiritual abuse."[11]

8. *A new gender sensitivity that recognizes and empowers women:* With the exception of South Korea, where Confucianistic principles of male domination are practiced in church government, Charismatic Christianity has played a vital role in changing the gender dynamics of the churches in the South Hemisphere. Jenkins (2002: 75), in demonstrating the effects of the movement in Latin America, reports that "the emphasis on domestic values has had a transformative and often positive effect on gender relations." In the African context, Oduyoye (1995: 5) notes that "women are religion's chief clients." Even though the African church has generally maintained a male dominated outlook and a form of gerontocracy (rule by male elders),[12] the spiritual gift of prophecy is recognized and encouraged among women in churches. Shenk sees a distinct role in the doctrine of the Holy Spirit and women empowerment in Africa:

> The sense of immediacy of the Holy Spirit ... has fostered an ethos in which women are free to acknowledge and exercise their gifts, including leadership roles in the churches. Pentecostal/Charismatic churches have long recognized the leadership of women. Indeed numerous prophetesses have founded churches. Now a shift is under way as women in these churches are being encouraged, in the freedom of the Spirit to forge their own style of ministry rather than fitting into the conventional patterns of ministry of the past. (2001: 102)

9. *A sociopolitical voice to transform the nation:* Eduardo Villanueva, known as Bro Eddie Villanueva, founder and leader of the Jesus is Lord Church in Philippines, was one of three mega church leaders who stood as a presidential candidate in the 2010 Philippines general election. In the same vein, Pastor Chris Okotie of the Household of

Love Church in Lagos, Nigeria, announced his intention to run for presidency linking his faith with his political ambitions. "... Okotie hinges his faith on his chances of winning a future presidential race on the divine: the whole concept of the presidential system comes from the bible, because God is our law-giver ..." (Okulaja, 2010, cited in Ihejirika, 2012: 186).

The Economist reports of a government official by the name of Bishop Margaret Wanjiru, who runs Jesus is Alive ministries in Nairobi, Kenya. The website of this ministry shows photographs of Margaret shaking hands with the president, the prime minister, and other Kenyan government officials. The church draws close to 100,000 worshippers to meetings (with nine services every week), but numbers rise considerably when a visiting preacher comes along (*The Economist*, 2012).

Freston argues that Christians in many nations of the South consider political involvement as part and parcel of the mandate of the church. He concludes that Brazil is a key nation to watch in setting the scene for the rest of the continent, and even Africa:

> Brazil as the major Third World democracy with a significant evangelical presence, and the second largest evangelical community in the world, could be a guide to what will happen if conditions are favorable [for evangelical political involvement] in some Latin American and African countries. (2001: 320)

Drawing on these nine standpoints, the authors in this book acquaint the readers with the culture and ethos of Southern Christianity—the Christianity of the future. Even though the book looks primarily at institutional Christianity (and not grassroots Christianity or the ministries arising out of small to medium churches) in the South, nevertheless there are several useful lessons to be learned from this book.

Whereas the stereotypes of flamboyance and hucksterism are clearly evident, this book offers a nuanced analysis by including the outreach and socioeconomic successes of these churches, which are located in nations where suffering, poverty, and hopelessness is the order of the day. We reveal how the ordinary members in these new Christian movements are involved in various endeavors that empower and encourage communities all around them. Professor James Wellman and his associates, in their groundbreaking study on mega churches in the USA, conclude that "the mega church message is more positive about being good or different people." Comparing modern mega churches to the fire and brimstone preachers of the old, Wellman and his associates say: "The pastors are not generating horror and terror and fear of the afterlife, but really positive sentiments" (cited in Hamilton, 2012). The same can be said of churches in the South.

The material in this book has been researched by a distinguished group of scholars who used case studies, thick description, and comparative analysis of mega churches in different regions in the Southern Hemisphere. The team includes historians, sociologists, theologians, marketing and communication scholars from Africa, Asia, Latin America, USA, UK, and Australia. The studies take a critical look at the forces at work in the realm of contemporary global Christianity: mega churches in the South, marketing techniques, Charismatic Christianity, and technology.

Chapter Summaries

In Chapter 1, Jesudas Athyal points out the cultural, theological, and political contexts of Southern Christianity, and paints a broad portrait of this new Christianity. This seminal chapter attempts to give the reader an overview of the norm-setting dimensions of the new Christianity so as to assist engagement with the studies to follow—representative mega churches from various parts of the South.

Chapters 2 and 3 look at the mega church phenomenon in Africa, where clearly the greatest growth in Christianity has taken place. Asamoah-Gyadu discusses the amazing rise and significance of the African and African-led mega churches in Africa as well as Europe. Using an example of the Kingsway International Christian Center, a Pentecostal Church led by a Nigerian pastor in London, Asamoah-Gyadu's study is a prime example of *missions in reverse*—how the South is reinvigorating and evangelizing the churches in Europe and the West through means of immigration and visionary church planting practices. Ihejirika and Okon situate their study of mega churches in Nigeria in the highly contested arena of Islam and Christianity, and point out that the rhetoric and activism of church leaders are increasing as the airwaves are being captured for the faith. What will be the religious fate of Nigeria? Will this nation continue as a nation open to diverse religions, or will these new Christian voices be eventually silenced?

In the chapters on Asia and the Pacific that follow, Kim (Chapter 4) explores the growth and impact of mega churches in South Korea (the home of the world's largest church), in the context of three vital issues: The Nevius principle,[13] the concept of *Jaebeol* (family-run corporations, such as Samsung), and the Confucian model of leadership. Kim argues that the much talked about churches in South Korea have compromised their public and prophetic roles because of their indiscriminate espousal of certain Korean norms and traditions. Yip in Chapter 5[14] examines the hugely popular Hillsong Church in Australia, well known for its creation of a new worship genre of song and praise now used in contemporary churches throughout the world, including churches with traditional and pietistic backgrounds. Yip portrays Hillsong as a religious institution that has rebranded itself in the secular marketplace, and in the process has *de-religionized* mainline Christianity in its practice, theology, and the perspective of the worshippers who are now considered as consumers. Wiegele in Chapter 6 demonstrates, using thick description, the sheer sense of community and belonging amongst the followers of Velarde, the founder of El Shaddai, and how this Catholic-cum-Charismatic populist movement eventually became a mega church in the Philippines with a US$20 billion worship structure within metropolitan Manila. Chapter 7, a study of mega churches in India, takes the folk culture approach in understanding the appropriation of the Christian faith in India. Reddy explains the ways in which, even in Hindu India, mega churches are providing a space for the urban, educated Indians by creating *communal shelters* and *imagined communities* in light of rampant contemporary fears concerning issues, such as job security, identity, the caste system, and the like.

The chapters on Latin America (Brazil and Peru) investigate the growth of Charismatic (Protestant) Christianity in a Catholic stronghold. Smith and Campos (Chapter 8) argue that Charismatic Christianity is not exclusive to the traditional Protestant denomination as mega churches, parishes (Catholic Church), and temples are flourishing in Brazil. They describe the example of how Father Marcelo Rossi, a singing priest, runs a Catholic mega church which can receive 100,000 people for mass. Rolando Perez in Chapter 9 reveals how Evangelical Christian leaders, largely from mega churches, are creating new spaces in Peru's public sphere in the course of evangelization and sociopolitical activism. Conversion in Peru is redefined to include the spiritual renewal of sociopolitical agencies and systems.

Taken as a whole, the book captures the dynamic shift of Christianity to the South and provides a composite portrait of institutional Christianity—a movement that promises prosperity, healing, empowerment, and gender equality by invoking neo-Pentecostal and Charismatic resources. It clearly demonstrates that the South as a region offers a location from which to question and revisits our assumptions about religion and religious practices.

Notes

1. *Global South* is a term coined by the United Nations, which is now used in mission as well as in political and economic nomenclature. For our purpose, the Global South is a missiological term which refers to Africa, Asia, and Latin America. What is rather remarkable is that the missionary *receiving countries* have a greater critical mass of Christians than the *sending countries*. For instance, in 1900, there were reportedly 8 million Christians in Africa, and today there are close to 500 million Christians. In China, when the missionaries left in 1949, there were approximately 2 million Christians; today the estimates are between 60 and 100 million. See http://www.worldchristiandatabase.org/wcd/. Retrieved on July 20, 2012.
2. Recently, another term has been introduced to keep pace with this growing phenomenon: *Giga churches*, churches with 10,000 attendees or more. See http://churchedge.blogspot.com.au/2007/10/giga-churches.html. Retrieved on June 18, 2012.
3. For useful definitions on Pentecostalism, neo-Pentecostalism, and the Charismatic movement, see Hunt (2002), James (2010), and McGaw (1980).
4. See http://closed1357246.wordpress.com/2011/07/19/hillsong-conference-2012-announcement/. Retrieved on September 4, 2012.
5. For an excellent treatment of the City Harvest Church in Singapore, see Tong (2008).
6. See Singapore Management University website. Retrieved from http://www2.socsc.smu.edu.sg/emailer/2012/ssh27072012e.htm on October 29, 2012.
7. See Mashable Social Media website. Retrieved from http://mashable.com/2012/07/31/churches-social-media/ on November 29, 2012.
8. See AFT website. Retrieved from http://www.revsam.org/?q=thechurch on November 24, 2012.
9. See http://www.lawrenceandpriscilla.com/latestnews13.html. Retrieved on November 20, 2012.
10. See http://www.omg.com.ng/2012/06/pasto-chris-okotie-end-marriage-with-stephanie/. Retrieved on November 25, 2012.
11. See http://www.cultwatch.com/AuthoritarianLeadership.html. Retrieved on November 26, 2012.

12. See Soothill (2007). She draws attention to the *First Lady Syndrome*, which refers to the role of the pastor's wife and to a female version of the *Pentecostal Big Man*. Her interpretation is different from existing scholarship, especially from Martin's (2001) understanding of the egalitarian nature of Charismatic Churches with regard to gender.
13. The Nevius principle is named after the American Presbyterian Missionary Strategist John Nevius, who worked in China in the 19th century and famously advocated a model of missions consisting of three principles: self-supporting, self-governing, and self-propagating.
14. An Australian mega church is intentionally included in this volume which needs clarification. Australia is located geographically in the Southern Hemisphere, although it is considered *Western*, just like the Northern nations, such as the USA and Canada. I felt that it was important to include the Hillsong Church in our studies, as this church has had a far reaching influence in a cross-section of churches in the Asia-Pacific region as well as in the rest of the world primarily through its redefinition of both the style and substance of contemporary Christian worship and praise. Hillsong's music is widely used in churches of all denominations, many without an awareness of Hillsong's theological practices, including the selective editing of Scripture to ensure marketability. The *consumer is king* ideologue of the marketplace, which Hillsong adopts, often omits God out of the equation.

Bibliography

Anderson, Allan. 2004. *An Introduction to Pentecostalism: Global Charismatic Christianity*. Cambridge: Cambridge University Press.
Asamoah-Gyadu, J.K. 2005. "Anointing Through the Screen: Neo-Pentecostalism and Televised Christianity in Ghana," *Studies in World Christianity*, 11(1): 9–28.
———. 2009a. "The Promise is for You and Your Children: Pentecostal Spirituality, Mission and Discipleship in Africa," paper presented at West Africa Consultation of Edinburgh, March 23–25.
———. 2009b. "Did Jesus Wear Designer Robes?" *Christianity Today Global Conversation*. Retrieved from http://www.christianitytoday.com/globalconversation/november2009/ on January 22, 2013.
Bird, W. (n.d.). "Global Mega Churches: World's Largest Churches." Retrieved from http://leadnet.org/world/ on August 21, 2012.
Freston, P. 2001. *Evangelicals and Politics in Asia, Africa and Latin America*. Cambridge: Cambridge University Press.
Hamilton, K. 2012. "Attending a Megachurch is Kinda like Doing Drugs, UW Study Finds." Retrieved from http://blogs.seattleweekly.com/dailyweekly/2012/08/attending_a_megachurch_drugs_uw.php on August 21, 2014.
Hunt, S.J. 2002. "Deprivation and Western Pentecostalism Revisited: Neo Pentecostalism," *PentecoStudies*, 1(2): 4–29.
Ihejirika, W.C. 2012. "From Televisuality to Social Action: Nigerian Televangelists and Their Socio-Political Agenda." In P.N. Thomas and J. Lee (eds), *Global and Local Televangelism* (pp. 173–199). Basingstoke: Palgrave MacMillan.
James, J.D. 2010. *McDonaldisation, Masala McGospel and Om Economics: Televangelism in Contemporary India*. New Delhi: SAGE Publications.

James, J.D. Unpublished. "The Objectification of the Body in Charismatic Teachings."
———. 2012. "The Global in the Local: The Ambivalence and Ambition of Christian Televangelism in India." In P.N. Thomas and J. Lee (eds), *Global and Local Televangelism* (pp. 108–125). Basingstoke: Palgrave MacMillan.
Jenkins, P. 2002. *The Next Christendom: The Rise of Global Christianity*. New York: Oxford University Press.
———. 2006. *The New Faces of Christianity: Believing the Bible in the Global South*. New York: Oxford University Press.
Martin, D. 2001. *Pentecostalism: The World Their Parish*. Malden: Blackwell Publishing Ltd.
McGaw, D.B. 1980. "Meaning and Belonging in a Charismatic Congregation: An Investigation into sources of Neo-Pentecostal Success," *Review of Religious Research*, 21(3): 284–301.
Oduyoye, M.A. 1995. *Hearing and Knowing: Theological Reflections on Christianity in Africa*. Maryknoll: Orbis Books.
Reynalds, J. 2012. "As Christianity's Center Shifts to Global South, Leaders Converge in Chicago to Pioneer Next Generation of Innovative Global Ministry Partnerships." Retrieved from http://www.firstfruit.org/news-resources/guiding_trends/global-trends/prominence-of-the-global-south-church on November 7, 2012.
Sanneh, L. 2008. *Disciples of All Nations: Pillars of World Christianity*. New York: Oxford University Press.
Shenk, W.R. 2001. "Recasting Theology of Mission: Impulses from the Non-Western World," *International Bulletin of Missionary Research*, 25(3): 98–107.
Smith, D.A. & Campos, L.S. 2005. "Christianity and Television in Guatemala and Brazil: The Pentecostal Experience," *Studies in World Christianity*, 11(1): 49–64.
Soothill, J. 2007. *Gender, Social Change and Spiritual Power: Charismatic Christianity in Ghana*. Leiden: Brill.
Strauss, J.D. (n.d.). "Worship Wars and a Post Modern Culture." Retrieved from www.worldvieweyes.org/resources/Strauss/WorshipWars6.doc on November 25, 2012.
The Economist. 2012. "Slain by the Spirit: The Rise of Christian Fundamentalism in the Horn of Africa." Retrieved from http://www.economist.com/node/16488830?story_id=16488830 on November 24, 2012. *The Economist*, July 2012.
Zengkun, Feng. (2014). Kong didn't want the crossover project to be openly funded. *The Straits Times*. Retrieved from http://www.straitstimes.com/the-big-story/chc-funds-case/story/kong-didnt-want-the-crossover-project-be-openly-funded-church-all on August 21, 2014.
Thumma, S. and D. Travis. 2007. *Beyond Megachurch Myths: What We Can Learn from America's largest Churches*. San Francisco, CA: John Wiley & Sons, Inc.
Tong, Joy Kooi-chin. 2008. "McDonaldization and the Mega-Church: A Case Study of City Harvest Church in Singapore." In P. Kitiarsa (ed.), *Religious Commodifications in Asia: Marketing Gods,* (pp. 186–204). London and New York: Routledge.
Walls, A.F. 1996. *The Missionary Movement in Christian History: Studies in the Transmission of Faith*. New York: Orbis Books.
———. 1997. "Old Athens and New Jerusalem: Some Signposts for Christian Scholarship in the Early History of Mission Studies," *International Bulletin of Missionary Research*, 21(4): 147.
———. 2005. *The Cross-Cultural Process in Christian History: Studies in the Transmission and Appropriation of Faith*. New York: Orbis Books.

SECTION I
Understanding Southern Christianity

1

Southern Christianity: Key Considerations and Characteristics

Jesudas M. Athyal

In the light of demographic evidence that during the last century, the centers of rapid Christian growth have shifted from the global North to the Southern Hemisphere, which Roberts (2011: para 3) asserts rather provocatively: "Christianity is fast becoming a non-Western religion." Commenting on the election of Cardinal Jorge Bergoglio of Argentina as the new pope (in March 2013), Donadio, contends that the election "sent a strong message of change: that the future of the church lies in the global south" (2013: para 1). There is no indication that Donadio was referring to *church* as non-Western. Yet the demographics seem clear enough. According to Crossing (2011: 1), "a century ago 66 percent of the world's Christians lived in Europe, but today it accounts for only 26 percent of the world's Christian population."[1] And when addressing a group of world church leaders at the Global Christian Forum held at Manado, Indonesia, Robert asserted, "Christianity has undergone one of the greatest demographic and cultural shifts in its 2000 year history."[2] *The Atlas of Global Christianity* (Johnson & Ross, 2010) focused on the shifting center of gravity of Christianity, aided by the enormous amount of data on religious demography that has been collected and analyzed over 25 years, including the *World Christian Encyclopaedia* (Barrett, 1982 and 2001). The Atlas corrected "the false impression that Christianity is a Western religion" and affirmed, "Southern Christians can rediscover the theological, ecclesiastical and missiological trajectory of the first Christian millennium, when Southern Christians were in the majority and the centre of gravity was in Western Asia" (Johnson & Ross, 2010: 51).

Notwithstanding such compelling statistics, I believe that claims about the Southward shift of Christianity calls for a closer scrutiny. In this chapter, I intend to address three questions:

1. What are the contours of the alleged shift? Are they merely demographical, or reflected also in content and culture?

2. In ecclesiology, are the Southern churches breaking out of the institutional–traditional framework of the West/North and evolving into forms that reflect local influence?
3. Is there a Southern perspective on *what is happening* in the South, or do we, once again, have to depend on Western interpretation of these changes?

In addressing these questions, mindful that the issues are complex and global, I strive for an interdisciplinary approach, drawing on theologians, historians, and social analysts from both the North and the South. I begin with an overview of the Christianization of the South within the historical context of mission and colonialism. While the Missionary Movement played a role in the spreading of the gospel, the post-colonial context is characterized by a self-confidence of the indigenous churches that reject the missionary model. Subsequently, the need to take seriously the complexities of the Asian–African–Latin American contexts and to locate Christian mission within a subaltern perspective is addressed. In such an approach, the marginalized people will not be the objects, but the subjects of the mission. The first section raises questions about some of the assumptions with regard to the Southward shift of Christianity and argues that political, cultural, and even demographic factors have not been sufficiently addressed while reaching conclusions. It is noted here that the growth or decline in the Christian population of a particular country is largely a function of growth or decline in the overall population of that country. Pentecostalism, which has experienced considerable growth in the recent decades, especially in the Global South, is subsequently considered. While the growth or potential of Pentecostalism cannot be denied, the inability of scholars to clearly define the term *Pentecostal* or to carefully scrutinize the methodology of Pentecostalism is an area that calls for further study. Considered next are the issues of gender and sexuality, perhaps the most explosive topics in global church in recent times. While the churches in the South are often portrayed to be conservative and traditional on matters of gender and sexuality, and also unable and unwilling to shake off their patriarchal mindset, the current demographic shift in Christianity needs also to be understood as a movement, in many cases, led by women. Subsequently, the *diaspora factor* in Southern Christianity is discussed. Even as the traditional churches in Europe and North America are on the decline, immigrant

Christians from the South that populate these places are rapidly emerging as *mainline Christianity* in the North. In conclusion, Southern Christianity is also viewed as a post-denominational movement in which Christians strive to overcome the denominational divide that characterized much of Christian mission in the past. A post-denominational approach also helps the Southern Christians to develop a faith-based response to the existential struggles unique to their contexts, such as poverty and oppression.

Mission, Colonialism, and Christianization of the South

It is interesting to note that in the first and early second millennium of Christianity, the church's center was actually in the Middle East, Asia, and Africa (ibid.).[3] However, the movement of Christianization to more Southern regions occurred much later, after centuries of Christianization in the Northern countries; this *new wave* in the South occurred with the spread of colonization, especially in the 18th and 19th centuries. A major criticism of the association between colonialism and Christianity was the way in which missionaries assumed that Western culture was integral to the gospel they preached, and indeed many missionaries colluded with Western colonial powers to gain dominion over the local people. This is eloquently stated by historian Dharmaraj (1993: xvi): "[G]un and gospel were carried on the same ship." And according to Bosch, colonialism was often seen as "the colonization of non-Christian peoples by Christian nations" (1991: 227). He went on to say:

> From the point of view of the colonial government the missionaries were indeed ideal allies. They lived among the local people, knew their languages, and understood their customs. Who was better equipped than these missionaries to persuade unwilling 'natives' to submit to the *pax Britannica* or the *pax Teutonica?* Whether they liked it or not, the missionaries became pioneers of Western imperialistic expansion. (Bosch, 1991: 303–304)

Whereas worldwide acknowledgment that Southern churches have *come of age* is a recent phenomenon, the emergence of Southern Christianity has long been recognized by the modern ecumenical movement. At the third

International Missionary Conference (IMC) held in Tambaram (India) in 1938, *younger churches* situated in pluralistic contexts were given due recognition. In his presentation on the topic of "The Christian Message in the Non-Christian World" at the IMC, Hendrick Kraemer asserted that the divine revelation in Christ transcended Western Christianity and that this transcendence made Asian and African incarnations of Christianity not only legitimate, but also imperative. As Kraemer put it, "The point that needs now to be made is that in principle and for reasons of history, new incarnations and adaptations of Christianity in the concrete Asian and African settings are natural and legitimate" (cited in Thomas, 1988: 394).

Reflecting on the emergent Southern Christianity in relation to the missionary movement, Thomas reports that: "... the new search by Asian–African churches for their selfhood freed from the paternalism and domination of missions should enable them to relate themselves to the emerging national selfhood of their peoples within the universality of the worldwide church" (ibid., 393).

The mood for self-reliance in Asian churches was so strong at Tambaram that the general secretary of the National Christian Council of India hinted that it was perhaps time for the missionaries to *go home* and leave the task to local churches (Ariarajah, 1994: 19). In tune with the national awakening and independence movements in most of the colonies, there was a strong plea there for the unhindered development of indigenous churches. Later, Emerito Nacpil of the Philippines also called on the mission societies to leave the churches in Asia alone so that they could discover themselves and devote their ministry to the people and cultures of Asia (cited in Ariarajah, 1994: 19).

As indicated in the previous paragraph, a key characteristic of the new self-confidence of the emerging churches in the South, therefore, was the rejection of the missionary pattern. Referring to a later period, Jenkins claims:

> By 1970, African churches in particular were calling for a moratorium on Western missions because they stunted the growth of local initiatives. The equation seemed clear: missions were an arm of colonialism, and once the colonial governments were withdrawn, so also should their religious manifestations. (2011: 54–55)

Even while acknowledging the role of *individual missionaries* who tried to work out the meaning of the gospel in collaboration with a specific culture, it can be asserted that the missionary churches generally felt that the missionary enterprise, as a whole, undermined the local cultures of the non-Western world.

A Subaltern Perspective

Even though there may be undisputed evidence of the nexus between colonial powers and missionary movements, I believe a more nuanced reading of the history of Christianity would reveal more of the complexities of the Asian–African–Latin American situations. For example, despite obvious collusion between the two parties, the relationship of missionaries with colonial powers was often far from cordial. The interest of the colonial powers was primarily mercantile, and, thus, it clashed with the concerns of the missionaries. As noted by Bosch (1991: 303), "… Dutch, British and Danish trading companies, at least in the early stages, usually refused to allow any missionaries in the territories under their jurisdiction since they saw them as a threat to their commercial interests."

Sanneh (1989), in his comprehensive study of Christianity in the South—especially Africa—questions the widely prevalent view that the missionary movement was a little more than *imperialism at prayer*. The main focus of Sanneh's monumental work was the recognition that the missionary movement played a key role in the liberation of the oppressed and the marginalized masses, and in the anticolonial independence movements in the South. The translation of the biblical and nonreligious literature and the consequent vernacular renewal were key factors in this process. Sanneh, thus, clearly distinguishes between missionary work and colonial interests:

> Missionary translation was instrumental in the emergence of indigenous resistance to colonialism. Local Christians acquired from the vernacular translations confidence in the indigenous cause. While the colonial system represented a worldwide economic and military order, mission represented vindication for the vernacular. Local Christians apprehended the significance of world events, and as such the purposes of God, through the familiar medium of mother tongues, with subject peoples able to respond to colonial events in the light of vernacular understanding. (1989: 123)

It follows that the commercial interests of the colonial powers in promoting Western languages clearly clashed with the missionaries' translation, which made the mother tongues of the indigenous people the centerpiece of cultural and social renaissance. Therefore, masses of indigenous people were somewhat emancipated, and in some cases empowered through their acquisition of literacy. With reference to Christian converts in Nigeria, Jenkins quotes Chinua Achebe who noted: "None of the converts was a man whose word was heeded in the assembly of the people. None of them was a man of title. They were mostly the kind of people that were called *efulefu*, worthless, empty, men ..." (Jenkins, 2011: 55). In India too, while the upper castes rejected the missionaries, the Dalits (untouchables) wholeheartedly embraced them (Devasahayam, 1992: 37). The historiography of the Church History Association of India (CHAI) gives particular attention to social and contextual factors in its ongoing multivolume project, *History of Christianity in India* (Grafe, 1990; Mundadan, 1983; and Thekkedath, 1982). Thus, the awakening of the marginalized masses to a new identity and self-dignity equipped them to struggle against oppressive structures, both within their socioreligious structures and outside.

The preceding text implies that the history of the missionary era needs to accommodate the perspective of the common people, including the oppressed and the marginalized, and not just the elite and the educated. Such a historiography has enormous relevance in today's context of neocolonialism aligned with globalization and universalization of Western culture. When all is said and done, the fact remains that the end of the colonial era marked the beginning of a period of intense growth for Christianity in the South, suggesting that colonialism was, at best, only one of the factors that aided the growth of Christianity.

Questioning the Narrative of Southern Shift

While multiple studies in the recent decades have claimed an increase in the Christian population in the global South—and a decline for the churches in the North[4]—scholars caution us against any sweeping judgments on the shifting demography of Christianity. Relying too much on descriptive claims of a paradigm shift in Christianity is indeed fraught with grave dangers. For example, how can one be sure about who is a Christian, and who is not? The history of Christianity is littered with *secret believers* and *hidden Christians*—people who, for political reasons or in theocratically oppressive regimes, are unable or unwilling to openly acknowledge their faith; and claim about demographic changes that rely on government-managed census data are especially problematic.

There are also cultural factors, especially in South Asia, where Christian converts often continue their affiliation with their old religions, thus holding dual religious identities. Thomas's (1969) and Samartha's (1974) exhaustive studies on how Hindu leaders and masses responded to the gospel of Christ revealed a long history of people whose lives were spiritually and religiously centered on the crucified Christ, but decided to stay outside the structured church of baptized believers. There were also leaders and scholars who felt strongly that "the new disciple should remain within his community, witnessing from there" (Kumari, 1995: 13) because the Christian church had become a civic community instead of a spiritual fellowship. In a survey conducted by the Gurukul Lutheran Theological College in the 1970s, it came to light that about 10 percent of the population in Chennai accepted Jesus Christ as their personal savior (whereas the government census showed a much smaller number of Christians); many of these *Christians* had chosen to continue with their religious, cultural, and caste communities without any formal conversion to the Christian church. Among them were those who maintained close spiritual fellowships with other Christians, and others "who pursued their devotion to Christ without such support" (Hoefer, 1979: 403). Therefore, in a context where people maintain fluid and multiple religious identities, "counting the Christians" indeed becomes highly problematic (ibid.).

Apart from political and cultural reasons, demography itself should keep us wary of claims about a recent shift in *the center of gravity* of Christianity. On the issue of *recency*, Wuthnow (2009) points out that as early as in the 1940s, the belief in God had declined in Europe, and that by 1970, 49 percent of the global Christian population already lived outside of Europe and the USA. His basic argument is that "growth or decline in the Christian population of a particular country is largely a function of growth or decline in the overall population of that country, and is in turn shaped by local conditions that affect longevity, morbidity rates, and decisions about fertility" (Wuthnow, 2009: 43). Wuthnow's argument that the shifting demography of Christianity is largely in tune with the larger population trends is substantiated by a comprehensive demographic study conducted by the Pew Forum on Religion and Public Life in 2010. According to the study, whereas the number of Christians around the world has nearly quadrupled in the last 100 years (from about 600 million in 1910 to more than two billion in 2010), the world's overall population also has risen rapidly: from an estimated 1.8 billion in 1910 to 6.9 billion in 2010. "As a result, Christians make up about the same portion of the world's population today (32%) as they did a century ago (35%)" (The Pew Forum on Religion and Public Life, 2011). This study, which covered more than 200 countries and represented nearly a third of the estimated global population, concluded that no single continent or region can indisputably claim to be the center of global Christianity.

The anomaly with regard to material and organizational resources is also a factor to be considered when assessing the Southward shift of Christianity. "Finances are still firmly in the global North. Sixty percent of Christians live in the South, but they have only 17 percent of Christian income."[5] Apart from the lingering material clout of the Northern societies on the rest of the world, there are also the missionaries. For example, in 2000, the USA had just 10 percent of the world's Christian population, but at the same time it accounted for "approximately a quarter of the world's foreign missionaries and a quarter of the total amount spent on foreign missions ..." (Wuthnow, 2009: 42). Furthermore, a substantial part of the academic work in Christian mission is still located in the North, or is done in the South with resources from the North. In short, despite a shift in the *location* of the Christian population from the North to the South, there was probably little concomitant shift in the *influence* of the North, a situation not reflected in statistical data. Addressing the question of the growing inequality between Northern and Southern societies, Nicks (2013: 24) argues that the Christian story is a global one and should expand our vision in more equitable ways, "not in terms of seeing every human as a potential consumer in a global market", but seeing "every person as a reflection of God's image endowed with human dignity."

The globalization of Western culture is yet another factor. Jonathan James, in his study of *the changing shape and form of Christian ministry* in the Indian church (2010), points toward the rapid inroads that have been made by televangelism, which might once have been thought of as entirely a creature of the USA or the West. Today, however, James argues, we need to recognize "mediated and commodified spheres of action and cultural practices that make modern religious meanings possible" (ibid., xii).

Beyond counting the number of Christians, we need to consider whether Western culture and values have permeated deep into the South, providing a lingering impact.

In short, we need to broaden our discussion on the global shift in Christianity to include cultural, political, and regional dynamics; demography itself needs to be seen in relation to the larger population trends. Questionable claims made by theologians on the numeric success of Christianity at the global level also point toward the need for interdisciplinary efforts that are likely to lead to more balanced and accurate findings.

The Pentecostalization of the South?

Much research in the recent decades have been devoted to the deep inroads Pentecostalism has made in the global South. Scholars affirm the Southward shift of Christianity as heralding a post-denominational experience that would transcend the traditional churches and usher in independent, indigenous, and Pentecostal forms of Christianity. Considerable literature has also been generated during the last few decades analyzing this phenomenon. For example, David Barrett predicted that Pentecostalism could, by 2025, account for 44 percent of the total number of Christians in the world: "The Pentecostals are the fastest growing movement within Christianity today, with almost 500 million adherents worldwide" (Barrett, 1997: 25). And Cox (1996: 83) referred to Pentecostalism as "the reshaping of religion in the twenty-first century." It is generally accepted that the roots of the modern Pentecostal Movement can be traced to the Christian revivals at the Azusa Street, California, USA, in 1906 (Anderson, 2013a). Furthermore, the roots of the modern Pentecostal Movement can be traced to the Christian revivals in the USA in the first decade of the 20th century; a century later, the movement started spreading rapidly in Asia, Africa, and Latin America. Anderson describes Pentecostalism as "predominantly a Third World phenomenon" (ibid.). A study conducted by the Pew Forum on Religion and Public Life concluded that Pentecostals now represent 12 percent, or about 107 million, of Africa's population and "has become an increasingly prominent feature of Africa's religious and political landscape" (The Pew Forum on Religion and Public Life, 2006).

A more recent study by Anderson (2013b) explored over a century of history across most of the globe, resulting in a description of the spectacular rise of global Pentecostalism and how it has changed the face of Christianity worldwide.

Pentecostalism has, in particular, appealed to the racial and ethnic minorities, and social classes of Asia and Africa who lack political or ideological power. According to Prior (2013), a missionary priest in Indonesia since 1973, Pentecostalism is an urban phenomenon and is likely to be a growing one with the urbanization of the Asian societies. Prior states, "People who have been uprooted from their village and culture," who are "somewhat insecure in the cities as migrants," join the new Charismatic and Pentecostal communities because there they find "warm fellowship" and "have a place" while "Catholic parishes in the cities are large, anonymous ... very ritualistic" (Prior, 2013: para 8).

The inroad of Pentecostalism into the traditional churches in the South has been a matter of considerable academic interest in the recent years. Jenkins acknowledges that Pentecostalism is a global phenomenon in the South, but cites statistical data to suggest that Pentecostalism is far from displacing the traditional churches: "Although African Independents today claim an impressive 100 million members; that represents only one-fifth of all African Christians" (2011: 71). According to Jenkins, traditional churches, such as Catholic and Anglican, continue to play significant roles in African Christianity. Jenkins (2011) contends that this is largely true in Latin America also where even after several decades of Protestant and Pentecostal growth, the Catholic Church continues to be the dominant religious institution. "If 60 or 70 million Latin Americans are Protestant (a fair estimate) then 490 million are not: most are, at least nominally, Catholic" (Jenkins, 2011: 71).

Overall, studies have revealed that the membership of the traditional churches in the South has not decreased substantially. According to a Pew survey in 2011,

> Catholics have made up a remarkably stable share of all people on Earth. In 1910, 'Catholics comprised about half (48%) of all Christians and 17% of the world's total population, according to historical estimates from the World Christian Database. A century later ... Catholics still comprise about half (50%) of Christians worldwide and 16% of the total global population.' (The Pew Forum on Religion and Public Life, 2013)

In short, the portrayal by Western scholars and journalists that the growth of Christianity in the South is essentially an explosion of Pentecostalism is far from reality.

The global Pentecostalism approach has also been closely scrutinized. Robert (2006: 186) questions its *multicultural* nature asserting that: "Putting older indigenous churches under the term *Pentecostal* raises methodological problems." Whereas the haziness of the term *Pentecostalism* has the advantage of portraying the phenomenon as a movement with open boundaries, it also becomes impossible to make any accurate descriptive claims about the number of Pentecostals in any region. But just as traditional churches are closely scrutinized, so there is the need to critically evaluate the positions and impact of the Pentecostals in the South. In his study of Christian fundamentalism and communication in India, Thomas wonders if Pentecostalism is contributing to the fracturing of national identities, and the creation of larger and wider allegiances. He asks pointedly: "Why is it the case that the message of conservative Christianity has greater interdenominational acceptability today?" (2008: 129). Apart from such critical voices, the focus today is also on the liberative and reformative roles the Pentecostals play with regard to the religious and wider social scene. A study by González and González (2007: 310) finds that both Liberation Theology and Pentecostalism "point to the changing role of Latin America within worldwide Christianity as an active protagonist in theology, in evangelism, and in the entire life of the church." There are clearly issues and questions that need to be researched as Pentecostalism emerges as a global Christian Movement, especially in the South.

The Gender Divide and Sexuality

Of all the topics that have caused tensions in global Christianity, gender and sexuality are the foremost. For example, whereas several Protestant Churches in the North have welcomed the increased role of women in leadership positions, in most churches in the South, women continue to play a secondary role to men. The churches in Asia and Africa, largely due to their traditional patriarchal social structures and proximity to people of other faiths, such as Islam, have been less eager to welcome women to leadership positions.

Probably, the most explosive topic in the global church in the recent times is the acceptance of homosexuality within the fold of the church. The initiative of the Episcopal Church in the USA during the last few decades to ordain openly gay people, initially to the priesthood and later as bishops, attracted global attention and threatened to disrupt the 2008 Lambeth Conference and rupture worldwide Anglican fellowship. However, the step taken by the Episcopalians was not an abrupt one; it was the natural consequence of the evolution that happened in the Anglican Church in the USA over half a century. As reported by Carroll: "Led by ministers and laity who had been sobered by the mid-century war, Episcopalians took seriously the great lessons of the civil rights movement, feminism, gay rights, and a new skepticism toward violence" (Carroll, 2008: para 27).

Yet the openness among the Protestant Churches in the North to embrace people of diverse sexual orientations has been angrily denounced by several churches in the rest of the world, particularly in Africa where today Anglicanism is stronger than in any other continent. In a letter addressed to the (then) Canterbury Archbishop Rowan Williams in 2005, Archbishop Peter Akinola of Nigeria and several other bishops of the global South acknowledged the dilemma faced by the Anglican communion, and yet wondered why the leadership was reluctant to confront the churches that accommodate homosexuality—a practice that, they asserted, was "contrary to the overwhelming testimony of the Anglican Communion and the Catholic Church."[6]

The global media has often portrayed churches in the South as conservative and traditional, unable and unwilling to shake off their patriarchal mindset, and allow women positions of power. The South, however, is far from homogenous. And despite enormous social and economic challenges, the Southern societies have, time and again, risen above stereotypical images to provide meaningful leadership. Such leadership was on display in 1951 when Sarah Chakko, a lay Christian of India, became the first woman president of the World Council of Churches. Jenkins (2011) cites the case of Alice Lenshina, who in 1953 formed an independent church in Africa and attracted hundreds of thousands of followers. As a candidate for baptism in the Presbyterian Church of Rhodesia, she had "received visions in which she was taken up to heaven and ordered to destroy witchcraft, which was seen as so pressing a danger in many African societies" (Jenkins, 2011: 65).

There are also clear indications that the recent explosion of Christianity in the South has brought women to the center stage, so that in several Southern societies, women could play significant roles in the churches, especially at the level of local congregations. Scholars, such as Robert (2006: 180), assert that "the current demographic shift in world Christianity should be analyzed as a women's movement, based on the fact that even though men are typically the formal, ordained religious leaders and theologians, women constitute the majority of active participants." Women's role as a catalyst in the conversion of the other members of the family should also be acknowledged.

It is important to note that the current crises in the churches in the North over gender—sexuality issues, such as sexual orientation within Anglican fellowship and sexual abuse by clergy in the Roman Catholic Church, are prompting the churches in the South to ask the question: How far should their issues be our priorities? The churches and communities in the South, on the other hand, are confronted by the existential problems of poverty, economic inequality, and political instability. These are clearly their priorities.

Southern Christianity Goes Global!

In his article titled "The End of Christian America," *Newsweek* (2009), Meacham argued that the historic foundation of America's Christian culture is cracking; Christians now make up a declining percentage of the American population, and this trend would lead to the marginalization of Christianity in the USA. The decline was based on the 2009 American Religious Identification Survey, which found that the number of those in the USA declaring themselves religiously *unaffiliated* had nearly doubled in two decades—from 8 percent in 1990 to 15 percent in 2009. Apparently, Christians are drifting away from organized religion to either new religious movements or a secular humanist worldview, noting that the trend was particularly prevalent in the northeast of the USA, the cradle of the faith in the New World.

In a rejoinder to Meacham's article, Rah (2013: para 2) highlights a significant point when he argues that what is declining in the country is not so much the Christian faith as *Europeanized* Christianity. In fact, Rah claims, "American Christianity may actually be growing, but in unexpected and surprising ways." His thesis is that immigrant Christian groups are rapidly filling the space traditionally occupied by the Europeanized Christians. Coming back to Meacham's point about the decline of Christianity, particularly in the northeast of the USA, Rah noted:

> Let's take for example the Northeastern city of Boston in a region of the country that Mohler believes we have "lost." In 1970, the city of Boston was home to about 200 churches. Thirty years later, there were 412 churches. The net gain in the number of churches was in the growth of the number of churches in the ethnic and immigrant communities. While only a handful of churches in 1970 held services in a language other than English, thirty years later, more than half of those churches held services in a language other than English. (2013: para 2)

A few years earlier, speaking on the *coloring of American Christianity*, Warner also remarked that a large number of the recent immigrants to the USA were Christians from Central and Latin America, Africa, and Asia. Whereas the immigrants from Central and Latin America were predominantly Catholic, the Asian Christian immigrants were mostly Protestant and Evangelical. According to Warner, "This means that the new immigrants represent not the de-Christianization of American society but the de-Europeanization of American Christianity" (2006: 233–255). This phenomenon is not typical of the USA alone, but is true for the most of Europe as well. As the population of the traditional Europeanized Christians has dwindled, they are rapidly being replaced by the immigrant Christians from the South.

In their northward migration, the Christians of the South are often called upon to strike a balance between the social and cultural realities of their new homes and the values they bring with them. The resulting cultural, social, and religious tensions are particularly pronounced as the immigrant groups settle down in their new homes, and the second and subsequent generations are born and brought up in the *diaspora*. Speaking specifically of the South Asian immigrant groups in the North, Judith Brown noted: "Anecdotal evidence suggests that South Asians who do become Christian either as individuals or in family groups face considerable social ostracism by those who remain within their traditions" (Brown, 2006: 95). A typical response to such challenges is for immigrant Christians to create ecclesiastical and cultural havens in an alien context, thereby creating islands of familiarity. As the fledging immigrant groups take root and become part of the local community, however, their religious institutions also undergo radical changes. Mega churches, such as the Korean Lakewood Church in Houston (Texas), and the African-diaspora churches in London and Kiev, can thus be considered as the next phase in the evolution of a migrant religious community. It seems that in and through it all, Christianity in the North is being challenged and transformed irreversibly by the influx of Southern Christians.

As the focal point of global Christianity is turning toward the South and the distinctiveness of Asian–African–Latin American forms of Christianity is increasingly recognized, the migration of faith communities assumes special significance. While segments of the traditionally Anglo-Saxon Northern communities are today shifting culturally to post-Christianity and undergoing varying degrees of secularization, intense and growing religiosity continues to define the identity of the Southern immigrant communities in the North. Like most other new religious groups, these communities are at the cutting edge of the rapid changes in culture, religiosity, and social values. In this sense, traffic across national borders is not merely a geographic reality, but also a social and spiritual one. Theologically, the church is the community of the dispersed—the people of God are scattered over the face of the earth to witness the great deeds of God. As Spindler (2002: 295) so aptly puts it: "The whole church shares Christ's ministry in the world and the effective exercise of this ministry must largely be by church members when they are dispersed in the life of the world."

Conclusion: Toward Relevant Patterns of Christian Witness in the South

It is by now accepted history that the missionary initiative in the Christianization of the South also introduced to the Asian–African contexts the denominational divide—a characteristic of Christianity in the South. While analyzing the history of Asian Christianity, Philip (1999) says that whereas the Western mission boards that brought Christianity to several parts of Asia originated as protest groups in the established churches in Europe, they slowly became denominational and planted German Lutheran, British Anglican, and such churches in the mission fields of Asia. "Thus denominational churches arose in the mission field. In several instances, this slowed down the early cooperation in mission" (Philip, 1999: 13). While Christianity as a whole had a liberative and unifying effect, the spirit of denominationalism, so alien to the ethos of most Southern societies, added a discordant note to Christian witness in pluralist contexts.

As a consequence, there have been several initiatives for the various denominations in a country to come together under a united church. These attempts gathered momentum in the 20th century, but often resulted in uniformity over unity. The challenges today are different. As Robert puts it:

> ... today's urgent need for Christian unity does not look like the 1950s and 1960s when self-satisfied Protestant leaders pushed for organic unity at the expense of diversity of witness. The growth that characterizes world Christianity today means that unity will be taken seriously only where mission is taken seriously.[7]

The link between the renewal of the church and her missionary mandate is indeed crucial: "The unity of the whole, along with the diversity among members" was also the challenge for the Three-Self Patriotic Movement of the Chinese Christians who attempted to set in motion an era of post-denominationalism. While defining the post-denominational era that was ushered in China, the Biblical imagery of the Lord as the head of the church with many members in the body, each with their own roles, was frequently invoked. According to Han, "the unity of the whole, along with the diversity among members ... is characteristic of the 'post-denominational' Chinese church today" (Han, 1998: 68–73).

Today when Christians in the South discuss the Christian mission in their contexts, their own identities as minority religious groups in most Asian–African countries is bound to color their response. What should be the form of the church in societies such as theirs? Ariarajah's question is pertinent: "Why are we in mission? Is it because God is present with our neighbour or because God is absent?" (1999: 129). During the long decades when the churches in Africa and Asia were founded and administered by the mission agencies and churches from the North, dialogue with people of other faiths was viewed with suspicion. The independence for the churches in the South, however, opened up new vistas for better relations with the neighbors of other faiths. After attending a meeting of the Christian Conference of Asia in Hong Kong in 2003, Cox noted:

> I was surprised to find that the central concern of the two hundred delegates was how best to work together with their non-Christian neighbors on issues of women's rights, ecology, and peace. It was also clear to me that they thought arguing over doctrines ... was too 'Western' and a little boring. Their idea of interfaith dialogue was to work with their fellow Asians of whatever religion to advance the Kingdom that Jesus had inspired them, as Christians, to strive for, regardless of what the others called it. (2009: 136–137)

The existential struggles of most people in the South too are bound to play a major role, as Christians there evolve their own patterns of mission. According to Aloysius Pieris S.J. of Sri Lanka, most Asian societies are characterized by religiosity and poverty, and, therefore, "this involves the church in a double-baptism, one 'in the Jordan of Asian religiosity' and the other 'on the cross of Asian poverty'" (Thomas, 1987: 119).

Following the Second Vatican Council and the Uppsala Assembly of the World Council of Churches in the 1960s, it was recognized by the churches that the liberation of the oppressed and the marginalized people of the Global South needed to be a programmatic priority for the worldwide church. These exhortations have become more urgent as the process of globalization and liberalization during the last few decades has pushed great masses in the South further into poverty and inequality. As J. Russell Chandran, who served for a number of years as a president of the Ecumenical Association of Third World Theologians (EATWOT) points out:

> ... true theology is not just a process of formulation of doctrines, but a process of doing, a process of participation in the real presence of Christ with two poles, one the sacramental participation and the other a contemporary re-enactment of the exodus-covenant experience for people suffering under different forms of oppression. (cited in Torres & Fabella, 1976: 171)

According to Philip (1999: 14), it has been the people engaged in mission in the world who have often raised fundamental questions about the nature of the church, its catholicity and unity. It is within this tension between mission to the world and openness to meaningfully transform their structures that Southern Christians today are actively involved seeking patterns of mission relevant for their times.

Notes

1. See http://www.pcusa.org/news/2011/10/17/world-christianity-has-new-address-new-look-and-ma/. Retrieved on April 19, 2013.
2. Ibid.
3. The main focus of this chapter is on the course and character of Southern Christianity in the recent decades. For a discussion on the early history of Christianity in the South, see Irwin and Sunquist (2001); Jenkins (2008); Koschorke et al., (2007); and Moffett (1998).
4. The decline of the mainline churches in the North is a debated theory. Scholars who have examined the rise of these churches to a position of cultural prominence in the North in the first half of the 20th century have argued that the liberal Protestants have used cultural capital and persuasive rhetoric to make a strong case for their own status, but that their influence was ultimately "more a social construct than a demographic reality." See Coffman (2013).
5. See http://www.pcusa.org/news/2011/10/17/world-christianity-has-new-address-new-look-and-ma/. Retrieved on April 19, 2013.
6. See "Global South Primates response to Archbishop Rowan Williams." Retrieved from http://www.globalsouthanglican.org/index.php/article/global_south_primates_response_to_archbishop_rowan_williams on April 8, 2013.
7. See http://www.pcusa.org/news/2011/10/17/world-christianity-has-new-address-new-look-and-ma/. Retrieved on April 19, 2013.

Bibliography

Anderson, Allan. 2013a. "The Origins, Growth and Significance of the Pentecostal Movements in the Third World." Retrieved from http://artsweb.bham.ac.uk/aanderson/Publications/origins.htm on April 3, 2013.

———. 2013b. *To the Ends of the Earth: Pentecostalism and the Transformation of World Christianity*. New York: Oxford University Press.

Ariarajah, S. Wesley. 1994. *Gospel and Culture: An Ongoing Discussion within the Ecumenical Movement*. Geneva: WCC Publications.

———. 1999. *Not Without My Neighbour: Issues in Inter-Faith Relations*. Geneva: WCC Publications.

Barrett, David B. 1982 and 2001. *World Christian Encyclopedia: A Comparative Study of Churches and Religions in the Modern World, AD 1900–2000*. New York: Oxford University Press.

———. 1997. "Annual Statistical Table on Global Mission: 1997," *International Bulletin of Missionary Research*, 21(1): 25.

Bosch, David J. 1991. *Transforming Mission: Paradigm Shifts in Theology of Mission*. Maryknoll, New York: Orbis Books.

Brown, Judith M. 2006. *Global South Asians: Introducing the Modern Diaspora*. Cambridge: Cambridge University Press.

Burrows, William R., Mark R. Gornik, & Janice A.McLean. 2011. *Understanding World Christianity: The Vision and Work of Andrew F. Walls*. Maryknoll, NY: Orbis Books.

Carroll, James. 2008. "A Double-scoped Vision of Religion and Liberalism." *The Boston Globe*, Boston, July 21.
Coffman, E.J. 2013. *The Christian Century and the Rise of the Protestant Mainline*. New York: Oxford University Press.
Cox, Harvey. 1996. *Fire from Heaven: The Rise of Pentecostal Spirituality and the Reshaping of Religion in the Twenty-first Century*. London: Cassell.
———. 2009. *The Future of Faith*. New York: HarperOne.
Devasahayam, V. 1992. *Outside the Camp: Biblical Studies in Dalit Perspective*. Madras: Gurukul.
Dharmaraj, Jacob S. 1993. *Colonialism and Christian Mission: Postcolonial Reflections*. Delhi: ISPCK.
Donadio, Rachel. 2013. "Entrenched Troubles at Vatican Await a New Pope." *New York Times*, New York, March 14.
González, Ondina E & Justo L. González. 2007. *Christianity in Latin America: A History*. Cambridge: Cambridge University Press.
Grafe, H. 1990. *History of Christianity in India*, Vol. IV. Bangalore: CHAI.
Han W. 1998. "Work Together with One Heart to Build Up the Body of Christ." *Chinese Theological Review*. Retrieved from https://www.google.com.au/search?q=Wenzao+Han.+1998.+%E2%80%9CWork+Together+with+One+Heart+to+Build+Up+the+Body+of+Christ%E2%80%9D.+Chinese+Theological+Review.+Vol.+12&ie=utf-8&oe=utf-8&aq=t&rls=org.mozilla:en-GB:official&client=firefox-a on May 7, 2013.
Hoefer, Herbert E. 1979. *Debate on Mission*. Madras: Gurukul Lutheran Theological College and Research Institute.
Irwin, D.T. & S.W. Sunquist. 2001. *History of the World Christian Movement: Earliest Christianity to 1453*. Maryknoll, NY: Orbis Book.
James, Jonathan D. 2010. *McDonaldisation, Masala McGospel and Om Economics: Televangelism in Contemporary India*. New Delhi: SAGE Publications.
Jenkins, Philip. 2007. "Christianity Moves South." In Frans Wijsen & Robert Schreiter (eds), *Global Christianity: Contested Claims* (pp. 15–33). Amsterdam: Rodopi.
———. 2008. *The Lost History of Christianity: The Thousand-Year Golden Age of the Church in the Middle East, Africa, and Asia—and How It Died*. New York: HarperOne.
———. 2011. *The Next Christendom: The Coming of Global Christianity*. Oxford and New York: Oxford University Press.
Johnson, Todd M. & Kenneth R. Ross. 2010. *Atlas of Global Christianity 1910-2010*. Edinburgh: Edinburgh University Press.
Koschorke, K., F. Ludwig, & M. Delgado (eds). 2007. *History of Christianity in Asia, Africa, and Latin America, 1450–1990*. Grand Rapids, MI: Eerdmans.
Kumari, Prasanna. 1995. *Liberating Witness*. Madras: Gurukul.
Meacham, Jon. 2009. "The End of Christian America." *Newsweek*, New York, April 4.
Moffett, S.H. 1998. *A History of Christianity in Asia: Beginnings to 1500*. Maryknoll, NY: Orbis.
Mundadan, A.M. 1983. *A History of Christianity in India*, Vol. I. Bangalore: CHAI.
Nicks, Douglas A. 2013. "Global Inequality." Retrieved from http://www.baylor.edu/christianethics/GlobalWealthArticleHicks.pdf. on April 8, 2013.
Philip, T.V. 1999. *Edinburgh to Salvador (Twentieth Century Ecumenical Missiology): A Historical Study of the Ecumenical Discussions on Mission*. Tiruvalla and Delhi: CSS and ISPCK.
Prior, John Mansford. 2013. "In Asia, the Pentecostals Are on the March." Retrieved from http://persecutedchurch.info/2013/04/17/in-asia-the-pentecostals-are-on-the-march/ on April 17, 2013.
Robert, Dana. 2006. "World Christianity as a Women's Movement," *International Bulletin of Missionary Research*, 30(4): 179–186.

Roberts, Matthew. 2011. "The Rise of Anti-Western Christianity." Retrieved from https://whitelocust.wordpress.com/category/islamic-socialism/page/2/ on April 20, 2013.
Samartha, S.J. 1974. *The Hindu Response to the Unbound Christ.* Madras: CLS.
Sanneh, Lamin. 1989. *Translating the Message: The Missionary Impact on Culture.* Maryknoll, New York: Orbis Books.
Rah, Soong-chan. 2013. "The End of Christianity in America?" Retrieved from http://www.patheos.com/Resources/Additional-Resources/End-of-Christianity-in-America.html on April 15, 2013.
Spindler, Marc. 2002. "Diaspora." In N. Lossky et al. (eds), *Dictionary of the Ecumenical Movement* (pp. 290–298). Geneva: WCC Publications.
The Pew Forum on Religion & Public Life. 2006. "Overview: Pentecostalism in Africa." Retrieved from http://www.pewforum.org/Christian/Evangelical-Protestant-Churches/Overview-Pentecostalism-in-Africa.aspx on April 20, 2013.
———. 2011. "Global Christianity: A Report on the Size and Distribution of the World's Christian Population." Retrieved from http://www.pewforum.org/Christian/Global-Christianity-exec.aspx on July 3, 2014.
———. 2013. "The Global Catholic Population." Retrieved from http://www.pewforum.org/Christian/Catholic/The-Global-Catholic-Population.aspx on April 20, 2013.
Thekkedath, J. 1982. *History of Christianity in India*, Vol. II. Bangalore: CHAI.
Thomas, M.M. 1969. *The Acknowledged Christ of the Indian Renaissance.* London: SCM Press.
———. 1987. *Risking Christ for Christ's Sake: Towards an Ecumenical Theology of Pluralism.* Geneva: WCC.
———. 1988. "An Assessment of Tambaram's Contribution to the Search of the Asian Churches for an Authentic Selfhood." *International Review of Mission.* 78(307): 390–397.
Thomas, P.N. 2008. *Strong Religion, Zealous Media: Christian Fundamentalism and Communication in India.* New Delhi: SAGE Publications.
Torres, Sergio &Virginia Fabella. 1976. *The Emerging Gospel: Theology from the Underside of History.* Maryknoll, New York: Orbis Books.
Warner, R. Stephen. 2006. "The De-Europeanization of American Christianity." In S. Prothero (ed.), *A Nation of Religions: The Politics of Pluralism in Multi religious America* (pp. 233–255). Chapel Hill, NC: University of North Carolina Press.
Wuthnow, Robert. 2009. *Boundless Faith: The Global Outreach of American Churches.* Los Angeles: University of California Press.

SECTION II
Mega Churches in Africa

2

Doing Greater Things: Mega Church as an African Phenomenon

J. Kwabena Asamoah-Gyadu

This chapter examines the mega church phenomenon as part of the African Christian experience. Christianity is now a non-Western religion, and in that sense greater things are happening in the Global South—the former recipient of Western missionary evangelization—with even ripple effects in the North. In other words, the accession of Christianity in the Global South has coincided with the recession of the faith in the northern continents of Europe and parts of North America. Mega churches of African origin and composition now exist in both the continents and the African diaspora in the West. In Nigeria, we have one of the world's largest meeting places for a church, David O. Oyedepo's Living Faith Church Worldwide, popularly known as Winners' Chapel. The Winners' Chapel auditorium in Lagos, the capital city, seats in excess of 50,000 people. In two other cases, also involving Nigerian pastors, one leads the most prominent and predominantly White mega church in Eastern Europe and the other leads a predominantly Black one in Western Europe. There has been what Shaw (2010) describes as a *global awakening* within Christianity since the early decades of the 20th century, and the mega church cultures of the late 20th century stand in continuity with those developments.

I will argue that although there have been large churches within Christianity in Africa in the last century, the description of churches in terms of *mega* is part of a new religious culture associated with contemporary Pentecostalism. On one Saturday in March 2010, a personal journey that was supposed to take a little over four hours from the Lagos Airport to the Nigeria Baptist Theological Seminary, in Ogbomosho ended up taking 12 hours. My plane touched down from Accra at 4:00 pm. I was picked up about two hours later, and arrived in Ogbomosho at 7:00 am on Sunday. The delay was primarily due to traffic buildup on a stretch of the Lagos–Ibadan expressway that houses the two contemporary Pentecostal

Churches, the Redeemed Christian Church of God (RCCG) led by Enoch Adeboye and Oyedepo's Winners' Chapel. Traveling that stretch should not have taken 30 minutes, and the time it took told something about the numbers these churches attracted. One of the two churches held a weekend program, and the human traffic that was generated as members crossed the expressway during a break in proceedings accounted for our over five hour delay on that stretch of road. We will encounter these churches again in this chapter, but suffice it to say here that they both belong to the stream of churches that I designate as contemporary Pentecostal.

New Paradigm Christianity

The African Pentecostal Churches that will concern us in this chapter belong to the same family as North America's *new paradigm churches* succinctly described by Donald E. Miller:

> These new paradigm churches ... are changing the way Christianity looks and is experienced. ... they have jettisoned aspects of organized religion that alienate many teenagers and young adults; and they provide programming that emphasizes well-defined moral values and is not otherwise available in the culture. In short, they offer people hope and meaning that is grounded in a transcendent experience of the sacred. (1997: 1, 3)

New paradigm Pentecostalism belongs to the stream of Christianity that privileges the experiential presence and power of the Holy Spirit in church life. As a religious expression, *mega* has become part of the nomenclature associated with this contemporary, usually urban-based Pentecostal Christianity, which Miller describes here as new paradigm churches. Thus, contemporary Pentecostalism or Charismatic Christianity, as the phenomenon is called in parts of Africa, is now a global culture, and designating churches as *mega* is one of its features (Poewe, 1994). The expression *mega church* is, therefore, fairly new and has a quantitative import to its meaning.

This chapter discusses the rise and significance of African and African-led mega-sized Pentecostal Churches in both Europe and Africa. It is impossible to understand the culture of mega churches without reference to the main features of these new churches which include their youthful, upwardly mobile congregations and the use of modern media. In Africa, as Paul Gifford (2004) argues from the Ghanaian perspective, the Charismatic sector of Christianity has eclipsed the historic mission denominations. Nobody in Ghana is unaware of the shift, Gifford rightly points out, because their prayer centers, all-night prayer vigils, evangelistic crusades, conventions, summits, Bible Schools, new buildings and car bumper stickers, posters and banners now dominate public space. The expression *mega* is not seen only in the size of the churches, but also in those activities carefully crafted to give practical expression to the fact they are on to big and influential things as part of a divine mandate. To that end, and almost without exception, each of the new paradigm churches has the words *international, global,* or *worldwide* included in its name.

The globe is arguably the most important item found in the designs of the logos of these churches. If a particular Charismatic Church is not yet megasized, it remains an aspiration toward which the leadership may be working. A useful indicator of this aspiration may be seen in the way that the eagle—symbolizing height, power, and achievement—has become the preferred symbol of the Holy Spirit in the African new paradigm communities. Additionally, the word *dominion* is an important part of the discourse of Charismatic Christianity because of its connotations of power, control, authority, and conquest. We referred to the shift in the demographic center of gravity of Christianity from the Northern to the Southern continents. My view is that the new Charismatic Churches under study here with their mega-sized churches and aspirations are paradigmatic of the types of the *pneumatic* communities (Sprit-led) leading the charge both locally and in the African *diaspora* worldwide.

Pentecost, Witness, and Growth

The title of the chapter is taken from a section of the pre-crucifixion admonitions of Jesus Christ, as outlined by the Gospel, according to John. The context is the assurance of Jesus that the ministry granted to him by God was going to continue in the work of the disciples. The admonishment of Jesus that those who believed in him will do *greater works* is interpreted in part to mean that they will attract large numbers as examples of successful ministry. The text reads as follows: "I tell you the truth, anyone who has faith in me will do what I have been doing. He will do even greater things than these, because I am going to the Father" (John 14: 12).

These were the words spoken to the disciples of Jesus who were empowered to continue with his ministry among the nations. Thus, an important characteristic of this Christianity is their perception that the leaders stand in continuity with that of the Apostles in terms of territorial expansion and the manifestations of the power of God. The salvation of souls and the growth of believing communities are, thus, important indicators of its success. The post-Pentecost experiences of Philip, who fled to Samaria during the early persecution of Christians in Jerusalem, are paradigmatic of the sort of growth and influence sought within historical Pentecostalism:

> Those who had been scattered preached the word wherever they went. Philip went down to a city in Samaria and proclaimed the Christ there. When the crowds heard Philip and saw the miraculous signs he did, they all paid close attention to what he said. With shrieks, evil spirits came out of many, and many paralytics and cripples were healed. So there was great joy in the city. (Acts 8:4–8)

Pentecostalism came into prominence at the beginning of the 20th century, and right from its origins, growth has been an important part of its self-definition. Early Pentecostals from the Azusa Street (Los Angeles, USA) Revival Movement of 1906 traveled across the world to preach Christ as a king who was returning soon to judge the world. In the process, many souls were won for the Kingdom of God, and large churches were established as a result. Contemporary Pentecostalism has taken the desire for growth and expansion a notch higher by giving it a certain existential interpretation. Thus, although the hope of heaven and eternal life still lurks somewhere in the Pentecostal imagination, there is now much more emphasis on self-improvement, exploration of possibilities, dreaming big, and doing greater works by building large, influential organizations including churches. This comes as part of the prosperity and possibility mindset of postmodern culture, where contemporary Pentecostalism has introduced its dominion theology.

The Mega Church: An African Perspective

In principle, the mega church idea, it must be understood, is not new to Christianity in Africa. Prior to the use of the word *mega* in relation to Christian congregations, there were churches in Africa that were already attracting 2,000 worshippers on Sundays. Thus, the church in Africa has had large-sized congregations since the early 20th century. This was when indigenous Holy Spirit or prophet-healing churches emerged, converting many and drawing into their fold hundreds of disenchanted members of existing historic mission denominations. In Ghana, the Musama Disco Christo Church (MDCC), also known as the Church of the Army of the Cross of Christ, started under the leadership of a local Methodist catechist, William Egyanka Appiah, in 1923.

Under persecution from the mother church, the followers of Catechist Appiah went on to find their own village called Mozano, a *heavenly* expression, meaning *my city*. They resettled there worshipping together as a single Christian community. Although the MDCC still exists and boasts of an impressive following, nobody describes it as a mega church. Historically, the MDCC belongs to the same category of religious innovation in Africa as Nigeria's *Aladura* (people of prayer) Movement and the *Balokole* (the saved ones or the chosen ones) Churches of Uganda. They are *pneumatic* churches (Spirit-filled), alright, but their modes of operation and traditional outlook do not simply belong to the postmodern ecclesial culture associated with contemporary Pentecostalism. The African Independent Churches (AICs), as these early 20th century Christian innovations came to be tagged collectively, became important not simply for their innovative Christian practices of religious enculturation, but also for the huge numbers that joined their fold.

For the purposes of this chapter, a mega-sized congregation would refer to any Christian church able to assemble between 2,000 and 3,000 congregants at a single location on *ordinary* or *normal* worship days. The stress on *ordinary* or *normal* is important. In Ghana, for example, a non-denominational prayer service takes place at the prayer cathedral of the Action Chapel International (ACI) in Accra. Jericho Hour, as it is dubbed, attracts about 4,000 people every Thursday morning from 9:00 a.m. to 12 noon (Asamoah-Gyadu, 2013). However, this prayer service, which has been replicated in other Charismatic Churches in the capital city, is not what makes ACI a mega church. Participants come from different churches, and they are attracted to Jericho Hour simply because of the *prophetic prayers* offered on Thursday mornings. The reference to Jericho Hour is to make the point that, to qualify as a mega church, the numbers attracted must be there on normal or ordinary worship days. This is because in urban Africa, events such as Christmas, Easter, end-of-year watch-night celebrations including weddings and funerals, could swell numbers attending services to mega-size proportions.

A number of Pentecostal/Charismatic Churches today may simply have large numbers at particular times in the year because they tend to be event-driven, which means, some mega churches only attract numbers that are temporal or event related. Many leaders who pastor actual mega-sized congregations, also constantly hold special miracle, prayer, anointing, and prophetic services. They organize non-denominational summits and conventions or monthly Holy Communion services that are advertised extensively. There is much circulation of people during these events, and the meetings can attract tens of thousands because of the special impact they make on people outside the normal worship periods. In other words, these are churches that could attract huge numbers either because there is a special healing or miracle service, or a preacher known for a particular prophetic ministry has been invited. Numbers tend to return to normal levels after such events. In most cases, the fact that the leader behind the event who leads a mega-size church, also, adds to the appeal of events he or she organizes.

This makes it imperative that the expression *mega* be restricted to churches able to attract certain defined levels of patronage when no such special events are in place. In Africa, there are many of these churches. With reference to developments in Uganda, Gifford talks about the new Pentecostals as churches that are "mushrooming in luxuriant fashion" (1998: 156). In Kampala alone (the capital of Uganda), there are churches with names, such as the Kampala Pentecostal Church, Rugbaga Miracle Center, Prayer Palace Christian Center, Victory Christian Center, and Abundant Life. The Kampala Pentecostal Church is housed in a converted cinema hall, and, as Gifford reports, the entire block of about 20 shops has been renovated to make it the most desirable real estate in the area (ibid., 158). In Ghana, the notable ones are: The Lighthouse Chapel International (LCI) led by Bishop Dag Heward-Mills, the International Central Gospel Church led by Pastor Mensa Otabil, Nigerian Enoch Adeboye's RCCG, David O. Oyedepo's Living Faith Church Worldwide (or Winners' Chapel), and Bishop Ezekiel Guti's Zimbabwe Assemblies of God Church, Africa. Each of the churches as listed, just like others located in various African cities, has two things in common. First, they are all new Pentecostal Churches, and, second, they all attract at least 5,000 worshippers to a single service of their multiple services on Sundays.

It must be noted that in many cases, building a mega-size church could also be a matter of choice. For example, there are churches, such as Ghana's Church of Pentecost (CoP), that have made a decision not to congregate large numbers at particular locations. The CoP, which belongs to the older Pentecostal religious tradition, has opted for a community-based church planting approach. Here, no single assembly—as their branches are called—is allowed by policy to go beyond 500 members. In a particular community, the CoP could have three or four assemblies within 300 meters of each other, and each with about 500 members. All this is to say that the whole mega-church idea is driven by a certain understanding of biblical discipleship making and a theological interpretation of what it means to be a community of God. Given the numbers that are usually in church on Sundays in urban Africa, a congregation of 2,000 worshippers may be considered successful, but not extraordinary. Thus, in this chapter and as noted earlier, the minimum number for a mega church is pegged at anything between 2,000 and 3,000, and this must be a number that is in church on *ordinary* Sundays.

Mega Churches in Context

That which grows in terms of numbers is what eventually develops into a mega-size community. Historically, Pentecostal Churches, in particular, actively seek to grow as an important testimony of successful ministries through the harvest of souls. The description of any particular church as *mega* may differ from place to place depending on the numbers attracted in proportion to the total population of Christians within particular geographical contexts. The expression *mega church* is a description for *out-of-proportion* congregations which have crept into Christian usage with the rise of contemporary USA-based conservative Evangelical Christianity. The category of conservative Evangelicalism, which I have in mind here, includes the newer Charismatic and Pentecostal Christian Churches of the last four decades which we have already described.

As a matter of clarification, the features of this new type of Pentecostalism include:

> A charismatic and often well-educated, gifted, articulate and professional leadership; mostly urban-centered mega-size congregations that appeal to

an upwardly mobile youth; worship styles that are exuberant, affective, emotionally-laden, expressive and dynamic; innovative uses of modern media technologies; extensive and evangelistic uses of media for advertising religious programs and mediating religious services and supernatural power; an internationalism that is evident in the names, choice of religious symbolism, the worldwide missionary peregrinations of the leadership, and the establishment of transnational networks including the formation of foreign branches; preaching of a Christian message that directly addresses contemporary concerns of upward mobility; seizing social, political and economic opportunities; and the application of certain social and biblical principles for the realization of success in this life. (Asamoah-Gyadu, 2010: 13)

Pentecostal/Charismatic Christianity is inherently evangelistic because of the relationship between the promise of the Holy Spirit and empowerment for witness. These contemporary, urban-based, and prosperity-preaching Pentecostal Churches have, since the last three decades of the 20th century, taken over from the eschatology- and holiness-preaching older Pentecostals as the representative face of Pentecostalism in many parts of the world. An important characteristic of the new Pentecostals is this passion to build mega-size congregations. On one hand, the growing sizes of these congregations are indications of their popularity but on the other hand, it is also meant to symbolically represent the message of prosperity which many of them preach.

The churches concerned are operating within a historically different context than their forbears, the historic mission denominations, whose ecclesial culture was built on Western missionary paradigms. The new churches are functioning within postcolonial contexts with increased choices in life facilitated by modern media technologies and in which anything that sounds *traditional* and *conservative* seems to be unattractive. In other words, traditional, liturgically conservative, older churches have lost their place to these newer members of the Christian family who are open to more contemporary, postmodern, and non-traditional ways of expressing faith. Miller's description of the North American new paradigm churches is relevant here too:

> The typical new paradigm church meets in a converted warehouse, a rented school auditorium, or a leased space in a shopping mall. These meeting places boast no religious symbols, no stained glass, and no religious statuary. Folding chairs are more common than pews. At the front is a stage, often portable, which is bare except for sound equipment, a simple podium, and sometimes a few plants .... What is surprising is how quickly these churches develop a

broad range of ministries in response to the spiritual as well as personal and recreational needs of converts. (1997: 12, 14–15)

The church building in now referred to as the auditorium, and it is set up to accommodate the demands of modern media culture. Except for special occasions, most preachers preach in ordinary but usually very fashionable and expensive clothes in keeping with the *prosperity gospel* mindset. In the new religious culture, preachers, for example, are not glued to a pulpit. They preach from platforms that facilitate much movement. They also minister in modern outfits and entertain the crowds in keeping with modern religious culture. After all, for many of the young people in contemporary Pentecostal Churches, these are seen as alternatives to secular entertainment centers that they got accustomed to in their former lives. Testimonies abound by many converts on how resources previously dissipated in wild living are now salvaged for constructive purposes, as a result of finding Christ in these conservative Evangelical prosperity-preaching churches.

Mega Churches and Postmodernity

The phenomenon of mega churches as a contemporary religious idea has become part of the experience of Global South Christians, although it emerged in North America. In his book, *Above all Earthly Powers: Christ in a Postmodern World,* Wells places the rise of American mega churches within the context of the culture of postmodernity. The changed American cultural context, he notes, "is producing spiritual seekers" (Wells, 2005: 269). "Spiritual seekers," Wells explains, are those "who seek spirituality without religion" and the communities of faith themselves offer spirituality without theology (ibid.). He notes:

> It is, most often, spirituality of a therapeutic kind, which assumes that the most pressing issues that should be addressed in church are those with which most people are preoccupied: how to sustain relationships, how to handle stress, what to do about recurring financial problems, how to handle conflicts in the workplace, and how to raise children. (ibid.)

Those Christian communities functioning as seeker churches, according to Wells, recognize that in the postmodern context, they function within a *marketplace* of choice even in religion, and what we find in this world "is increasingly a buyer's, not a seller's market" (ibid., 270). It is a common place to find large billboards in urban Africa advertising Pentecostal/Charismatic events, and as with economic markets, it is the availability of choices that necessitate commercial advertising. "Just as there is choice in the mall," Wells continues, "so there is choice in religion" (ibid.).

The shopping *mall* started as part of American capitalism and just as it has become a global phenomenon, so have the churches that function to meet postmodern needs. Mega church is now a description reserved for extraordinarily large congregations, and indeed many have adopted *mall-like* architectural designs with worship auditoriums, basketball courts, and eateries within the same space. In the Global South, the Yoido Full Gospel Church (YFGC) in Seoul, Korea, and several African Pentecostal/Charismatic Churches, some of which are named in this chapter, have become paradigmatic of the mega church tradition. Pentecostal/Charismatic Churches in the rest of the Global South now tend to be inspired by the South Korean example. Their total congregation of 700,000 worshippers spread over multiple Sunday services clearly makes the YFGC the largest in the world (Anderson, 2004: 1–4).

Mega Churches, World Christianity, and Africa

The rise of mega churches within the Global South informs us of three main developments within world Christianity. First, it is illustrative of the coincidence of the recession of Christian presence in the North with the accession of the faith in non-Western contexts: Africa, Asia, and Latin America. I have argued elsewhere that at a time when cathedrals are metamorphosing into Hindu temples and mosques, and not in a few cases even restaurants and brothels, warehouses, and former entertainment spots and cinema houses are being *baptized* and turned into churches in Africa (Asamoah-Gyadu, 2005). Africa has emerged as a major Christian heartland, and that process was made possible partly by the phenomenal growth of Evangelical Christianity of the Pentecostal/Charismatic kind.

Secondly, the rise of mega churches is illustrative of the collapse of denominational loyalties that the historic mission denominations took for granted for close to a century. There are obviously things about contemporary Pentecostal Churches that raise critical theological questions regarding their modus operandi. In spite of this, I am not as dismissive of the spirituality of African mega churches as Wells is of their American versions. He criticizes them as places where people do not come to find those historical truths that have defined the church down the centuries. That may be so in the USA but in Africa, the historically older churches became too denominationally oriented to the point of neglecting the deeper spiritual needs of their younger converts. In many African countries, young people became Methodist, Presbyterian, or Catholic simply because they were educated in institutions owned by these historically older denominations. The slow response to change and the inability to accommodate the needs of younger generations means that today, young people, in particular, are making religious choices different from those handed down to them through formal education or by parents and guardians. Thirdly, as I will argue, the rise of mega churches is linked to the prosperity gospel associated with contemporary Pentecostalism because *size* is an important indicator in this new interpretation of success.

Taking New Territories in Prosperity

In the opening paragraphs, I referred to how a Nigerian pastor led the biggest single church in Western Europe. The Kingsway International Christian Center (KICC), based in London and led by the Nigerian Charismatic pastor, Matthew Ashimolowo, has as its slogan—"taking territories and raising champions."[1] *Territories* in this context can mean several things. It includes attracting numbers into church, and such growth naturally implies the acquisition of larger spaces. Ashimolowo attracts more than 10,000 worshippers every Sunday, mostly Blacks, and in a country in which most cathedrals are virtually empty and losing their sacred value. In terms of the claim to physical territories, consider the following observation made by British Sociologist of Religion Peel, in a foreword to Asonzeh Ukah's study of Enoch A. Adeboye's RCCG:

> The center of all RCCG's activities is the Redemption Camp, a 10 square kilometer site on the Lagos-Ibadan expressway. Since 1983, this has grown to the scale of a small town with all modern facilities, a high school and a university, its own drainage system, electricity and water supplies, banks

and supermarkets, houses built by wealthy members...and at the center of it an auditorium that will seat half a million people. Here takes place every month the famous Holy Ghost Night, at which divine miracles and blessings are outpoured. A place where God reveals his dominion, a place where the *kingdom of heaven* is reproduced on earth ... (2008: xxi,xiii)

It needs to be pointed out that mega-sized growth is not simply a natural feature of this new type of Pentecostalism, but it is something that is aggressively coveted as part of a new understanding of prosperity.

Many African church leaders from the independent Pentecostal/Charismatic Churches, including Bishop Heward-Mills, founder and leader of Ghana's LCI, have attended church growth conferences in Seoul to learn about the principles of building mega-size churches (Anderson, 2013: 236). LCI does not only advertise itself as a mega church, but its television program, which is available in other parts of Africa, is also known as *Mega Word*. The founder has written a book on how to grow a congregation into mega size. We will examine his thoughts as outlined in that material presently. When they started in Africa in the middle of the 1970s, contemporary Pentecostal Churches quickly abandoned the idea of denominationalism associated with historic mission Christianity. Many claimed that the establishment of church branches and assemblies was not biblical, and that a church must grow in a single location. Thus, the mega church idea was introduced into African Christianity by the contemporary Pentecostals, and, as I point out, it is not unrelated to the prosperity gospel which many of the leaders promote.

The larger the size of a pastor's congregation, the more he/she is seen as bearing the fruit of prosperity. Founders, pastors, and leaders of contemporary Pentecostal Churches, therefore, competitively refer to the growing sizes of their congregations as marks of success, indicative of divine approval and favor. There has, therefore, been a consistent attempt on the part of the leadership to grow their main branches to mega-size levels. There is a mindset among contemporary Pentecostals that the absence of numerical growth in church life is seen as a sign of failure of mission. Jimmy Bakker's (of the PTL Club, USA) fall from grace, a casualty of this new mindset, is fairly well known even in African Christian circles, yet African churches still consider size as an index of spiritual progress (Bakker & Ken, 1996). In Africa, even in denominational churches, several branch churches remain mega-sized. The terrain has, therefore, become competitive. The numbers attracted usually depend on several factors, including the gifts and graces of the leadership, the dynamism of worship, and the extent to which members feel that their spiritual and physical needs are met through the prayerful interventions of the leadership.

Jenkins has said that when the declining strength of Christianity in Europe is measured, it must be kept in mind that the statistics would have been much leaner without immigrants and their children (2007: 116). Many of these immigrants in Europe and North America have been Africans who have established large churches in the former heartlands of the Christian faith. A useful example of an African immigrant mega-sized church in the North is the KICC, established in 1995, which as noted earlier, was established by Nigerian Pastor Matthew Ashimolowo. Its total worshipping community of almost 10,000 worshippers per Sunday makes the KICC the single largest Christian church in Western Europe. In Kyiv, the capital of Ukraine, another Nigerian, Sunday Adelaja, leads a 25,000 member church, the Church of the Embassy of the Blessed Kingdom of God for all Nations. The main church in Kyiv has more than 10,000 worshippers per Sunday with satellite churches across the country. Whereas KICC has attracted Africans and Black British Christians, *God Embassy* is virtually Eastern European in membership. What this means is that in both Western Europe and Africa, Africans lead some of the largest congregations in world Christianity.

In the African continent itself, the numbers attending mega-size churches can be staggering. One of the first contemporary Pentecostal Churches to undertake a mega-size project is the Church of God Mission International, established by Archbishop Benson Idahosa (1938–1998) in Benin City, Nigeria. The church was founded in 1972 as virtually the first contemporary Pentecostal Church in sub-Saharan Africa with the aim to build a mega-size congregation. Benson Idahosa was a strong advocate of the prosperity gospel, and he made a conscious attempt to be a living embodiment of his message whether in his choice of clothing, titles, or in the religious empire he created through his international networks and worldwide peregrinations. The *Miracle Center* that was erected by Archbishop Idahosa in Benin City had a seating capacity of 10,000. It became the model for subsequent initiatives because a lot of founders of such churches from the middle of the 1970s, including Archbishop Duncan-Williams of ACI, in Ghana, trained directly with Idahosa.

The RCCG, led by Enoch A. Adeboye, we have noted, is one of Africa's most influential mega churches. The RCCG is rooted in the older AIC tradition, but Pastor Adeboye, a former lecturer in mathematics, took over in 1980 from the original founder, Josiah O. Akindayomi. Pastor Adeboye has within the period of his service as the general overseer grown the RCCG into an international church with many transnational networks. The RCCG holds a monthly Redemption Camp that attracts numbers reaching half a million people. Based in Nigeria, David O. Oyedepo started the Living Faith Worldwide Church in 1981. In the same location as the RCCG on the Lagos-Ibadan expressway, he has erected a 50,000 seat auditorium called Faith Tabernacle, which may be one of the largest church buildings in the world. The site boasts of a number of other structures for religious, commercial, and social purposes known as *Canaan Land*. Finally, in South Africa, Mosa Sono's Soweto-based Grace Bible Church has over 10,000 members with other congregations in major urban areas, including some poor communities.

Building a Mega-Sized Church

Anderson cites a Nigerian Charismatic preacher as submitting against the backdrop of Africa's difficult socioeconomic circumstances: "[A] church that preaches a message that gives people hope, encouragement and healing will never lack attendance" (2013: 243). In Anderson's commentary on the matter, the remarkable growth of Pentecostalism in Africa in the midst of harsh economic and political realities, including devastating natural disasters, means that there is something about these churches that has much to teach others. In his words: "What is happening in Africa is happening throughout the majority world, with new Pentecostal mega-churches springing up wherever large cities and relative religious freedom are to be found" (ibid.). In Ghana, the growth of the LCI with its impressive infrastructure and very successful mission outreach across Africa and beyond, and has attracted much interest among those interested in contemporary Pentecostalism in Africa.

The founder of the LCI, Dag Heward-Mills, virtually publishes every sermon he preaches and has recently written a book on mega churches to meet the needs of those who want to know his secrets. Bishop Heward-Mills is of Ghanaian parentage on the paternal side with a Swiss mother.

He founded the LCI, which qualifies by our criteria of a mega-size church in about 1987. Lighthouse started in the canteen facilities of Ghana's premier teaching hospital, Korle Bu, where Bishop Heward-Mills trained. He started serving Lighthouse full time in 1991. About five years ago, Lighthouse moved to *The Quodesh,* the Lord's Hill, and an old industrial estate which was purchased and transformed into the headquarters of the LCI. The church is actively engaged in mission and has managed to plant branches not only across Ghana, but in many countries in Africa, Europe, and North America.

Every sermon preached by Bishop Heward-Mills is potentially a book. In one of his most sought-after publications, *The Mega Church: How to Make Your Church Grow,* Bishop Heward-Mills outlines 25 reasons behind "why you must have a mega church" (Heward-Mills, 2011). It is worthy of note that the endorsement for this book was provided by David Yonggi Cho, who signs as the chairman of the Church Growth International. He refers to the work and the person behind it in the following terms:

> Dr. Heward-Mills is committed to the Lord Jesus Christ and the work involved in the evangelization of the world. He is a great leader and role-model for all those in ministry, and we were at "Church Growth International", are very honored to know and call Dr. Dag Heward-Mills a friend and co-worker in the great harvest fields of the world. (Cho, cited in Heward-Mills, 2011)

The references to the *evangelization of the world* and the *great harvest fields of the world* are important because those are the principal mindsets behind the building of mega churches. There are many other reasons why churches want to have mega-size congregations. According to Heward-Mills, pastors must desire to have mega churches because:

> ... that is the most appropriate vision and goal for a pastor; the desire for a mega church leads you on a journey of church growth; the prophetic destiny of every church that the Lord builds is to have a greater end than the beginning; most pastors are deceived into thinking that the work is being done when it is not being done; God's will is that "his house may be filled"; your harvest field is the world; the biblical example of churches had thousands of members; having a large church means that more souls have been won to the kingdom; in a mega church more workers and laborers are released to work for God; through a mega church more ministers of the gospel, full-time pastors and bishops are appointed and released into the harvest field; more people are involved in prayer against the power of the

prince of the air; a mega church generates large crowds and large crowds create great expectation; in a mega church you have a greater manifestation of miracles because of the greater crowds and greater expectation; more evangelism is possible through a mega church; a mega church has a larger and greater income that can be used for the work of God; special ministries which take care of special needs will develop within a mega church; it shows that you have made full proof of your ministry; in a mega church there are more "beloveds" (potential marriage partners); in a mega church more marriages and more weddings take place; there are more contacts and connections through the people in the mega church; in a mega church there is always a large pool of employers who can help the church members; all the different needs of the congregation can be met through the mega church; a mega church is more likely to accomplish the 25% biblical quota of souls won from the community; a mega church is a force to reckon with and it becomes a nation within a nation; the glory of the end-time Church will be greater than the glory of the early church. (2011: 1–19)

There must obviously be advantages in having a mega church. It is evident from the 25 reasons given by Bishop Heward-Mills that in addition to the Pentecostal desire to win souls and attract numbers, many of the reasons are simply for practical, financial, and other material advantages, including being *properly connected* and raising more financial resources. On the whole, however, the impression is created in this list that building a mega church once coveted is bound to happen. Biblically, it is the Lord who added to the numbers of believers being saved daily (Acts 2: 47). The mere fact that a pastor has attracted large numbers must not necessarily be taken to mean success in church life because Christian ministry is more than numbers. Mega churches create public recognition and attraction for their leaders, making them important in society. In Africa, leaders of mega churches play important roles in the lives of political authority both because of their spiritual services to vulnerable heads of state and for the sheer numbers they command in terms of following.

Biblical and Theological Foundations

The chapter began with a reference to the words of Jesus to his disciples that those who believe in him will do *greater works*. For those who pursue the idea of building mega-size churches, this is something that is seen to have both biblical and theological connotations. Theologically, this is an idea that is closely tied to the prosperity gospel. According to the principles of prosperity preaching, when God is in something, it grows big which in this context is synonymous with success. This theological idea is founded on the *blessings of Abraham,* as understood within the preaching on prosperity. A part of the Abrahamic covenant story, particularly cherished in mega-church discourse, is when he parted with his nephew, Lot. Their workmen were fighting over limited grazing land, and Abraham gave Lot the option to choose any part of the territory for resettlement. The Lord said to Abraham after Lot had parted from him:

> Lift up your eyes from where you are and look north and south, east and west. All the land you see I will give to you and your offspring like the dust of the earth, so that if anyone could count the dust, then your offspring could be counted. Go; walk through the land, for I am giving it to you. (Genesis 13: 14–17)

In prosperity preaching, almost anything that the Christian touches, based on the understanding of passages, such as the aforementioned one, must blossom, and the expansion of territory is an important aspect of such success. Thus, in addition to the blessings of Abraham (mentioned in the Biblical account in Genesis), the Jabez story on the expansion of territories is one that is also used extensively to underscore the fact that God provides increase for his children, including granting them numbers under their pastoral leadership. We encounter Jabez in I Chronicles 4: 9–10 where his name simply means *born in pain*. He cries out to God in prayer: "[B]less me and enlarge my territory," and God grants his request. This story and that of Abraham, dealing with the expansion of territory, is very important in contemporary Pentecostal hermeneutics, and they are used to explain that God grants the requests of those who seek bigger things in Christian ministry.

In terms of the establishment of churches, the ability to build a large congregation is an important index of the gospel of prosperity because it is a mark of a successful ministry. This means that there is an important correlation between striving to build a mega church and the prosperity gospel. Christian presence may have shifted to the Global South and East; however, contemporary Christian culture still bears the marks of influence from North American Evangelicalism with its idea of the *mega* as indicative of success. Much of this influence comes through the use of media in church life. The media facilitates wide circulation and dissemination of ideas and cultures well beyond the geographical origins of these churches. To that end, there is no context with greater influence on contemporary Christian cultures than the USA. North American Evangelicalism has changed the face of Christianity through its integration of popular cultural ideas, marketing strategies, and consumerist values into church life and worship (Wells, 2005).

Conclusion

The point to note is that the idea of a mega church is closely tied to a certain Evangelical religious culture. Certain classical Pentecostal and historic mission denominations that have existed in urban Africa for more than a century do not necessarily embrace the mega-sized church idea. The argument against the mega-sized church is that it tends to make church administration a bit unwieldy. In the case of Methodist Churches, for example, the method, right from the time of the Wesley brothers in the 18th century, has been to build small communities of faith for effective personal fellowship and pastoral care; that has remained the case in most of Africa. African churches that work toward mega-sized congregations seem without exception to belong to the Pentecostal/Charismatic streams of Christianity. This is because, as noted previously, building huge cathedrals and filling them with people have become an important index of the workings of the prosperity gospel associated with these churches. Thus, the expression *mega-size church* has come to refer to contemporary Pentecostal Churches that are promoting and integrating postmodern values into church life, in which size is usually a sign of divine favor and blessing. The church in Africa is rich with examples of mega churches both in the continent, and also in the Global North (led by Africans), thus heralding a new era in world Christianity.

Note

1. See http://www.kicc.org.uk/. Retrieved on March 25, 2013.

Bibliography

Anderson, Allan. 2004. *An Introduction to Pentecostalism: Global Charismatic Christianity.* Cambridge: Cambridge University Press.

———. 2013. *To the Ends of the Earth: Pentecostalism and the Transformation of World Christianity.* Oxford: Oxford University Press.

Asamoah-Gyadu, J. Kwabena. 2005. *African Charismatics: Current Developments within Independent Indigenous Pentecostalism in Ghana.* Leiden: Brill Academic Publishers.

———. 2010. *Taking Territories and Raising Champions: Contemporary Pentecostalism and the Changing Face of the Christianity in Africa 1980–2010.* Accra: Asempa Publishers.

———. 2013. *Contemporary Pentecostal Christianity: Interpretations from an African Context.* Oxford: Regnum Oxford International.

Bakker, Jimmy & Ken Abraham. 1996. *I was Wrong: The Untold Story of the Shocking Journey from PTL Power to Prison and Beyond.* Nashville, TN: Thomas Nelson Publishers.

Gifford, Paul. 1998. *African Christianity: Its Public Role.* Indianapolis, IN: Indiana University Press.

———. 2004. *Ghana's New Christianity: Pentecostalism in a Globalizing African Economy.* Indianapolis, IN: Indiana University Press.

Heward-Mills, Dag. 2011. *The Mega Church: How to Make Your Church Grow.* Accra: Parchment House Publishers.

Jenkins, Philip. 2007. *The Next Christendom: The Coming of Global Christianity.* Oxford: Oxford University Press.

Miller, Donald E. 1997. *Reinventing American Protestantism: Christianity in the New Millennium.* Berkeley/Los Angeles/London: University of California Press.

Peel, John D.Y. 2008. "Foreword." In Asonzeh Ukah (ed.), *A New Paradigm of Pentecostal Power: A Study of the Redeemed Christian Church of God in Nigeria* (pp. xix-xxiv). Trenton, NJ: Africa World Press.

Poewe, Karla. 1994. *Charismatic Christianity as a Global Culture.* South Carolina: University of South Carolina Press.

Shaw, Mark. 2010. *Global Awakening: How 20th Century Revivals Triggered a Christian Revolution.* Downers Grove, IL: Intervarsity Press.

Wells, David F. 2005. *Above all Earthly Powers: Christ in a Postmodern World.* Grand Rapids, MI: Wm. B. Eerdmans

3

Mega Churches and Megaphones: Nigerian Church Leaders and Their Media Ministries

Walter C. Ihejirika and Godwin B. Okon

Introduction

The religious demography of Nigeria is a much contested issue, especially between the two dominant religions in the country—Christianity and Islam. The 2009 Annual US State Department Report on International Religious Freedom rightly noted that there is no agreement on the total number of Christians or Muslims in Nigeria. The report concluded: "[I]t is generally assumed that the proportions of citizens, who practice Islam and citizens who practice Christianity are roughly, equal" (Akande, 2009). For political reasons, the Nigerian government, since independence, has excluded religious questions in any census since its first one was conducted in 1963. Thus, even the Nigerian government cannot point to specific numbers in regard to the population of Christians and Muslims.

In terms of the geographical distribution of the major religious groups, it is generally agreed that the North is largely Muslim dominated; that there are large numbers of both Muslims and Christians in the middle belt and in the West, especially in the Yorubaland. The South and South-eastern regions are generally acknowledged as predominantly Christian with a small majority who are practitioners of traditional beliefs.

What is, however, not contested is the vibrancy and increasing visibility which the Christian religion has demonstrated in Nigeria over the last two decades, especially in the southern part of the country. A visit around major cities, such as Lagos, Ibadan, Port Harcourt, Owerri, and Calabar, provides ocular evidence of this phenomenon. There are sign posts and billboards of various sizes and shapes, mounted along the road and on street corners, gigantic church buildings, colorful posters and banners announcing crusades, vigils, and other religious gatherings in all these cities (Ukah, 2008a).

There is also an overwhelming presence of many of these leaders in the nation's airwaves. The increased vocal involvement and activism of some of the Christian leaders in the nation's socio-political arena is yet another evidence of the vibrancy of Christianity in Nigeria (Ihejirika, 2012).

The growth, vibrancy, and increased visibility of Christianity in Nigeria, especially the new wave Pentecostal Movement, has received some scholarly attention. This chapter adds to the literature on the current state of Christianity in Nigeria by presenting a comparative study of 10 Christian leaders who lead, what we could effectively call, mega churches. As Kalu noted, the rise of the mega churches is one the characteristics of African *new wave* Pentecostalism (2008). These mega church pastors are so characterized because they are the leaders of Christian churches and ministries which have very large followership (both physically and virtually); they conduct regular religious activities which attract massive crowds, upward of 10,000 people; they have built or are in the process of building gigantic structures which can accommodate huge congregations, and are very active in the mass media which are used as *megaphones* to proclaim their teaching and project their image.

Based on our local knowledge of Christianity and the major leaders in the country, we intentionally selected the following leaders who we believe qualify as mega church pastors: Enoch Adeboye of the Redeemed Christian Church of God (RCCG), T.B. Joshua of the Synagogue Church of All Nations, David Oyedepo of the Living Faith Church (Winners' Chapel), Chris Oyakhilome of Believers Loveworld Incorporated (Christ Embassy), Ayo Oritsejafor of the Word of Life Bible Church, Ejike Mbaka of the Catholic Adoration Ministries, David Ibiyeomie of the Salvation Ministries, F. Kumiyi of the Deeper Life Bible Church, Lazarus Muoka of the Lord Chosen Charismatic Renewal Ministry, and Daniel Olukoya of the Mountain of Fire and Miracle Ministries.

The phenomenological research we carried out on these leaders and their ministries was aimed at highlighting the vibrancy and visibility of Christianity through the media in contemporary Nigeria. In line with the standard phenomenological tradition (Gubrium & Holstein, 2000; Moustakas, 1994), we attempt to accurately describe this religious phenomenon from the perspective of the people involved. We rely on data derived from personal observations, information from these churches as published in both the traditional and the new media, as well as studies from other scholars.

Our design entails a comparative look at the mega church pastors to tease out elements of similarities and differences in an attempt to highlight the vibrancy and visibility of Christianity in Nigeria. The following comparative categories are used: main theological themes, size of followership and reach of ministry, grandiose infrastructure, media ministries and social visibility, and controversies involving the leaders and their ministries.

Main Theological Themes

In the absence of reliable data, the growth of Christianity in Nigeria was measured by non-quantitative indices and assessed by the vitality of practice, as well as high visibility in the public space, especially in the mass media. The branch of Christianity which has exhibited most of these traits is the Pentecostal Movement, specifically modern African Pentecostalism or *new wave* Pentecostalism. Apart from Ejike Mbaka, who is a Catholic priest, the other nine church leaders we have selected belong to this dominant strand of Christianity.

The term *modern African Pentecostalism* refers to the indigenous Protestant Christian denominations which emphasize salvation by faith in the atoning death of Jesus Christ through personal conversion, the authority of Scripture in matters of faith and Christian practice, and clear manifestation of the signs of the Spirit's radical transforming power, especially the Pentecostal signs of faith healing and speaking in tongues (Asamoah-Gyadu, 2005; Ihejirika, 2006 and 2009). The theological mooring of these leaders revolves around the belief that divine intervention in the lives of believers and those who accept Jesus is inevitable when faith is activated. In their ministries, these leaders accentuate the supernatural and insist that true religion should be evidenced by the unmistakable signs of the Spirit's radical transforming power, especially Pentecostal signs, as mentioned earlier. Barret articulates this belief system as thus:

> ... all Christians should seek a post-conversion religious experience called baptism of the Holy Spirit, and that the Spirit baptised believer may receive one or more of the supernatural gifts known in the early Church: instantaneous sanctification, the ability to prophecy, to practice divine healing through prayer, to speak in tongues (*glossolalia*), or to interpret tongues, singing

in the Spirit, praying with upraised hands, dreams, visions, discernment of spirits, words of wisdom, words of knowledge, emphasis on miracles, power encounters, exorcisms (casting out demon), resuscitations, deliverances, signs and wonders. (1988: 124)

Mbaka, though a Catholic priest, is Charismatic in orientation and like all members of the Catholic Charismatic Movement, teaches and preaches similar messages as the Pentecostal pastors, especially topics, such as the expectation of the manifestation of supernatural powers. The difference between the Pentecostal leaders and Mbaka is: Mbaka does not teach the doctrine of a second baptism or being *born again*, as it is professed by the others. Also, unlike the Pentecostals whose ministries are hinged on the Scripture alone (in line with their Protestant orientation of *sola scriptura* [by scripture alone]), Mbaka projects the Scripture, the traditions of the Catholic Church, and the Eucharistic adoration as bedrocks of his ministry. In fact, the defining characteristic of his ministry is the adoration of the Eucharist. Finally, unlike the others who are independent leaders, at the helm of ministries they founded, Mbaka, like most Catholic Charismatics, is rooted in the Catholic Church and is obedient to his ecclesiastical superiors. His ministry is the result of a splinter group from the Catholic Church, as is often the case with the Pentecostal Movement, but a ministry within the Catholic Church denomination.

The major theological emphasis of the Pentecostal pastors is faith healing and other forms of divine intervention in the lives of people. Unlike earlier missionary Christianity which laid more emphasis on post-death reward, the new wave Pentecostalism and Charismatic Christianity indicate that the reward for believers begins here on earth before the final one is received in the afterlife. This belief system resonates with the traditional African world view.

Africans always expect power to emanate from religious forms. A religion is useful and worthy of profession if it embodies and imparts this power; otherwise, it is to be rejected and a *power-full* alternative must be sought. The Pentecostal insistence on divine intervention in the lives of believers is similar to the aforementioned African view on religion. The Pentecostal Movement not only presents the Christian God as capable of doing what the Supreme God and other deities are expected to do in the African world view, but it actually goes a step further to purport that the Christian God is more powerful than the African deities. In the Pentecostal belief system, African traditional beliefs and practices are in a way refashioned or modernized and in a sense *re-dimensioned*. It is within this context that we situate the Pentecostal emphasis on miracles, healing, and exorcism.

Another aspect of the African world view that is evident in Pentecostalism is the *harmatological* (the doctrine of sin) dimension that stipulates instant divine punishment awaits sinners. This teaching also runs deep within the Pentecostal belief system, as it is believed that individuals who are suffering from social or financial setbacks are in that condition because of their sinfulness. They are advised to look into their lives and even that of their ancestors to discern any non-expiated sins. *Breaking ancestral curses* is a major theme of many Pentecostal sermons and revival meetings.

The main theological themes of these mega church pastors could be summarized as thus:

1. Holiness of life through total commitment to the Savior Jesus Christ and conformity to the God's teaching in the Bible;
2. Belief in a more powerful God who intervenes miraculously in peoples' lives by dispensing cures for various forms of ailments and brings about other spectacular acts;
3. Prosperity theology—the emphasis on the material well-being of believers;
4. Emphasis on the power of the devil and evil spirits to harm human beings;
5. Exorcism as a remedy to evil attacks;
6. Public confession and being *born-again* as a prerequisite for receiving God's blessings.

Size of Followership and Reach of Ministry

As with the general religious statistics of Nigeria, it is difficult to state with certainty the numerical strength of the ministries under study. Records of members are not kept and if they are, they are hardly made available for study. Again, most of these ministries, like others in the Pentecostal Movement, experience frequent splintering with members drifting over to new factions. There could also be cases of multiple memberships, where some people attend programs organized by one group while still identifying with another. For instance, non-Catholics participate in Fr Ejike Mbaka's Adoration programs, as do some Catholics who attend revivals and crusades organized by the Pentecostal pastors.

One thing that can be said for all the church leaders is that they are consumed by a driving force and missionary vision to win as many souls as possible for Christ. They proclaim the need to *plant* churches in every corner of the globe. Thus, new branches are opened up both in the country and outside the country. The pastors are constantly invited to conduct crusades and other forms of spiritual ministries in every part of the world. Outside the country, these ministries attract not only Nigerians and Africans in the diaspora, but also believers from other parts of the world. A comparison, revealing the followership and reach of the ministry of the 10 mega church leaders, is presented in Table 3.1.

In spite of the absence of verifiable numerical data regarding the membership of the churches and ministries under study, the ubiquity of their churches both within and outside Nigeria is undeniable. The presence of affiliate churches in many Western countries is indicative of the growing strength of these churches, and it lends credence to the trend which has been called *reverse evangelization* or church shift, that is, Africans who were initially evangelized by Europeans, now are taking the gospel back to them, a form of re-evangelization.

Grandiose Infrastructure

Another ocular evidence of the growing profile of Christianity in Nigeria is the grandeur of physical structures erected by some of the denominations within the religion. As we noted earlier, these gigantic structures are another defining characteristic of the mega churches.

The 10 church leaders who are the subjects of this study have erected structures which deserve the tag *mega church* buildings. A comparative examination shows two patterns of erection: First, as a single imposing church, and second as an expansive complex comprising various facilities. The church leaders who built single imposing church buildings are T.B. Joshua, Ayo Oritsejafor, Lazarus Muoka, Williams Kumiyi, and David Ibiyeomie, while Enoch Adeboye, David Oyedepo, Daniel Olukoya, and Ejike Mbaka have built or are in the process of building sprawling complexes.

Table 3.1:
Comparative Table of the Missionary Vision and Spread of 10 Mega Churches in Nigeria

Ministry/Church	Leadership	Year Founded	Missionary Vision	Countries	Mega Religious Activity	Attendance	Membership
The RCCG	Pastor Enoch Adeboye (converted in 1973, assumed leadership in 1981, and initiated a transformation of the church)	1952	To have a member of RCCG in every family of nations, plant churches within five minutes walking distance in every city and town of developing countries and within five minutes driving distance in every city and town of developed countries	100 countries[a]	Holy Ghost Service, held every first Friday of the month	The Service attracts 300–500 participants, while the Congress attracts up to 3 million participants from 34 countries.[b]	Estimated to be between 2 and 5 million[c]
Synagogue Church of All Nations	Prophet T.B. Joshua (founder and leader)	1987	One way; one job. The way is Jesus Christ; the job is to talk about Him to others	4 countries	Weekly Sunday Deliverance Service	Between 15,000 and 20,000 participants	Not determined
Living Faith Church (Winners' Chapel)	Bishop David Oyedepo (founder and leader)	1985	The Living Faith World Outreach Center (LFWOC) is a Christian missionary organization, whose primary objective is the general development and upliftment of mankind by stirring up the God-given potentials embedded in people of all races and nations through the propagation of the gospel of Jesus Christ	The Winners' Chapel network of churches is present in over 300 cities in all states of Nigeria, as well as in over 63 cities in 32 African Nations, Dubai, the United Kingdom and the United States of America.	Shiloh (four-day crusade)	Between 300,000 and 500,000 participants	Not determined

Church	Leader	Year	Vision	Location	Program	Participants
Believers Loveworld Incorporated (Christ Embassy),	Pastor Chris Oyakilome (founder and leader)		A vision of taking God's divine presence to the nations of the world, and to demonstrate the character of the Holy Spirit	Not specified	Night of Bliss (held in different countries)	Depending on country, participants can be in the hundreds of thousands.
Word of Life Bible Church	Pastor Ayo Oritsejafor; (founder and leader)		*Take my Word to the World*	He is more of an international speaker	Weekly Sunday Services and periodic healing crusades	10,000–15,000 participants in Services.
AMEN	Rev. Fr Ejike Mbaka (founder of ministry, but under the authority of the Catholic Church)	1996	To draw as many people as possible to Jesus present in the Holy Eucharist because in the presence of the Lord, there is fullness of joy and in his presence, impossibilities are made to be possible	Ministry followers are found in many countries, mostly as virtual communities	All night Adoration (every Friday)	Between 100,000 and 200,000 participants
Salvation Ministries (Glorious Chapel)	Pastor David Ibiyeomie (founder and leader)	1997	A divine mandate *to establish the Kingdom of God here on earth*	Mostly in Port Harcourt	Days of Divine Encounter (first week of every month)	20,000–30,0000 participants
Deeper Christian Life Ministry	Pastor William F. Kumiyi (founder and leader)	1973 (as Deeper Life Bible Church)			Monthly Revival and Miracle Program	100,000–200,000 participants nationwide
						Not determined
						Not determined

(Table 3.1 Continued)

(Table 3.1 Continued)

Ministry/Church	Leadership	Year Founded	Missionary Vision	Countries	Mega Religious Activity	Attendance	Membership
Lord Chosen Charismatic Renewal Ministry	Pastor Lazarus Muoka (founder and leader)	2002	Ten billion souls mandate—this mandate is bigger than the world population; this means that we and our descendants will continue to evangelize until Jesus comes	63 countries	Weekly Crusades organized in different cities	25,000–30,000 participants	
Mountain of Fire and Miracle Ministries (MFM)	Pastor Daniel Olukoya (founder and leader)	1994	MFM evolved a strategy of a network of branches in every state capital, local government headquarters, senatorial district, and locality	On every continent, MFM is profoundly visible.	Prayer Rain (First Friday) and Power Must Change Hands Program (First Saturday of the month)	30,000–35,000 participants	

Source: Authors.
Notes: [a] See Rice (2009).
[b] The official website of the church does not have specific data on its membership. This estimate was provided by Apologetics Index, the website which provides research resources on religious movements, cults, sects, world religions, and related issues. Retrieved from http://www.apologeticsindex.org/210-redeemed-christian-church-of-god March 25, 2013.
[c] Ibid.

Pastor Adeboye conceived and built the Redemption Camp or Redemption City. This is a sprawling 10 square kilometer project along the Lagos–Ibadan expressway. This is a religious town with all modern facilities, including drainage system, electricity and water supplies, bank, supermarkets, schools (nursery, primary, and secondary), the Redeemers University and the Redeemed Bible College, housing estate, and hotels. At the center of the city is the Congress Arena, a huge space measuring about three square kilometers which hosts the annual Holy Ghost Congress, in December each year, attracting an estimated crowd of three million people.

Outside the shores of Nigeria, the church is replicating the Redemption Camp in the USA. It paid more than US$ 1 million to acquire 500 acres of land in Floyd, a rural northern town of Texas. The project, which a redeemed pastor described as a *Christian Disneyland*, when completed will have a 10,000-seat sanctuary, a conference center, two elementary school-size lecture centers, a dormitory, several cottages, a lake, and a Christian-themed water park (Farwell, 2005; Romero, 2005).

David Oyedepo's Canaanland is very similar to the Redemption Camp. Conceived, according to Oyedepo, through a divine revelation, the city was opened in 1999 on a 560-acre (2.3 square kilometer) piece of land. It has since expanded to more than triple the original size. It includes the headquarters of the Living Faith Church Worldwide, the church building itself known as Faith Tabernacle, Covenant University, Faith Academy Secondary School, and Kingdom Heritage Nursery/Primary School. Several business ventures operated by the church are located within the Canaanland complex, including Dominion Publishing House, Hebron Bottled Water Processing Plant, a bakery, various restaurants and stores, four banks, and several residential estates that provide for the over 2,000 church employees and 9,000 students that live there. The 50,000 capacity Faith Tabernacle, which was built within 10 months in 1999 is reputed to be the world's largest church building. Inside, the Tabernacle has a total space of 3.5 hectares, and it is quite a spectacular sight.

Daniel Olukoya also has a sprawling facility called Prayer City, though not as grandiose as the Redemption Camp or Canaanland. A huge expanse of land has been donated to Ejike Mbaka by the indigenous people group of Emene in a suburb of Enugu for the construction of the permanent site of his Adoration Ground. When completed, it will have a stadium-like church which will accommodate more than 70,000 people at the same time.

The International Gospel Center, Ajamimogha Warri, is a 35,000-seater church auditorium built by Ayo Oritsejafor. Prophet T.B. Joshua's Synagogue Church of All Nations in Lagos is another mega church, as is David Ibiyeomie's Glorious Chapel which is nearing completion in Port Harcourt. It is a state-of-the-art architectural masterpiece cathedral with hi-tech facilities.

The erection of these mega structures is indicative of the large followership of these pastors. More importantly, it is also indicative that the pastors are getting ample financial support from their members because the costs of building these structures run into billions of naira (Nigerian currency). Anyone who sees these mega structures will come to the conclusion that Christianity is indeed alive and active in Nigeria.

Media Ministries and Social Visibility

The grandiose facilities erected by these Christian religious leaders symbolically communicate the vitality and vibrancy of Christianity in Nigeria. This is accentuated by the leaders' direct engagement with the means of communication. In Nigeria, as in other parts of the world, any discussion of religious belief and praxis which does not incorporate the media component is definitely looked down upon. Scholars have realized that the study of religion and the media cannot be adequately carried out in isolation. Televangelism has brought a great deal of visibility to Christianity and the church leaders who propagate it. Today, the Christian message is widely circulated in both the traditional and new media.

It is agreed that one of the defining characteristics of Pentecostalism is the appropriation and use of modern media technologies as part of their religious ritual practice (Hackett, 1998). The mass media are used for the purpose of disseminating the *word of God* to the masses in order to consolidate the faith of believers and reach the nonbelievers. It is also a reflection of the globalizing aspirations of the Pentecostal Movement as well as a calculated attempt to transform and Christianize popular culture, so that it is safe for consumption by *born-again* Christians. Rosalind Hackett puts it succinctly: "In short, the modern media are deemed an acceptable weapon for God's army in the battle against Satan" (ibid., 258).

Huge amounts of money are expended by the church leaders to promote their media ministries. One can safely say today that a good percentage of the internally generated revenue of both private and government broadcast media houses in Nigeria come from televangelism. Studies have documented that a huge portion of donations accrue to Nigerian mega televangelists for their media ministries (Ihejirika, 2006; Ukah, 2008a and 2008b). Televangelism is a major gold mine for revenue in the form of donations for the operating costs of the Christian broadcast industry as well as general income for the various ministries.

The leaders are actively involved in both traditional and new media. By means of Table 3.1, we will show the evolving media skyline, that is, an overview of the range of media usage by these Christian leaders.

This comparative table clearly shows the active involvement of the church leaders with the mass media. It is evident that of all the 10 leaders, only the Catholic priest is not very active with the mass media. This supports the earlier findings which indicate that the Catholic Church and other mainline churches are very slow to embrace the mass media as tools for evangelization and ministry (see Ihejirika, 2008).

New media is providing an avenue for the church leaders to evade current Nigerian broadcasting laws which prohibit religious bodies from operating broadcasting stations. Both live streaming of radio and television signals are transmitted online, and the television channels are now cleverly established on the satellite platform. Apart from spreading their messages, the new media also offer an ample forum for interaction among members for counseling matters, and also making donations to the churches. To circumvent the existing laws that prohibit the ownership and use of local Nigerian TV channels for religious use, mega church leaders, such as Oritsejafor (see Table 3.2), have also launched satellite stations outside Nigeria. The ABN satellite channel, broadcasting from London under Oritsejafor, has a coverage spanning across the whole of Africa, Asia, Middle East, Australia, America, and some parts of Europe.[1]

The content of the broadcast programs of all the church leaders are very similar—they buttress the need for commitment to the moral teachings of Jesus Christ and to live upright lives. But the most important element in all the programs is the manifestation of divine power in healings, deliverance from satanic forces, and testimonies of wellbeing and various forms of divine intervention in peoples' lives.

Table 3.2:
A Comparative Overview of the Media Skyline of 10 Church Leaders in Nigeria

Name of Ministry	Leadership	Traditional Media					New Media				
		Print (Posters, Handbills, Newspapers, Magazines, and Books)	Radio	Television	Music/Tape Ministries	Website	Social Media	Satellite TV	Webcasting	Cinema/Video Films
The RCCG[a]	Pastor Enoch Adeboye[b]	Church posters and stickers, publishes *Redemption Light*, *Redemption Times*, as well as books	Church-run radio programs	Adeboye's messages broadcast in over 28 state and private TV stations	Dove Music markets, Church tapes, DVDs, and VCDs.	www.rccg.org. Retrieved on March 15, 2013.	Facebook, Twitter, and devotional SMS	Dove Vision, 24-hour TV channel	Liveway Radio and Liveway TV.	Dove produces numerous video films featuring actors from Nigeria's movie industry—(Nollywood)
Synagogue Church of All Nations	Prophet T.B. Joshua	Books, publishes magazine *Faith Cometh*	Not visible	Teachings aired in selected private television stations	DVDs and VCDs of preaching and healing sessions	www.scoan.org. Retrieved on May 1, 2013.	Facebook, Twitter, YouTube, video podcast, and The Joshua Blog	Emmanuel TV, a 24-hour TV channel	Emmanuel TV streams online via Faith Streaming platform	Not visible

Church	Leader	Publications	Visibility	Television	Visibility	Website	Social Media	Visibility	Radio/Other	Visibility
Living Faith Church (Winners' Chapel)	Bishop David Oyedepo	Dominion Publishing House; Extensive range of books by Oyedepo; A magazine—*Ministers Digest*; tracts, Winners Hotline, and Healings at Winners' Chapel	Not very visible			www.davidoyedepoministries.org. Retrieved on May 1, 2013.	Facebook and Twitter	Not very visible	Domiradi—web radio, on media flash	Not visible
Believers Loveworld Incorporated (Christ Embassy)	Pastor Chris Oyakhilome	Posters and handbills, many books by Pastor Chris, publishes monthly inspirational book—*Rhapsodies of Reality*	Has a teaching program on radio	Very visible on Nigerian television channels, programs called *Atmosphere for Miracles*	Not very visible	www.christembassy.org. Retrieved on March 15, 2013.	Facebook, Twitter, YouTube, and Yokoos. Online apps for both Apple and Andriod smartphones	Launched first Satellite TV channel in Africa—LoveWorld Sat. Runs LoveWorld UK and LoveWorld Plus	Both radio and video streaming	Not visible
Word of Life Bible Church	Pastor Ayo Oritsejafor	Several books published by Pastor Oritsejafor	Not visible	Second prominent televangelist in Nigeria after Idahosa. Started *Hour of Deliverance*, on over 20 TV channels.	Not very visible	http://www.ayo-oritsejafor.org/. Retrieved on March 25, 2013.	Facebook and Twitter	Owns the African Broadcasting Network, a satellite TV channel. Also available on God TV channels	Live video streaming	Not visible

(Table 3.2 Continued)

(Table 3.2 Continued)

Name of Ministry	Leadership	Media Skyline								
		Traditional Media				New Media				
		Print (Posters, Handbills, Newspapers, Magazines, and Books)	Radio	Television	Music/Tape Ministries	Website	Social Media	Satellite TV	Webcasting	Cinema/Video Films
Adoration Ministries Enugu Nigeria (AMEN)	Rev Fr Ejike Mbaka	Posters, handbills, almanacs, and devotional books	Not visible	Not visible	Active music ministry. Has over 20 music CDs and VCDs on sale	No official website[c]	Blogs	Not visible	Not visible	Not visible
Salvation Ministries (Glorious Chapel)	Pastor David Ibiyeomie	Posters, handbills, and books	Not very visible	Vibrant TV ministry. *Hour of Salvation* program on 24 stations in Nigeria.	Not very active	http://www.salvationministrieshs.org. Retrieved on March 25, 2013.	YouTube and SMS for testimonies	*Hour of Salvation* on: Daystar TV Network, The Word Network, KICC TV UK, Ben TV, Inspiration TV, God TV, and ACBN, Kingdom Live Network, WJYS, and MCTV Channels in Chicago	Live streaming, podcasts	Not visible

Ministry	Pastor	Print	Radio	TV	Other media	Website	Social media	Satellite	Streaming	
Deeper Christian Life Ministry	Pastor William F. Kumiyi	Tracts and pamphlets and a devotional—*Daily Manna*	Radio program *Restoration Hour*	*Restoration Hour* on 10 channels	Music, cassettes, and CDs	http://www.dclm.org/. Retrieved on May 1, 2013.	Facebook, Twitter, YouTube, and SMS	MyTV satellite channel	Live streaming	Not visible
Lord Chosen Charismatic Renewal Church	Pastor Lazarus Muoka	Posters, handbills, and books	Not very visible	Not very visible	Not very visible	http://www.thelordschosenworld.org. Retrieved on May 20, 2013.	Live broadcasts available on smartphones	Not visible	Internet television—*Chosen Revival TV*	Not visible
Mountain of Fire and Miracle Ministries	Pastor Daniel Olukoya	Posters, handbills, and books. Owns Christian Battle Cry Publishing.	Not very visible	Owns MountaintopLife TV aired on 12 channels.	Music—Mountaintop Music School	http://www.mountainoffire.org/#. Retrieved on March 15, 2013.	Facebook, Twitter, YouTube, etc.	Owns a satellite channel MFM TV	WebTV; webstreaming, and video on demand	Not visible

Source: Authors.

Notes:
[a] See https://www.facebook.com/davidoyedepoministries. Retrieved on August 22, 2014.
[b] For a detailed presentation of Adeboye's media ministry, see Ukah (2008b).
[c] Fraudsters have cashed in on this lack of official presence. Some often open Facebook pages with his picture, and post prayers and blessings purportedly from him. When thousands of people sign up to the page, they then begin to demand donations.

These media ministries no doubt have brought a lot of visibility to Christianity. The church leaders have become *celebrities* of sorts, easily recognized in any part of the country and even beyond. This visibility has made some of them notable players in the nation's socio-political scene. Political office holders at different levels pay them visits and court their friendship. Today in Nigeria, some mega church pastors, who are also televangelists, have become veritable *kingmakers* whose endorsements and predictions can bring about victory or defeat to politicians.

Controversies

While the activities of these church leaders exemplify the vitality and growth of Christianity in Nigeria, there is a flip side to their ministries which may be a drawback to the spread of the gospel. Some of the controversies have revolved around their lifestyles, others on some aspects of their teaching, while others have to do with insinuations of pecuniary misdemeanors.

It has been noted that the prosperity gospel is one of the main tenets propagated by the new wave Pentecostalism in Nigeria. The pastors ostensibly manifest this divinely bestowed prosperity in the way they live. They live in palatial mansions, ride the best cars, don designer clothing, and generally enjoy the good things of life (Ajaero, 2007). This issue of the flamboyant lifestyle of the pastors was brought to the fore by wide discussions in the social arena regarding the growing number among them who spend huge sums of money to acquire private jets. *Forbes* magazine reported that Nigerian pastors spent US $225 million to acquire private jets (2011). Pastor Adeboye and Bishop Oyedepo are reported to own more than two jets, while Pastor Oritsejafor claimed that he got one as a birthday gift (Eyieyien, 2012). Many people have wondered how this ostentatious manifestation of wealth can be justified in the light of the general poverty which is representative of most of Nigeria's populace.

Again, aspects of the teachings and religious praxis of some of the pastors have also been controversial. Prophet T.B. Joshua is accused by his fellow pastors for his lack of orthodoxy in the ministry. They see him as being more of a traditional healer than a Christian pastor. In 2001, The Pentecostal Fellowship of Nigeria, headed by Bishop Mike Okonkwo, denounced Joshua as an imposter. The group, which is the umbrella body of all Pentecostal Churches in the country, had warned of the dangers of infiltrators who modernized cultism by injecting the name of Jesus Christ into their largely unbiblical practices. The group indicted the Synagogue of All Nations as falling into this category. When Chris Oyakhilome paid a visit to Joshua's Synagogue, he also incurred the wrath of his fellow pastors. After warning Oyakhilome in a letter that he must renounce all ties with Joshua, Okotie appeared on national television and announced that Oyakhilome was sold out to the devil by accepting money from Joshua to buy TV airtime (Eyoboka, 2010; Grady, 2001).

A video clip showing Bishop Oyedepo slapping a woman during a deliverance session in his Faith Tabernacle, which was circulated over the YouTube channel in 2009, brought a critical searchlight on the modus operandi of Christian healers and exorcists. Many pastors have been accused of indulging in unethical acts in the name of performing deliverance, such as having sexual relations with women who come to them for miracles of pregnancy or those in search of spouses. There have also been outlandish claims of miraculous interventions by some of the pastors, such as bringing dead people back to life and curing those suffering from HIV/AIDS and other such diseases.

Chris Oyakhilome, who thrives on the performance of miracles, has been accused of stage managing his healing sessions and of planting people in the crowd whom he eventually *heals*. He is also accused of offering money to his congregants who allegedly pose to be ill and wheelchair bound at their healing schools. Oyakhilome supposedly then heals these individuals at his *Night of Bliss* event (Ekenna, 2002). With constant publicity through all forms of media for crusades that promise signs, wonders, deliverance, and healings, many people have wondered why widespread problems still exist in the nation.

The financial activities of some of the pastors and their churches have also become sources of controversy. Two board members of the Redeemed Dove Media enterprise belonging to the RCCG—Cecilia Ibru and Erastus Akingbola—are deeply implicated in the banking scandal which rocked the Nigerian financial institutions in 2008. Some pastors have been accused of coercing members to make large donations to the church even though they may be poor, while some have come under investigation by the Nigerian financial crime police and the Economic and Financial Crimes Commission for allegations of money laundering.

The continued splintering and often violent litigations experienced among the churches is another controversial dimension of the manifestation of Christianity in Nigeria. An example is the one between Pastor Lazarus Muoka of Lord's Chosen Charismatic Revival Ministry and Pastor Nnamdi Ofoegbu of the Christ Chosen Generation Revival Ministry. Ofoegbu claimed that Mouka short-changed him to the tune of N317 million being what he contributed to the growth of the church since its inception till the time he left the church in 2006. He claimed that it was an *investment plan* based on an unwritten agreement he reached with Muoka to invest all he had with the hope of reaping bountifully at the time of harvest. Unfortunately, when it was time for him to enjoy the fruit of his labor, Muoka allegedly sidelined him (Emperoh, 2008).

Conclusion

This chapter has shown that Christianity is very much alive and thriving in Nigeria, and is even being exported to other countries of the world. This growth has tremendous religious and social implications for Nigeria. One area which is becoming pronounced is the increased tension in the relationship between Christianity and Islam. Many Christian leaders believe that the upsurge in Islamic militancy in the country, especially with the Boko Haram group, is an Islamic reaction to the penetration of Christianity into the northern parts of the country which are generally considered Muslim territories.

However, neither this inter-religious tension nor the controversies surrounding some of the churches and their leaders vitiates the observed dynamism of Christianity in the country. Based on the non-quantitative indicators we have highlighted in this chapter and given the size of her population, it stands to reason that Nigeria will remain one of the major pillars supporting the global Christian edifice.

Note

1. See ABN website (http://www.abnchannel.net/about.php). Retrieved on June 16, 2013.

Bibliography

Ajaero, C. 2007. "Pastoral Empires." *Newswatch*, Monday, August 20.
Akande, L. 2009. "U.S. Heightens Debate on Nigeria's Christians, Muslims Population." Retrieved from http://www.nairaland.com/346015/u.s-heightens-debate-nigerias-christians on March 10, 2013.
Akukwe, O. 2012. "Bishop Oyedepo Shiloh Slap, Jesus Witch And Diaspora Nigerians." Retrieved from http://www.modernghana.com/news/384179/1/bishop-oyedepo-shiloh-slap-jesus-witch-and-diaspor.html on March 15, 2013.
Asamoah-Gyadu, J.K. 2005. *African Charismatics: Current Developments within Independent Indigenous Pentecostalism in Ghana*. Leiden: Brill.
Barret, D. 1988. "The 20th Century Pentecostal/Charismatic Renewal in the Holy Spirit, With its Goal of World Evangelization," *International Bulletin of Missionary Research*, 12(3): 119–129.
Ekenna, G. 2002. "Oyakhilome's Miracles: Real or Fake?" *Newswatch*, April 15.
Emperoh, 2008. "Muoka vs Ofegbu: War in the House of God." Retrieved from http://www.nairaland.com/105831/muoka-vs-ofoegbu-war-house on April 5, 2013.
Eyieyien, E. 2012. "Nigerian Pastors and Private Jets." *The Nation*. Retrieved from http://thenationonlineng.net/new/comments/nigerian-pastors-and-private-jets on March 25, 2013.
Eyoboka, S. 2010. "War of Pastors: Okotie Attacks T.B. Joshua Again." Retrieved from http://www.codewit.com/religion-and-philosophy/3670-war-of-pastors-okotie-attacks-tb-joshua-again on August 22, 2014.
Farwell, S. 2005. "Africa's Largest Evangelical Church Plans a New Home in Rural Texas." *The Dallas Morning News*, Wednesday, July 20. Retrieved from http://www.utexas.edu/conferences/africa/ads/938.html on May 1, 2013.
Forbes. 2011. "Wealthy Nigerian Pastors Spend $225 Million on Private Jets." Retrieved from http://www.forbes.com/sites/mfonobongnsehe/2011/05/17/wealthy-nigerians-pastors-spend-225-million-on-private-jets/ on March 25, 2013.
Grady, J.L. 2001. "Nigerian Pastors Take Stand Against Occult Leader." *Charisma Magazine*, December 19.
Gubrium, J.F. & J.A. Holstein. 2000. "Analyzing Interpretive Practice." In N.K. Denzin and Y.S. Lincoln (eds), *Handbook of Qualitative Research* (2nd edn) (pp. 214–248). Thousand Oaks, CA: SAGE.
Hackett, R.I.J. 1998. "Charismatic/Pentecostal Appropriations of Media Technologies in Nigeria and Ghana," *Journal of Religion in Africa*, 28(3): 258–277.
Ihejirika, W.C. 2006. *From Catholicism to Pentecostalism: Role of Nigerian Televangelists in Religious Conversion*. Port Harcourt: University of Port Harcourt Press.
———. 2008. "'In-Line Religion': Innovative Pastoral Applications of the New Information and Communication Technologies (NICTS) by the Catholic Church in Nigeria," *Politics and Religion Journal*, 2(2): 79–98.
———. 2009. "Current Trends in the Study of Media, Religion and Culture in Africa," *African Communication Research, A Journal of Information on Current Research in Africa*, 2(1): 1–60.
———. 2012. "From Televisuality to Social Activism: Nigerian Televangelists and Their Sociopolitical Agenda." In T.N. & P. Lee (eds), *Global and Local Televangelism* (pp. 173–199). London: Palgrave Macmillan.

Kalu, O.U. 2008. *African Pentecostalism: An Introduction*. Oxford: Oxford University Press.
Moustakas, C. 1994. *Phenomenological Research Methods*. Thousand Oaks, CA: SAGE.
Rice, A. 2009. "Mission from Africa." *New York Times*, April 8. Retrieved from http://www.nytimes.com/2009/04/12/magazine/12churches-t.html?hp&_r=0 on June 16, 2013.
Romero, S. 2005. "A Texas Town Nervously Awaits a New Neighbor." *New York Times*, August 21. Retrieved from http://www.nytimes.com/2005/08/21/national/21church.html?pagewanted=1&_r=0 on March 25, 2013.
Ukah, A. F-K. 2008a. "Roadside Pentecostalism: Religious Advertising in Nigeria and the Marketing of Charisma," *Critical Interventions: Journal of African Art History and Visual Culture*, 2(Spring): 125–141.
———. 2008b. *A New Paradigm of Pentecostal Power: The Redeemed Christian Church of God in Nigeria*. Asmara: Africa World Press.
———. 2008c. "Seeing is More than Believing: Posters and Proselytization in Nigeria." In R.I.J. Hackett (ed.), *Proselytization Revisited: Rights Talk, Free Markets and Culture Wars* (pp. 167–198). London: Equinox Publishing Limited.

SECTION III

Mega Churches in Asia and the Pacific

4

Mega Churches in South Korea: Their Impact and Prospect in the Public Sphere

Sebastian C.H. Kim

In the Korean context, mega churches are those with over 10,000 members. Out of the 50 largest churches in the world, Korea boasts of a record number of 23 (Suh, 1994: 153–161; Kim, 2013: 5). Protestant Churches in South Korea grew rapidly during the 1960s–1980s under the military-backed governments, and one of the key aspects of this rapid growth was the rise of mega churches in major cities in the 1980s and 1990s.

In order to understand the Korean Protestant Church, one has to examine the characteristics of mega churches, since their influence on the lives of Protestant Christians as well as on the wider contemporary Korean society is significant. This chapter will examine three critical questions:

1. In what way is the rise of mega churches associated with the growth of the Protestant Churches in Korea in the context of sociopolitical and economic developments?
2. How do mega churches establish themselves, and what are the implications of their presence in the Korean churches and wider society?
3. How do the leadership and the congregations of mega churches relate to the public sphere of the Korean society?

This chapter will discuss the growth of Protestant Churches in South Korea during 1960s–1980s, the socioeconomic and ecclesiological reasons for the rise of mega churches and their characteristics, and issues around mega churches within contemporary Korean Christianity and the wider society. I will argue that although mega churches demonstrate the dynamism and enthusiasm of Korean Protestants and have contributed to the growth of Christianity by adapting to the norms of the Korean society in

86 Sebastian C.H. Kim

their leadership and operations, however, their public and prophetic roles have been significantly compromised by their close association with those holding powerful positions in society.

I have mainly used published materials on the history of Korean Christianity, surveys done by Christian and secular organizations on various aspects of Christianity, sociopolitical analysis of Korean Protestant Churches, and relevant sociopolitical and economic developments in modern Korean society.

Christian Korea, the Nevius Method, and Mega Evangelistic Campaigns

The growth of mega churches needs to be discussed in the context of the overall church-growth process in South Korea, since these phenomena are entwined in terms of historical and ecclesiological contexts. Outside observers often mention mega churches as the hallmark of Korean church growth or even of the Korean Protestant Church as a whole. It must be noted, however, that the vast majority of Korean churches are small or medium-sized churches and mega churches are not necessarily representative of Korean Christianity, although the influence of mega churches is a significant consideration. Among the various explanations for the rapid church growth which has contributed to the significant presence of mega churches in Korea is the strong desire to make Korea a Christian nation through the use of the Nevius method (which will be explained later). A series of national mega-Evangelistic campaigns is another explanation for the rapid church growth in the nation.

The desire for the numerical growth was strongly put forward by church leaders and Christian politicians right after liberation from the Japanese colonial occupation, in August 1945. After independence, North and South Korea were placed under separate controls: The USSR controlled North Korea and the USA controlled South Korea. This was meant to be a temporary measure. In a time of political uncertainty, Protestants in South Korea were actively involved in politics by forming political groups and organizations both within and outside the church. Most churches also strongly supported the US military authority, and some of the church members held various high ranking positions in it. The US administration and the Christians in the South shared a common perceived threat to democracy and freedom of religion, which was communism. Public opinion in Korea at that time was largely socialist, but the Protestant Church leaders were overwhelmingly capitalist or right-wing (IKCHS, 1989: 39).[1] During this turbulent time, Protestant Church leaders (along with their right-wing supporters) opposed others on the issues of the trusteeship of the Korean peninsula[2] and the attempt of Syngman Rhee, later elected as the president, and his party to establish a separate government in South Korea.

In this political climate, there was a strong movement toward making South Korea a Christian nation, especially between the years 1945 and 1948. This was expressed when the three most prominent political leaders—Kim-ku, Kim Kyu-sik, and Syngman Rhee—delivered a talk at Jeongdong Church in November 1945, in which they suggested that Korea should be built on the basis of the Bible and on *Christ, the Rock*. In particular, Rhee introduced Christian rituals into the official government ceremonies and after he was elected as the president, significant numbers of Christians were appointed to the government. Out of the 208 members of the first parliament, there were 44 Protestants (21 percent), which was a very high proportion compared to the number of Christians in the nation (5 percent of the population). There was an even higher number (38 percent) of Christians among the government ministers and deputy ministers in the first government. Christian leaders repeatedly emphasized the Christian spirit as the foundation of the new nation (IKCHS, 1989: 44).

After the Korean War (1950–1953), Protestant Churches in South Korea continued to exhibit their close association with the government, and, in turn, the government provided various favors to the Protestant Churches. One of the best examples was the adoption of military chaplaincy, which was introduced in February 1951, and, as a result, the number of Christians among the military personnel increased significantly.[3] Church leaders regarded President Rhee as having a key role in achieving *Christian Korea* and a democracy free from the communist threat. So, they openly supported his re-election campaign and presidency until Rhee's regime was overturned by a student demonstration due to corruption and fraudulent elections in 1960. This political turmoil was soon followed by a military coup by General Park Chung-hee, in 1961, which was the beginning of successive military-backed governments that lasted until 1988.

From the Protestant point of view, the achievement of *Christian Korea* was perceived to be by numerical church growth and this was part of the deliberate strategy toward the wider goal of evangelizing the whole nation. In the context of democracy in South Korea, Christians needed a majority to claim that Korea was Christian, to defeat communism, and implement the Christian program in Korea: "freedom, justice, prosperity, and peace" (Han, 2002: 86, 296). The aim of increasing the Christian population and the practice of target setting for numerical growth had been well established since the missionary period but in the new context of South Korea, self-propagation became the chief interpretation of the mission of the church. Evangelism was no longer left to the revivalists and bible women, but church members were the main means of evangelization and were mobilized into a variety of activities toward this end.

Some of the activities which led to church growth were corollaries of the nature of the Protestant Churches. In 1891, the Presbyterian missions adopted the *three-self method* of church planting (self-propagation, self-governing, and self-supporting) which had been formulated for China by the foreign missionary, John L. Nevius (Clark 1937: 86–96; Nevius, 1886). It aimed to establish a strong, independent native church which was missionary in its own right, and not dependent on the foreign mission. The Nevius method has been immensely influential for the growth and operation of local churches, as it encouraged the local congregations to be independent at as early a stage as possible. One of the legacies of this method is church communitarianism (a term that emphasizes the importance of community in the functions of life). This sense of community was especially conducive to local church growth (Lee, 2000: 177–186). Members of local congregations are very committed to their own church community, even to the extent of displaying their allegiance on their doorposts. They are encouraged to bring newcomers along to church and are highly praised when they do so. Members persuade their families and friends to attend and bring along those facing problems expecting that the church can solve them. Other people are reached through door-to-door visits in the neighborhood, street preaching, or social work (Park, 1983: 208–210). Korean Protestant Churches have been earnestly self-governing and self-supporting to the extent that this method became a stumbling block for ecumenism and the sharing of resources. The numerical strength and financial sustainability of Protestant Churches are largely a product of the zeal of Christians who have taken the three-self principle seriously.

Numerical growth was also partly due to new strategies for evangelism at a national level in the post-Korean War period. In addition to existing methods dating from the revival period of distributing tracts, visiting homes of unbelievers, and holding seasonal revival meetings, the 1950s brought chaplaincies not only in the armed forces, but also in police departments and prisons, and the use of new media, such as radio, which continued strongly for the next decades (see Kim, 1983a: 146–155). The 1950s also saw the introduction of national and inter-denominational Evangelistic campaigns, and these increased in frequency and scaled up toward the end of the 1980s. Not only were they more sustained and inclusive of different churches than earlier campaigns organized by missionaries (Lee, 2010a: 90), but these campaigns were more in the tradition of *kibock sinang*, that is, focused on seeking blessings from God, and populist in their revivalistic style and in their emphasis on the power and gifts of the Holy Spirit (Kim, 2003: 139, 157). Furthermore, whereas earlier campaigns aimed at the growth of the church community, the new ones had a nationalistic agenda. The organizers focused on the *total Christianization of this nation*. *Total evangelization* is a stark reference to the intention of converting the whole nation, and thus saving it from communism (see Adams, 1995: 13–28). Total evangelization when achieved would bring, according to the leaders, the "the amazing blessing promised in Deuteronomy 28:1–4" (Kim, 1983b: 23). Mass rallies were a characteristic feature of Protestantism in this period which encouraged the faithful as they demonstrated the popularity and power of the Christian movement.

The first nationwide evangelization campaign took place in 1965. It was initiated by Helen Kim, the president of Ewha Women's University, who invited 75 church leaders, including Kyung-chik Han and Hong Hyun-seol, principal of the Methodist Seminary, to mark the 80th anniversary of Korean Christianity. Eventually, 17 denominations were involved, even though theologically there were deep divisions within some of these groups. Even the Pentecostals, and more remarkably, the Catholics and Anglicans (the only time this happened in history) joined hands. The organizers met regularly at the Young Men's Christian Association (YMCA). The slogan for the campaign was *30 million to Christ*, the figure representing the population of South Korea at that time. The campaign took place in several phases with more than 2,000 preparatory meetings in different locations across the whole country in both rural and urban areas, also involving schools and colleges. Hong Kong Evangelist Timothy

S.K. Chao was invited for the main event which lasted for 46 days during May–June with more than 100 revival meetings in different cities. After that the campaign continued throughout the rest of the year, concluding with a rally at the Seoul Stadium on November 5. The campaigners counted a total attendance of 2,294,159, of whom 40,000 made a commitment to Christ (Clark, 1971: 416–423; Lee, 2010a: 92–93).

Such large gatherings became a feature of the 1970s, the main venue being Yoido *Plaza* on an island in the Han River, in Seoul. At first, this was an emergency military airfield. Later, the military authorities allowed Christians to use the place for Christian purposes, and people could put up tents for meetings and accommodation. The next big event was the 1973 Billy Graham Crusade with the theme—*Find a New Life in Jesus Christ*. This was a cooperative venture of almost all the Korean Protestant Churches and the Billy Graham Organization (USA), coordinated by South Korean Evangelist Billy Kim (Kim Jang-hwan). The target was *Fifty Million to Christ*: a figure intended to signify the intention to evangelize North Korea as well. In the lead-up to the main event, meetings in other cities were addressed by Billy Graham Crusade revivalists. Graham rated this as the largest evangelistic rally in the history of the church, and the organizers claimed that 1.1 million people attended the final night rally. 4,000 people stayed overnight to pray on each one of the four nights of the event—the authorities suspended the curfew in that area to make this possible. 44,000 people made *first-time decisions for Christ*. There were other mega evangelistic campaigns in the 1970s, such as *Explo '74* organized by the Campus Crusade for Christ and the *Holy Assembly for the Evangelization of the Nation* in 1977, and both drew nearly a million participants each.

These large gatherings for Protestant Christians were a demonstration of the confidence of Christians that they could make Korea a Christian nation, but it also revealed an agenda to deal with the political crisis during the time of military-backed governments in the 1960s and 1970s. Under the military-backed government dictatorship, ordinary South Koreans found it extremely difficult and dangerous to express their political views. In this context, Christians were forced into separating politics from church life. Revival and church growth were dominant concerns for church leadership. Their method was to save individuals, and they believed this would eventually lead to the salvation of the whole nation both in terms of its spiritual and political life. The reluctance of Protestants to be politically involved was both the result of deliberate and collective decisions, and also due to the historical situation brought upon them. Dichotomies in philosophy, theology, and politics contributed to this reticence toward political involvement as well (Yi, 2001: 506–508). During this time, South Korean Protestant Christianity was overwhelmingly mystical, seeking material or physical blessings and spiritual gifts through revival meetings and various prayer mountain movements. The majority of pastors saw the human rights issue under the military government as a simple matter of the *process* of development, whose goals they applauded, while they concentrated on church growth. The vision for making Korea a Christian nation, the Nevius method, and the mega evangelistic campaigns were significant factors which laid the foundation for the growth for mega churches along with sociological and demographical factors, which I will discuss next.

The Urban Demographic Changes and the Increasing Presence of Mega Churches

Perhaps, the first *mega* church in Korea was the Youngnak Presbyterian Church, which was established in the center of the capital city, Seoul. Reverend Han Kyung-chik was one of the key leaders in North-west Korea who took refuge in the South, and, in December 1945, founded the Bethany Evangelistic Church in Seoul with 27 other Sinuiju refugees (Youngnak Church, 1998: 64–68). Already by spring 1946, it had 500 members. By 1947, the site of the Bethany Church, now called the Youngnak Church, was filled with various activities. The church supported an orphanage, student hostels, and mobilized the young people to preach and offer practical help in refugee camps, slums, and rural areas. Since it was clear that there was no immediate prospect of return to the North, the congregation began work on a permanent building, using funds mainly raised by the refugees themselves. The congregation eventually constructed with their own labor, a 2,500-seat stone building in the Gothic revivalist style. Soon the sanctuary was filled to capacity at the morning service: so to cope with the demand of the growing worshipping community,

Youngnak became the first church to hold more than one service on a Sunday morning. Han maintained his vision that the church should be "a center for the evangelization of the Korean people ... a stronghold of liberal democracy ... and a source of social renewal" (2010: 377).

The spectacular growth of the Protestant Churches in Korea has naturally attracted a great deal of attention from missiologists and sociologists of religion. Chief among the theories are those that suggest that Christian growth and economic growth in South Korea from the 1960s onward were not coincidental and that both were due to the background of social change and market competition. Durkheimian theorists point out the turmoil of colonization and rural-urban migration which contributed to the destruction of traditional hierarchies and the weakening of the extended family structure, leading to rootlessness and the need for community support (Kim, 1985: 59–72). The 1960s, especially, saw a widening gap between the rich and the poor, and frequent fluctuations in the economic growth together with political instability and authoritarian rule (Lee, 2000: 177–186). In a hostile and *cut-throat* economic environment, the churches provided social facilities, practical help, welfare support, advice, healing, and encouragement, especially for new arrivals from the countryside. Amidst the widespread "unrest, chaos, tension and instability, the churches gave self-identity, offered a haven of stability and functioned as a reference group" (Jang, 2004: 140; Kim, 1985: 69; Lee, 2010a: 89; Park, 2003: 45–46). Most of all, churches engendered a sense of togetherness in striving and suffering. In Protestant Churches, this was especially felt through the dawn prayer meetings and in the Friday night prayer vigils which lasted throughout the period of military curfew.

While theories of *anomie* (a term referring to a condition of instability resulting from a breakdown of values or ideals) suggest that the churches grew as the masses sought refuge from the negative effects of economic policy, supply-side theories portray the churches as positively benefitting from the immersion in the market. After the end of the comity arrangements, without a parish system and in the context of urbanization and social Darwinism, the Protestant Churches were increasingly situated *cheek by jowl* and in competition with each other for members. In the religious marketplace created by the city and urban transport infrastructures, popular churches could potentially attract people from across a whole conurbation and easily become mega churches (Lee, 2005: 94–124). Furthermore, from the 1960s to the early 1980s, religious demand was met by an increasing supply and this convinced some that this competition actually produced growth. This supply was driven by religio-economic entrepreneurship on the part of the clergy who expected to plant, market, and grow churches for consumers of religious goods and services (Han et al., 2009: 333–360). Some theological seminaries even made planting a new church by students a graduation prerequisite.

By 1970, Korean Christianity was predominantly urban (Biernatzki et al., 1975: 28). The appearance of mega churches was facilitated by the context of urbanization (Lee, 2005: 30–38). Between 1960 and 1990, the urban population of South Korea grew from a little more than a quarter to three-quarters of the total population (28 percent to 74 percent), and the number of cities rose from 27 to 73 mainly due to migration from the countryside (Lee, 2010a: 88). In an urban setting, due to advanced transport infrastructures, large churches were not just drawing people from their own districts. The city creates a religious marketplace where religious people are turned into consumers. Churches can potentially attract people from across a whole conurbation. Not surprisingly, the growth of mega churches is often achieved by *poaching* from other churches, as people are free to exercise their preferences from one church to the other and make *horizontal moves* through incentives and benefits (Han et al., 2009: 345–346). Large churches may offer several attractions over small ones. The perceived quality and popularity of the pastor's sermons are the main attractions, together with the variety and quality of the church's pastoral and educational programs. Large churches develop their own distinctive characteristics and membership benefits conferring status, similar to that gained by membership in a *prestigious club*, or employment in a *Jaebeol* or family-run mega company (Lee, 2005: 94–124).

In the 1970s, family-run mega companies called Jaebeols dominated the economy, as Protestant pastors also looked to develop mega churches and church campaigns for growth-paralleled government plans for economic growth. The churches experienced the *bigness syndrome* in which size was measured both in numbers of members and also the size of church buildings (Kim, 1985: 71). Urban churches invested heavily in the latter with the expectation that this would pay dividends in terms of people's growth. That this expectation was not always fulfilled, it accounted for the number of empty concrete shells of church structures in Seoul and other cities by the 1980s. Church growth had become an end in itself. The motive for church growth was not only in order to achieve the goal of Korean or world evangelization, but also because, by reference to the biological sense, growth was purported to be a sign of a healthy church, and growth would ultimately ensure that the church does not die. During this period, large congregations were also sought after uncritically as a sign of divine blessing and spiritual success.

The most spectacular example of growth in a single congregation is the Yoido Full Gospel Church (YFGC). By 1965, Cho Yonggi's Full Gospel Church congregation had reached 4,000 members and was second only to the Youngnak Church in physical size. But in 1969, Cho began a new church building on a large plot on Yoido Island. From its opening in 1973, growth accelerated to 100,000 in 1979; 200,000 in 1980; 500,000 in 1985; and 600,000 in 1986. By the 1970s, YFGC had taken leadership of the Pentecostal denomination in the Korean church—both in terms of the Pentecostal Churches and also the *kibock sinang* (the emphasis on blessings) that pervaded the other Protestant Churches. The influence of YFGC on other churches can be partly measured by the prevalence of speaking in tongues across the Korean churches by 1970 (Kim, 2003: 137–138, 157). In 1976, the church established a publishing company (Yongsan) which launched the *Full Gospel News Weekly* church bulletin in 1978. The church started a TV program in 1980 and opened a TV studio in 1983. And in 1988, it began publication of *The People's Daily* (*Kukmin Ilbo*), a national newspaper.

Although YFGC is on a different scale from other mega churches, it still shares many characteristics common to Korean Protestant Churches. It uses the same version of the Bible and hymnbook, and follows a very similar order for Sunday worship. It uses the same practices of Bible study and prayer inherited from the early Korean revivals. However, YFGC differs from other churches in that it sees itself as a continuous revival movement—*365-day revival*. The YFGC has a distinctive emphasis on *salvation of the spirit* involving faith centered on the word of God, experience of the Holy Spirit, and participation in world evangelization as a *Jesus-witnessing movement*. It emphasizes the patterns of *triple prayer* and Spirit-baptism with tongues-speaking, regarded as the most common evidence of it, and divine healing as an integral part of the movement. In 1973, the church built a mountain retreat or *fasting prayer house* in

Osanli Hills, which became a defining feature of the church's ministry (Kim, 2003: 167–168), a pattern that was later followed by most of the other mega churches.

Yonggi attributes the growth of YFGC to the cell system of church organization. Although the practice of meeting in small local groups for *family worship* was widespread in Korean Protestant Churches, Yonggi adapted and systematized these as *cell groups*, as a way of devolving responsibility. Each member was included in a group in their locality, and each group had five to seven families. They meet once a week in each other's homes under a leader with an assistant. Cells are conceived as house churches after the pattern of the book of Acts in the New Testament. They meet for worship services which include the following: prescribed Bible study, prayer for new members, Spirit-baptism, healing, sharing personal problems, and prayer. The groups are used for discipleship training, pastoral care, and also as the base for various proselytizing activities. When the group reaches 10 families, it would divide and the assistant leader would take on the new group. The city of Seoul is divided into districts overseen by pastors, sub-districts with sub-pastors, and sections also with leaders (Kim, 2003: 136–137; Lee, 2004: 15).

Mega churches continued to grow numerically even after the overall Protestant numbers began to decline in the 1990s. These churches were wealthy, sophisticated in their organization, and centered on a powerful senior pastor whose sermons were disseminated online and through tapes and books. They embraced the new information technologies of the 1990s, defining themselves through their websites in ways which enhanced the status and profile of the pastor and their business-like organization. They also grasped the possibilities of new technologies as tools for evangelism, using aggressive websites, cell phone technology, and social networking systems as a means of strengthening the church networks and of penetrating deeper into members' lives (Kim, 2007: 208–224). In the first decade of the 21st century, YFGC still ranks as the largest church not only in Korea but also in the world; it has a university (Hansei) and has successfully negotiated the transition from founder–minister Cho Yonggi to second-generation Pastor Lee Yeong-hoon.

Cho Yeong-muk, the younger brother of Cho Yonggi, is the senior minster of Eunhae wa Jinri (Grace and Truth) Church in Anyang city. Incheon Full Gospel Church, pastored by Choi Sung-kyu, is also a mega church with 60,000 members. Choi makes a point of relating Christian ethics to filial piety and established Sungsan Hyo (Filial Piety) University. The largest Presbyterian Church is Myungsung Church, in Myeongil-dong, Seoul; a member of the *Tonghap* (the Korean name of a denomination, known formally in English as the Presbyterian Church of Korea) denomination boasts of 90,000 registered members in 2010 with 40,000 people attending regularly. The congregation is predominately young—80 percent are below 40 years of age—and its worship style is Charismatic. Pastor Kim Sam-hwan began the church in 1980 on the then fringes of urban development and as the area developed, three churches were built successively on the same site in 1983, 1990, and 2011 to cater to the growing numbers. The church is known especially for its early-morning prayer meetings which start every hour in the hours from 5.00 am until 9.00 am and are said to attract 50,000 in total on any single day. Kim Sam-hwan's message is popular and intended to encourage the congregation in their personal and daily life, and like most mega churches, Myungsung has a large social work and mission program. Another very large and prominent Tonghap denominational church is Somang Church, which is former President Lee Myung-bak's home church and is situated in the elite Gangnam area of Seoul. In contrast to Myungsung Church, under the ministry of Kwak Sun-hui (succeeded by Kim Ji-cheol), the worship is very restrained, and the church intentionally does not engage in evangelistic or revival meetings. The largest single congregation in the Hapdong denomination is Sarang-ui Church, Seoul, founded by Ok Han-heum, who was succeeded by Oh Jeong-hyeon. In 2009, it claimed 80,000 registered members. It puts particular emphasis on the training which lay people as disciples in an evangelistic way. Of the Methodist Churches, the largest is the Kumnan (Geumran) Church in Seoul, which grew out of a tent fellowship that started in 1957 by Kim Hwal-ran in a poor area, north of Seoul. Its pastor Kim Hong-do, who joined in 1968 as the main pastor, was the second of four brothers (all of whom are engaged in Christian ministry). Two others, Kim Seon-do and Kim Guk-do pastor two other Methodist mega churches, and the youngest Kim Geon-do has a church in Los Angeles, USA. Kumnan Church has 130,000 registered members and the new church building completed in 2000 was designed to seat 10,000 people, making it the largest Methodist church building in the world.

Characteristics, Impact, and Criticism of Mega Churches

As we have seen, mega churches have grown along with Protestant Church growth in postwar South Korea. In particular, mega churches share distinctive characteristics of Korean Protestant Churches: The ideological aim of making Korea a Christian nation through numerical growth; a conservative and Evangelical vision for a democratic and free society for religious freedom against communist threat from the North; an emphasis on the importance of local churches; the Nevius principle of self-governing, self-propagating, and self-supporting churches; enthusiasm toward evangelism with a competitive spirit; creating and maintaining various programs and groups within the church; systematic evangelism among young people, students, and conscripted soldiers; and the growth of numbers seen as a visual demonstration of success and blessing, influenced by the *church growth* school.

In addition to the rationale for the aforementioned church growth, a number of studies suggest that the presence of mega churches is largely an urban, middle-class phenomenon, reflecting individuality, anonymity, status consciousness, and being seen as on the side of the powerful class of society. Mega churches provide all these for the South Korean believers. In her study of mega churches in Seoul, Lee Kwang-soon divided the capital city into four areas: The old city center, the Gangnam area (south of Han River), the Gangdong area (east of Han River), and the Bundang area (a satellite city, south of Gangnam). She suggests that one of the key reasons for the rapid growth of mega churches in the 1970s was the fact that the Gangnam area was developed according to government policy, and this caused a mass transfer of population, along with educational institutes and commercial centers from the northern parts of Seoul to the south. Gangnam, therefore, became a very desirable and affluent residential and commercial area not as a satellite city, but as the expansion of Seoul. Lee argues that there was a close relationship between the rise of the predominantly middle or upper-middle class community in this area and the rise of mega churches in this period. The traditional churches remained in the center of *old* Seoul, for example, Youngnak Church, Jeongdong Church, and Saemunan Church; Namdaemun Church, Yeondong Church, and other Methodist Churches still maintain their prominence, but with the exception of Youngnak Church, they have remained as large churches rather than becoming mega churches (Lee, 2005: 94–124). In the same vein, Suh Woo-seok examines the rise of mega churches more specifically and makes some comparisons between two types of mega churches from a sociological perspective: middle class mega churches mainly in the Gangnam area and mixed-class congregations in the other parts of Seoul. He lists the common attractions of all mega churches as: having a modern and well-equipped building, church choirs on par with professional choirs and an orchestra, and ministers who are well known and well educated. He argues, on the basis of a survey, that whereas the congregations of the mixed-class mega churches tend to join for the sermon of the main minister, middle-class mega churches attract membership for more complex reasons, including distance from home, family opinion, anonymity, the social levels of other congregations, and the quality of various church activities (Suh, 1994: 167–171). According to Suh, the most important factors for joining mega churches are status consciousness and the individuality of religious activities.

Both Lee and Suh are right in that the mega churches are an urban phenomenon, and there is ample evidence of the establishment of mega churches in newly developed areas. However, there are some difficulties with their assertions. While the aforementioned studies provide some insights into the rapid growth of mega churches in urban areas, especially in the newly developed parts of Seoul (which could be counted as three to four mega churches), these hardly explain the characteristics of the rest of the mega churches (about 23 or more) in other parts of Seoul and other cities, nor are these best described as *middle class*. Even in what are called *middle class* mega churches in the affluent Gangnam area, there is a mixed class of people drawn from surrounding areas of Seoul. The suggestion of the shift of the population of *old* Seoul to Gangnam could explain a couple of mega churches there, but this hardly explains the majority of mega churches which were not started in newly developed residential areas. Even in the case of some mega churches which relocated to newly developed areas for space for bigger church buildings, their congregations largely consisted of their original members, since Korean Christians tend to have strong attachment to their particular church. Since mega churches draw their congregations from large areas within their respective cities (and even from other cities), the consistence of the congregation is much more complex than the aforementioned studies suggest. A key component of the growth and sustenance of mega churches seems to be the strong sense of belonging and being a part of a community which has a public presence, and therefore provides a sense of collective pride not only in spiritual, but also in public life. Although Lee and Suh assert that individuality and anonymity are characteristics valued by members of mega churches, members usually belong to a house group or geographically divided local unit (*gyogu*) and are very active in their social and spiritual sharing. These groups are key points of contact for most members for evangelistic activities and social work in their areas, supervised by assistant pastors or elders. Although the sermon of the senior minister and the various facilities provided by mega churches are important factors, as Lee and Suh suggest, the community bond of the members of mega churches is also a key factor of the growth and sustenance of mega churches, especially in the context of the internet era when people can easily access video-taped sermons of well-known pastors.

Mega churches contribute to various aspects of the life of the Korean churches, chiefly to overseas mission, social activities, and Christian non-governmental organizations (NGOs). The growth of the Korean missionary movement went hand-in-hand with the growth of mega churches. The financial contributions of mega churches to overseas mission, either through mission organizations' denominations or their own, have been very significant, although medium to large churches also make significant contributions. In 1979, there were just 93 Korean cross-cultural missionaries. This had climbed to over a thousand a decade later. It rose by an average of 25 percent per year through the 1990s to more than 8,000 in 2000 and nearly 15,000 in 2006 (Moon, 2008: 59–64). In 2011, there were more than 19,000 Korean Protestant missionaries sent out by a recognized agency, a figure which included slightly more men than women (Moon, 2012: 84–85). In 2010, South Korea was fifth in the rankings in both total missionary numbers and missionaries per capita (Todd & Ross, 2009: 259). Mega churches have been leading in the support of missionaries as well as making financial contribution to large projects, such as hospitals, educational institutions, church buildings, and social projects overseas. In the domestic scene, mega churches have been supporting churches in rural areas, ministries in industrial areas, and providing support for foreign workers through Christian NGOs. In particular, mega churches have made significant contributions to support various large humanitarian projects in North Korea, including the support of North Korean refugees who are settled in the South.

With the advent of civil society, the churches became public institutions and following democratization, new standards of accountability began to be expected in public life and merit tended to be preferred over inheritance (Han et al., 2009: 348–350). From the 1990s, there were many scandals surrounding high profile clergy and prominent church elders with a range of charges, including corruption, extravagance, nepotism, and hypocrisy (Lee, 2010b: 148; Lee, 1998: 241–243). As many studies on Korean church growth demonstrate, a key factor for the attraction of mega churches is the senior minister of the church. Consequently, even though senior ministers are highly respected, they are also subject to critical scrutiny by the general public, secular media, and especially by their own congregations. Several high profile senior ministers (such as the leader of Sarang-ui Church) were dealt with for wrongdoing by the congregation members themselves. Although the press seizes on such dramatic examples of clergy failures, there are many more counterexamples of Protestant ministers of mega churches serving their congregation and community faithfully and with integrity. In 2000, Reverend Kyung-chik Han died at the age of 98. He had been the elder statesman of the Protestant Christianity and highly respected for his simple lifestyle, humble attitude, vision for ecumenical movements, and concern for the people of North Korea. His service to society was recognized in 1992, when he was awarded with the prestigious Templeton Prize.

As the growth of mega churches is part and parcel of Korean Protestant Church growth, the criticism of mega church needs to be examined in the context of the Protestant Church in general. As part of a self-critical evaluation, a survey was conducted by the Christian Ethics Movement of Korea in October 2008.[4] To the question of *how much do you trust the Protestant Churches*—18.4 percent people said they trusted them (*trust* and *strongly trust*), but 48.3 percent of people said they did not trust them (*distrust* and *strongly distrust*). Furthermore, the response among non-Protestants to the same question was even more, marked at 7.45 percent and 57.24 percent respectively.[5] Among the major religious groups, the overall ranking of trust was: Catholics (35.2 percent), Buddhists (31.1 percent), and Protestants (18.0 percent). The main criticisms were the problem of discontinuity between words and deeds among Protestant Christians (50.8 percent), between the sermons and lifestyles of ministers (43.3 percent), and between the message and operation of the churches (34.3 percent). On the question of what needs to be changed in order to improve credibility, top on the list are church leaders (25.5 percent), followed by the operation of the churches (24.4 percent), church members (17.2 percent), evangelism (16.2 percent), and social activities (15.4 percent). The answers to the question of what the church should do in order to improve trust were: consistency of words and deeds (42 percent), tolerance toward other religions (25.8 percent), improved social services (11.9 percent), and financial transparency (11.5 percent). The survey concluded that Protestant Churches are distrusted, isolated, and facing a crisis of lack of interaction with the wider society.

Though the survey applied to Protestant Churches in general, the criticisms are applicable to mega churches as well. In particular, Kim (2013: 16) criticized the growth of mega churches as seeking the gospel of success and *cheap grace* and being a consumer community, and not the community of sharing individuals. He further argued that mega churches tend not to seek a public faith for the common good of other congregations and wider society. Instead, they seek self-expansion and self-interest regardless of the needs of others. This, he suggests, is the result of growth without depth in conjunction with faith, seeking blessing, class distinctions, materialism, individual sectarianism, competition, lavish and selfish operation of financial expenditure, and lack of Christian discipleship (Kim, 2013: 23). Kim (2005: 68) was even more critical and accused mega churches of worshipping power and possessing fundamentalist moral standards, which cause more harm than good to Korean society as a whole. Although popular among their members, mega churches are resented by many others. The Protestant mega church dominance in Korean society is not received as a blessing for all. Numerical success led to *jingoism* in Protestant rhetoric with claims that demographic advantages and political power were a blessing from God. Many had a *survival-of-the-fittest* theology which celebrated the victory of ideological Christianity over communism, its religious supremacy over other contenders, and its political dominance (Shine, 2006). Most leaders of mega churches tend to hold anti-communist, pro-American, right-wing political views, along with Evangelical and Charismatic theological perspectives and conservative attitudes to social and moral issues. Other characteristics include optimistic and dynamic preaching styles. Though the members of mega churches are sincere and dedicated in their ministry within their churches and toward wider society, they often tend to have an attitude of holding *a powerful position* and are, therefore, resented by those outside these prestigious bodies. Perhaps, the problem is not so much to do with the existence of mega churches—they are the result of God's grace and also of the dedication of the leaders and congregation—it has, I would suggest, more to do with the problem of creating a cultural environment among Protestant Churches in which numerical growth is the key sign of God's blessings—one which must be pursued at all costs.

Conclusion

The vision for a Christian Korea, which was conceived by the postliberation Christian leaders, was pursued by mega evangelistic campaigns, and this vision and practice led to the growth of dynamic mega churches. The rapid development of urban populations in major cities of South Korea, and also the rise of the middle class, accelerated the growth of mega churches with a strong sense of Korean religiosity—of belonging to a *respectable* community. These factors have made the growth and sustenance of mega churches possible. Mega churches are part and parcel of Korean Protestant Christianity, and they have made significant contributions to the life of Protestant Christianity and also to the wider segments of society, although there are serious criticisms that should not be overlooked.

Moltmann, in his book, *God for a Secular Society: The Public Relevance of Theology*, argues that theology must publicly maintain the universal concerns of God's coming kingdom because:

> ... there is no Christian identity without public relevance, and no public relevance without theology's Christian identity, [and] as the theology of God's kingdom, theology has to be *public* theology in the mode of 'public, critical and prophetic complaint to God – public, critical and prophetic hope in God.' (1999: 5–23)

According to Moltmann, the church should be an instrument of critical, prophetic, reflective, and reasoned engagement of theology in society to bring the kingdom of God to the community. The public presence of mega churches in South Korea is clearly demonstrated through the size of their buildings and the numbers of their congregations, but their public role of bringing the kingdom of God in their midst has to be constantly and critically examined. Mega churches, because they are *blessed* through God's grace, as the members claim, must also exhibit God's spirit of sharing blessings with others (not merely seeking blessings), and this area of public engagement could be a key threshold for their future prospect in South Korean society.

Notes

1. A survey in 1949 shows the following preferences among the general public: capitalism—17 percent, socialism—70 percent, and communism—13 percent.
2. The USA, the USSR, and the UK were negotiating the trusteeship of the Korean Peninsula by four nations for a maximum of five years. Syngman Rhee and his party established a separate government in South Korea.
3. The chaplaincy started with 39 ministers from the Presbyterian, Methodist, Holiness, and Catholic Churches, and in 1955, their numbers reached 352. In 1955, 26 percent of the military personnel were Christians.
4. The Christian Ethics Movement of Korea was established in 1987 by a group of 38 Christians. The five core values of the movements are: honesty and integrity; accountability and responsibility; justice and fairness; peace and communication and; care and hospitality.
5. According to the 2005 census, the number of those who are affiliated in any religious group is 24,970,000 (53.1% percent of population). Three major groups are Buddhists (22.8% percent), Protestants (18.3% percent), and Roman Catholics (10.9% percent). The majority of Protestants are Presbyterians, but there is also a strong presence of Methodist, Baptist, Holiness Churches, and Pentecostals; altogether there are 230 different denominations and groups.

Bibliography

Adams, Daniel. J. 1995. "Church Growth in Korea: A Paradigm Shift from Ecclesiology to Nationalism." In Mark R. Mullins & Richard Fox Young (eds), *Perspectives on Christianity in Korea and Japan* (pp. 13–28). Lewiston, NY: Edwin Mellen Press.

Biernatzki, William E., Luke Jin-Chang Im & Anselm K. Min. 1975. *Korean Catholicism in the 70s: A Christian Community Comes of Age*. Maryknoll, NY: Orbis Books.

Clark, Allen D. 1971. *A History of the Church in Korea*. Seoul: Christian Literature Society.

Clark, C.A. 1937. *The Nevius Plan for Mission Work*. Minneapolis: E.C. Heinz Press.
Han, Gil-soo, Joy J. Han, & Andrew Eun-gi. Kim. 2009. "'Serving Two Masters': Protestant Churches in Korea and Money," *International Journal for the Study of the Christian Church*, 9(4): 333–360.
Han, Kyung-chik. 2002. *May the Words of My Mouth: A Memorial Collection of Rev. Kyung-chik Han's Sermons*. Seoul: Youngnak Presbyterian Church.
Han, Kyung-chik. 2010. "Christianity and the Foundation of the Nation." In Kim Eun-seop (ed.), *Kyung-chik Han Collection: Sermons 1* (pp. 408–420). Seoul: Kyung-chik Han Foundation.
Institute of Korean Church History Studies (IKCHS). 1989. *A History of Korean Church I*. (in Korean) Seoul: Christian Literature Press.
Jang, Suk-man. 2004. "Historical Currents and Characteristics of Korean Protestantism after Liberation," *Korea Journal*, 44 (4): 133–156.
Kim, Byong-suh. 1985. "The Explosive Growth of the Korean Church Today: A Sociological Analysis," *International Review of Mission*, 74(293): 59–72.
Kim, Ig-jin. 2003. *History and Theology of Korean Pentecostalism: Sunbogeum (Pure Gospel) Pentecostalism*. Zoetermeer: Uitgeverij Boekencentrum.
Kim, Jay-kwon. 1983a. "The Impact of Mass Communication." In Bong-rin Ro & Marlin L. Nelson (eds), *Korean Church Growth Explosion* (pp. 146–155). Seoul: Word of Life Press.
Kim, Jin-ho. 2005. "Pro-Americanism of Korean Protestant Church: Its Colonial Unconsciousness" (in Korean), *Historical Critique* 70(Autumn): 64–88.
Kim, Joon-gon. 1983b. "Korea's Total Evangelization Movement." In Bong-rin Ro & Marlin L. Nelson (eds), *Korean Church Growth Explosion* (pp.17–50). Seoul: Word of Life Press.
Kim, Kirsteen. 2007. "Ethereal Christianity: Reading Korean Church Websites," *Studies in World Christianity*, 13(3): 208–224.
Kim, Seong-geon. 2013. "The Korean Protestant Church after Its Rapid Growth: A Sociological Study of Religion" (in Korean), *Korean Christianity and History*, 38:5–45.
Lee, Kwang-soon. 2005. *Growth and Undergrowth of the Korean Church* (in Korean). Seoul: Mission Academy.
Lee, Timothy S. 2010a. *Born Again: Evangelicalism in Korea*. Honolulu: University of Hawaii Press.
Lee, Won-gue. 1998. *What is it all about the Korean Church?* (in Korean). Seoul: Methodist Theological Seminary Publishing.
Lee, Won-gue 2000. *Where is the Korean Church Going?* (in Korean). Seoul: Christian Literature Society.
———. 2010b. *The Crisis and Hope of Korean Church from the Perspective of Religio-Sociology* (in Korean). Seoul: Korean Methodist Church.
Lee, Young-hoon. 2004. "The Life and Ministry of David Yonggi Cho and the Yoido Full Gospel Church", *Asia Journal of Pentecostal Studies*, 7(1): 3–20.
Moltmann, Jürgen. 1999. *God for a Secular Society: The Public Relevance of Theology*. London: SCM Press.
Moon, Steve Sang-cheol. 2008. "The Protestant Missionary Movement in Korea: Current Growth and Development," *International Bulletin of Missionary Research*, 32(2): 59–64.
———. 2012. "Missions from Korea 2012: Slowdown and Maturation," *International Bulletin of Missionary Research*, 36(2): 84–85.
Nevius, J.L. 1886. *Methods of Mission Work*. Shanghai: American Presbyterian Missions Press.
Park, Cho-choon. 1983. "The Dynamics of Young Nak Presbyterian Church Growth." In Bong-rin Ro & Marlin L. Nelson (eds), *Korean Church Growth Explosion* (pp. 208–210). Seoul: Word of Life Press.

Park, Chung-shin. 2003. *Protestantism and Politics in Korea*. Seattle: University of Washington Press.
Shine, Yun-shik. 2006. *Korea Church Power I & II*. Seoul: Christian Council of Korea.
Suh, Woo-seok. 1994. "A Sociological Study of Middle Class Mega Churches" (in Korean), *Korean Sociology*, 28 (summer): 151–71.
Todd, M. Johnson & Kenneth R. Ross (eds). 2009. *Atlas of Global Christianity, 1910-2010*. Edinburgh: Edinburgh University Press
Yi, Mahn-yeol. 2001. *Korean Christianity and the National Unification Movement* (in Korean). Seoul: Institute of the History of Christianity in Korea.
Youngnak Church. 1998. *Fifty Years of History of Youngnak Church, 1945-1995* (in Korean). Seoul: Youngnak Church.

5

Marketing the Sacred: The Case of Hillsong Church, Australia

Jeaney Yip

Introduction

Religions have been argued to be *faith brands* (Einstein, 2008) that have blurred the line between marketing and religion. The concept of branding churches as a marketing activity is recent (Twitchell, 2004), although the proposition of religion being commodified and secularized is not novel. Rather than confirming this established proposition, the question becomes exactly *how* does the marketing discourse transform religious organizations into the business of branded religion. Religion by nature is not commercial; therefore, the proposal that a religious faith can be turned into a consumable and marketable good deserves scrutiny.

Using a highly successful Australian mega church as a case study—*Hillsong*—globally known in the contemporary worship music genre, I demonstrate how the church is able to strategically draw upon the marketing discourse, embedded in discursive practices and mediated by organizational, linguistic, and socio-cultural resources in order to construct its form of branded religion. Given the phenomenal growth and success of Hillsong in the Australian Christian landscape amidst a national decline (some *terminal* according to Bouma, 2006) of church membership in traditional Christian denominations, this case offers a site of investigation that is insightful to the scholarship of mega churches in the South.

I argue that in engaging with the marketing discourse, mega churches do not resist, but reify and reproduce ideologies related to the market and business which transform their own identities. This deliberate process of engagement changes the structure and substance of organized religion. Hillsong is able to destabilize traditional conceptualizations of religion and church by attaching familiar, secular images and signs from popular culture which have references to associated feelings and desires. This is evident in the production of artifacts so central to its own brand of religion that it reproduces these feelings and desires by offering the opportunity and agency to create a personal, individualized, and practical synthesis of Christian theology. Rather than resisting the ideologies and practices of the marketplace, this church embraces them and instead chooses to strategically distance itself from shared cultural understandings of religion's traditional past practices and doctrines. Hillsong Church in fact *de-religionized* organized religion into a spiritual product with its own brand.

Marketing and Mega Churches

There is a burgeoning interest in the connection between marketing and religion (Mottner & Ford, 2010). Despite interest in and established connection with mega churches, marketing and religion *is* an unusual cultural development (Bauman, 1998; Lyon, 2000). Religion by nature is *not commercial* (Strasser, 2003: 3). When religion adopts market logics, the result is religious commodification which "turns a religious faith or tradition into consumable and marketable goods" (Kitiarsa, 2010: 565). This development suggests that religion and the market are not at war with each other (Einstein, 2008). It is also an established observation that mega churches represent a secularized form of traditional religion (Ostwalt, 2003). To explore this, I turn to the marketing discourse for insights about its perpetuating influence in terms of how it structures, reproduces, and dominates in increasingly *non-business* spheres.

Marketing is best understood as a set of practices and discourses that reflects, produces, and is constituted by a particular kind of society (Brownlie et al., 1994; Hackley, 2003; Morgan, 2003). Marketing uncritically supports the existing structure of consumption, which only serves management interests and focuses on the consumer "only when the consumer enters a buying situation in the market" (Firat and Dholakia, 1982: 14). The notion of marketing as discourse can be approached in two ways: First, marketing as a form of managerial discourse, and, second, marketing and its effects on consumption (Skålén et al., 2008). The former focuses on management's prescription to be a *marketing-oriented* organization, and the latter focuses on the need to understand the *market* (that is, the customers). These two perspectives are interrelated and complementary—together they help to explain how marketing discourse functions as a *facilitator of consumerism* (O'Shaughnessy and O'Shaughnessy, 2007). Marketing as a form of discourse therefore is not neutral, and can shape practices that serve its own purposes while centralizing the individual consumer.

This chapter is built upon a critical perspective in terms of how the marketing discourse leaves its mark, and traces not only in language but in church practice. The chapter does not attempt to ascertain whether mega churches should market themselves or not. It explores how Hillsong Church uses elements of religious traditions and other familiar, appealing discourses to produce artifacts and experiences that resonate with contemporary consumption ideals. Using organizational discourse analysis (Grant et al., 2004), I specifically demonstrate this through the church's music business operation, branding, and drawing of consumerist discourses in order to make Christianity *marketable*. The artifacts and textual data presented here are predominantly based on the period between 2003 and 2010, from both an *emic* and *etic* perspective.[1]

Hillsong Church: Big and Successful

The Hillsong brand name originated from the church itself and through its best-selling product, its music label; in 1983, it was known as the Hills Christian Life Centre. It was an extension of the Sydney Christian Life Centre, which was started by Pastor Frank Houston in 1977, who passed away in 2004 (Gibbs, 2004). The current senior pastor and son of Frank Houston, Brian Houston, and his wife Bobbie, took full control of the church and rebranded it as Hillsong Church in 1999 (Clark, 2004). Hillsong currently has five *campuses* operating in Australia: Sydney city, a Sydney suburb called Baulkham Hills, a southwest campus in Campbelltown on the outskirts of Sydney, a Brisbane campus which was added in 2009 after a take-over of a local existing church, and Melbourne. *Extension Services* are located throughout Sydney, usually based on particular ethnic cultures. Apart from its campuses, Hillsong has become a family of brand names, which is an umbrella to its various ministries, including Hillsong Music,

Hillsong Kids, Hillsong Women (renamed the Colour Sisterhood), Hillsong Men, Hillsong Conference, Hillsong Citycare, Hillsong Leadership College, Hillsong TV, Hillsong Performing Arts Academy, and Hillsong Health Centre. Multiple services (up to eight in the City campus and five in the Hills campus) are held simultaneously over the weekend, featuring a suite of various pastors/speakers. Its messages are professionally and sophisticatedly scripted, while its pastors are highly Charismatic and *telegenic*. The senior pastor of the organization, Brian Houston, has a high public profile and is the face of Hillsong.

Hillsong Church is regularly cited as Australia's largest independent church with over 25,000 attendees (Payne & Cheng, 2007; Riches & Wagner, 2012; Zwartz, 2006). Although it is connected to the Pentecostal denomination of the Assemblies of God (AoG Movement, grouped in Australia as the Australian Christian Churches or ACC in which Hillsong's Senior Pastor Brian Houston was the former president), Hillsong does not make a direct link to this movement explicitly in its corporate communications. This connection is evidenced implicitly by practice and theology (Charismatic worship/preaching style, belief in miracles, emphasis on the Holy Spirit, experiential-focussed), rather than by an explicit label (AoG is not mentioned, referred to, or identified in any Hillsong artifacts, including the *About Us* section of the corporate website). Its de-affiliation with any denomination or movement suggests a market positioning that is based on its own brand, differentiated from any traditional churches or denominations.

Hillsong estimates that it earned AUD$60 million in 2008, half of which came from its congregation (Marriner, 2009), but the issues of transparency and accountability have always been closed and sensitive while subjected to media scrutiny (Ferguson, 2006). This has led to much scrutiny and criticism to which the church routinely responds:

> There's no doubt that our church breaks Australia's perception of Christianity. Hillsong church today has facilities valued somewhere near $100 million. In our last accounting period, the total income was fifty million dollars. I think that the idea of a church being big and successful and effective threatens some people. And there are certain people who point at motives and try to make them shallow or try and marginalise our motives. I just don't feel like I can be ruled by that. I feel we have to stay committed to what we're called to do. (cited in *The Life of Brian*, 2005c)

Bobbie Houston's excerpts below equate the church to a King's home, in a regal and worldly sense, which should be full of *lush and lavish things*. She argues that it is the *enemy* (aka the devil) that has blocked this kind of big thinking and left the church *contained and impoverished*. Theologically, this misalignment is rather obvious, but organizationally it is legitimized into a positive purpose as summarized as follows:

> I know this is a bit-in-your-face, but someone has to say it. For too long, the enemy has kept huge pockets of the Church contained and impoverished through small thinking. Sadly, this is not a true representation of our incredible King. This may come as a shock to some, but I don't think God has a problem with lush or lavish things. Now I'm certainly not suggesting you can make 'lush and lavish things' an idol in your life, but I'm talking about the splendours of our King finding a home in our lives. (Houston, 2001: 156)
>
> I understand that there is a perception about wealth or personal wealth, you know, I understand that does exist out there. But again, it's all about resourcing people's lives to actually make a difference. And the truth is, you know, there is so much need in our city, and our nation, and you know, if you have nothing, you can actually do nothing about it. And so the whole heart of our church is to seriously be resourced so that we can actually make a difference. (cited in *Interview with Bobby Houston*, 2005b)

An analysis of this statement, *to seriously be resourced* implies that one has the ability to *have everything* as this is juxtaposed with *nothing* ("if you have nothing, you can actually do nothing about it"). While *resource* is abstract, its meaning here is positive and empowering. In addition, *resource* is the term used to label the products and merchandise that the church offers, of which music is an integral part of its business operations.

Through its branding and market expansion strategies, Hillsong Church is intentionally and strategically building its *mega* identity. It is mega because of the size of its attendance, which is created by offering attractive artifacts, which is appealing to the current religious consumer. It is mega, and therefore seen as successful by other churches who may be struggling with attendances. A mega-congregation reproduces mega-outcomes in other areas of the church operations, such as tithing and donations, volunteering in church ministries and programs, and presenting a sizable market for other potential endeavors, such as conferences, events, seminars, and its products. By using popular music that acts as the magnet for attendees and revenue, the church is able to sustain and even grow its *mega* identity. Given its market expansion strategies to widen its distribution base, Hillsong music is undoubtedly a major artifact that the church constantly uses in enacting and perpetuating its brand of religion.

The Business of Music and I

For Hillsong Church, its music label is undoubtedly a central part of its worship practice, and thus is an important signifier of the church's identity. Moreover, because of its commercial success and high profile, it is a key identity artifact for the church as illustrated in the following quote from its senior pastor, Brian Houston: "I could write about many areas of our church, but the best known would be Hillsong's praise and worship. Over the years our music has been accredited with more than thirty gold and platinum sales awards worldwide and is distributed in some eighty nations" (2008: 30).

Music is the church's major business operation. Hillsong Music Australia is the church's music label that produces contemporary Christian music, sung in many churches worldwide. It produces praise and worship albums for church (Hillsong Live) and youth ministries (Hillsong United), as well as a children's album. Hillsong is a market leader in this genre of music in Australia and it plays a big role not only in promoting this form of music, but also in capitalizing its popularity for its own identity and corporate goals. Hillsong's influence worldwide is not to be understated as can be seen by this comment made in a Christian magazine published by Matthias Media (a publishing company affiliated with the Sydney Anglican Church):

> ... whether you travel across the urban areas of Asia, Africa, North America or Australia, everywhere you go, increasingly, the singing in the church—both the songs that are sung and the style of music—is the same. It's the McDonaldization of our world. And in every church you visit across the world, the music is just the same. I'd describe it as the '*Hillsongization*' of music except that it's such a clumsy word. (Raiter, 2008: 13)

The popularity of Hillsong's church music exemplifies the church's success in penetrating the global Christian music industry. This phenomenal music success has been analyzed elsewhere (McIntyre, 2007; Riches, 2010; Riches & Wagner, 2012); its internationalization and expansion strategy was consolidated in 2010, when it entered into an arrangement with the EMI Christian Music Group (CMG) label to market its music in the USA, Canada, and Latin America markets, a distributor position previously held by Integrity Music for 14 years. EMI recognizes Hillsong as "one of the world's fastest growing evangelical ministries and a global force in Christian music."[2] This global growth and presence was enhanced in 2012 through the release of *The Global Project*, in which a collection of its songs was recorded in nine languages (Spanish, Portuguese, Korean, Chinese, Indonesian, German, French, Swedish, and Russian) through partnership with local churches.

At the level of language, analysis of Hillsong artifacts reveals an individual-based theology that consistently focuses on the individuals and their personal relationship with God. This was evident in the dominant usage of *leitourgic*[3] (Woods et al., 2007) songs that express praise to God from the individual believer. They are usually unidirectional (from believer to God), couched in personal language that tend to be egocentric in that the focus is *me*, the individual expressing response, praise and/or request to God (Pass, 2007). In Hillsong songs, leitourgia is facilitated by the heavy use of personal pronouns, such as *you, I*, or *me*. The *you—me* address to God is also personalized, which contrasts with nominalization of God as *God* or *The Mighty One*, for example. God is, thus, constructed in relation to the individual believer in a highly personalized form. The intimacy of *you and me* introduces a spirit of closeness, warmth, and approachability that is meant to communicate difference from the traditional stereotype of religion that denotes doctrines, authority, and rules. The music is, thus, created to invoke a subjective, personal, and emotional outpouring of worship between *Jesus and me*, which occurs in a collective mega setting.

Fairclough (1989: 37) terms this as a form of synthetic personalization which is "a compensatory tendency to give the impression of treating each of the people handled 'en masse' as an individual." This mode of communication is prevalent in the advertising genre, in which a direct address to *you* refers to consumer authority (Keat et al., 1994). Therefore, synthetic personalization is actually a form of manipulation of interpersonal meanings for strategic and instrumental purposes (Fairclough, 1994). It is a discursive strategy used to build rapport and to make the individual feel special and important amidst a large and generic audience that is otherwise impersonal and anonymous. In effect, the individual believer is treated as a religious consumer in order to invoke their identity in a special kind of *simulated intimacy* (Baudrillard, 1998: 13), which is complemented by the *we* of church as a community of believers. This intimacy is simulated because the context where the form of synthetic personalization is occurring is a mass setting. The challenge for this branded church is to appeal to the masses in order to sustain its mega church identity, and yet convey intimacy in its execution and address to the religious consumers for them to feel that their spiritual needs are being met. One of the ways of achieving this is through strong use of individualist language and discourse in its artifacts and execution. Linguistically and discursively, this is used to invoke individual agency and create a personalized atmosphere at the same time that it can be experienced immediately in the midst of the church service. A *personal relationship* is, thus, constructed albeit in a simulated setting. Leitourgic songs tend to move in a seamless flow toward building up an awareness of the manifest presence of God, the intended atmosphere to be experienced by the church-goer in the mega church. This notion of *the presence of God* constructs an experiential form of moment in worship that is emotionally intense. Because the *presence of God* is abstract and ethereal, it can only be experienced by the church's construction of the worship atmosphere which the mega church creates through its music. The *atmosphere of worship* that is inundated with the presence of God is distinctive of Hillsong Church, and this form of worship is present in all church services and gatherings of any kind. The practice of worship, therefore, becomes a conduit for self-expression, while the church becomes the facilitator and enabler for this practice through its music and atmosphere.

Through the use of leitourgic songs which emphasize God and I, repetition and a memorable tune invokes this experience of the presence of God in a trance-like manner. Therefore, the presence of God which is ethereal is framed into an emotional experience that can be experienced subjectively by the individual in a congregation through the music. Music is considered one of the most powerful triggers of strong emotions (Gabrielsson, 2001) and can be used to elicit or even modify emotions (Rickard, 2004). In this view, it is relatively easy to understand the reasons behind the use of leitourgic music as it is more likely to elicit higher emotional relatedness which in turn facilitates experiential highs during worship. The mega church's production team works toward *creating* this spiritual presence through the deliberate orchestrating of tempo, rhythm, lyrics, lighting, stage effects, and gestures of performers on stage. This experiential form of worship is a Hillsong specialty that has become the standard of worship emulated by other churches nationally and globally.

Through leitourgia, it is demonstrably evident that Hillsong's music is predominantly created to allow for self-expression, thus elevating the individual—a central tenet in marketing discourse as part of its customer-centeredness. This form of self-expression is understandably important in a mega-sized congregation in order to individualize the experience. The prominence of Hillsong's music is not solely deployed for so-called worship purposes, but is a sophisticated major element of the church's business operation. The church produces this music in order to sing and sell, thereby taking into account the "perceived needs of the congregation" (Riches, 2010: 118) in *making* this music. The church then uses this music as an atmosphere builder and a conduit for self-expression. The music assures the success of the church service experience, for without the music there is no Hillsong experience. This music enacts what Hillsong Church is, and it is its music that it is globally most well known for.

Branding a Church

Branding *is* a marketing strategy, but it is also a part of management practice (Schultz et al., 2005) as well as being a tangible identifier of the organization. Therefore, the values, ideologies, ethos, people, products, and basically *anything* the organization wants to be identified with is enacted and communicated explicitly through the brand. A corporate brand sketches the organization's external profile (Kapferer, 2002: 187); it is also a "conscious distillation of identity" (Leitch & Motion, 2007: 72) and an "explicit covenant" (Balmer & Greyser, 2003) between the organization and its audiences. This covenant is a powerful (albeit informal) form of contract in that customer and other stakeholders often have a "religious-like loyalty" to the corporate brand (ibid., 737). Therefore, the practice of branding is a strategic tool designed to build loyalty toward the whole corporation. This is a specific strategy that, when successful, can be leveraged to other market strategies, such as launching new products and diversifying to other markets. After all, brands are "meticulously produced in order to make profits" (Kornberger, 2010: 13). Seen in this strategic way, branding is a highly managed practice that is expected to produce certain outcomes, and not an organic or natural evolution, as claimed by Riches and Wagner (2012). By virtue of branding practice, an organization uses and expects its brand to deliver results, which Hillsong Church has successfully demonstrated.

While Christianity is a belief system, Hillsong is a monolithic corporate brand where its name is used on all of its offerings. Hillsong Church is explicit about engaging with marketing practices. It is a client of BMCFerrell, a US-based church marketing consultancy firm that specializes in media placement, message impact development, and identity development. They are featured in the company's website[4] as *the church that never sleeps*, along with predominantly American churches. Domestically, Hillsong has also employed a creative design firm as part of its brand building strategy.[5] This explicit use of a marketing strategy appears to have resulted in positive outcomes for the church, for it is considered one of the top Australian brands (Marcus, 2008). It is also considered a "true BE brand" (Hammond, 2006), which creates a sense of belief and belonging that fosters loyal behavior from its customers. The church has even been labeled as "Australia's most powerful brand" by a marketing website.[6] It is interesting to note the senior pastor's explicit use of the language of branding as exemplified as follows:

> One of the things we haven't really tried to do is establish the Hillsong brand everywhere. There's only three Hillsongs in the world. We've got one in London, we've got one in Kiev and we've got the one here in Sydney. We have a relationship with churches and we've planted churches in many, many other places, but that name Hillsong we haven't sort of allowed to go out and be used everywhere. (*Interview with Brian Houston*, 2005a)

Since this interview, the church brand has expanded to include a current total presence in the following locations: London, Paris, Kiev, Cape Town, Stockholm, Moscow, Konstanz Germany, New York, Amsterdam, Copenhagen, and, domestically, Brisbane and Melbourne. Brian Houston has also explicitly mentioned "Europe" (Marriner, 2009) for future expansion. Given these market expansion strategies to widen its distribution base, Hillsong Church is undoubtedly taking an active role in employing practices that perpetuate its brand. Hillsong's branding strategy also sophisticatedly involves the idea of *storytelling*, advocated by advertising and branding practitioners as a powerful tool that can influence, shape, reinforce, and engage audiences toward a brand.[7] The storytelling provides an additional *touch point* for consumers to interact with the brand, which Hillsong developed through its blog page.[8] This page offers *stories* written by Hillsong leaders and staff which *inspire and encourage everyday people*, including a tactical section on why *digital storytelling* is important as *your content defines you*—"The content you create and publish shapes how people perceive you; it shapes your brand".[9]

Hillsong's branding and market expansion strategies so far appear to be achieving a hegemonic status in contemporary church practice, evidenced by Hillsong's success and the emulation of its style by smaller churches all over Australia. This is part of a more general dominance of marketing ethos increasingly used in the spiritual marketplace. Hillsong's size and market dominance, in both music and church practice, have resulted in *me–too* or follower strategies by the smaller churches striving to emulate, what is perceived as, a successful role model. This is supported by Houston's comment; he sees it as a mandate that the Hillsong's order of practice be the example for smaller churches to follow. This is a significant effect that is a consequence of its successful corporate brand, further reinforced by its website,[10] to "develop a unified digital brand and user experience."[11] Because of its success, size, and stature, Hillsong Church perceives itself as *the* brand to not only emulate, but to build the Church generically.

> I don't want to just build a Hillsong Church; I want to be a builder of 'The Church'. So I definitely want a Church that is impacting, and we will certainly from time to time spread our wings and start a new initiative. But I see our mandate as not just starting millions of Hillsong churches everywhere; it's really about championing the cause and the local churches. In other words, I would like to think we can be an example to help smaller churches grow. (Houston, cited in Clark, 2004)

By being non-denominational and producing music using its own brand, Hillsong is able to expand its market reach which has resulted in churches of various denominations singing its songs in various languages. This is consistent with the philosophy of corporate branding in that it aims to foster loyalty to the corporation in the long term in order to build the brand which can be subsequently extended to other kinds of offerings progressively. Apart from selling merchandise, the church runs a Bible college, a performing arts academy, a health center, and offers developmental courses (ranging from *Christian Discovery* to *Divorce Care* to *How to Manage your Frustration*), all on a fee-paying basis. Marketing, by its very nature, draws upon popular culture and market appeal in order to sell merchandize, and, in this context, the music, books, and recorded sermons/messages/events (that is, the corporate artifacts), form a major part of this mega church's business operations. In fact, its business arrangement in 2010 with EMI CMG as a strategy of expanding its music in the USA, Canada, and Latin America markets extends to the church's *resources*, which includes its books and basically any other type of resource produced by the church and its leaders. The church, therefore, is on a strategic mission to expand the business and distribution of its corporate artifacts internationally.

Appealing to the Consumer: Choosing and Having

Brands exist in the mind of the consumer, and its strategy involves the deliberate scripting of particular meanings, associations, and aspirations that the brand wants to be known for, in the mind of the consumer. Hillsong is a brand of religion that promises individuals the ability to make material and empowering changes for the better in their lives. Rather than denigrating contemporary consumerism and material aspirations, Hillsong frames these as worthy expressions of Christian faith by mixing references with consumption and popular culture. This reference involves ideas and values which are related to consumption or consumer culture, such as choice, desires for material possessions, wants and instant gratifications, as well as omission of negative connotations deemed *unappealing* to consumers. The notion of choice is present biblically as the verse in Deuteronomy (30: 19, NIV) demonstrates: "This day I call heaven and earth as witnesses against you that I have set before you life and death, blessings and curses. Now choose life so that you and your children may live."

Some have interpreted this biblical position on the notion of choice to imply free will; God gave people the option to choose Him. The choices, though, are presented by God (life, death, blessing, and curses) and commanded by Him for individuals to *choose life*. So, while individuals are given the option to choose, it is from preselected alternatives ultimately determined by the "will of God" (Ezra 7: 18). In fact, this notion of choice emphasizes God's sovereignty, rather than the individual's (for example, Proverbs 16:9 states that "in his heart a man plans his course, but the Lord determines his steps"). Therefore, the biblical notion of choice is not the kind of choice that completely renders sovereignty to the individual. On the contrary, it is God declaring ultimate sovereignty when it comes to choice in John 15:16 (NIV): "You did not choose me but I chose you and appointed you to bear fruit—fruit that will last."

In contrast, choice is also a classic consumerist ideology which characterizes our modern lifestyle (Slater, 1997). This type of choice is one that completely liberalizes the authority of the consumer. The exercise of free personal choice is central practice in consumer culture that not only renders the consumer sovereign, but implies unconstrained free will that the individual consumer can exercise in the market in order to make any kind of consumption choices deemed meaningful to the individual. These meaningful choices may serve needs, construct personal identities, aestheticize lifestyle, or enhance well being, but it is the act of choosing that is central. Slater (1997: 27) states, "[T]o be a consumer is to make choices: to decide what you want, to consider how to spend your money to get it." This is a compelling connection to freedom that implies choice as given in the pursuit of private comforts, desires, and aspirations through whatever means or resources that are deemed to be meaningful by the consumer. How a consumer makes these choices is a separate matter, but it is the very notion of choice that accentuates free will in consumption.

The economic rhetoric of the *marketplace* speaks of a free market and a consumer who is free to choose; a stance which is familiar in a modern consumer society. This familiar stance is reproduced here. Through this consumerist discourse, Houston uses choice to frame it as an entirely individual agency as the excerpt as follows demonstrates:

> Every choice we make has a consequence, so how we choose to use our money can have positive or negative results. Deuteronomy, Chapter 30, brings our life down to basic choices. It talks about blessing and cursing, and brings it right back to choices. God doesn't choose it for you—YOU make the choice. You choose whether money will bless or damage your life. (Houston, 1999: 43)

This notion of choice and the act of choosing imply that there are options which shift the sovereignty to the believer as consumer. Choice in this excerpt is also linked to money. Even though Houston cited Deuteronomy 30, which is the verse that presents God's offer of choice to individuals, he replaced the choices presented by God as "life, death, blessings and curses", as stated in the original verse to encourage individuals to choose their attitude toward money instead. Also in the Bible verse, God *commanded* the choice for individuals to make ("now choose life so that you and your children may live"). But in this excerpt, Houston reframed the verse to simply one that is about choice and shifts the center of choice to the individual ("God doesn't choose it for you—You make the choice"). He is invoking the authority of the consumer and its subject position of exercising free personal choices when it comes to how they want to spend their money. This is a classic consumerist notion of choice which always implicates the self and is contrary to the biblical notion of choice.

Another explicit demonstration of the consumerist discourse is seen in a 2002 (revised in 2008) book written by the pastor's wife, Bobbie Houston, *I'll Have What She's Having*, which is titled after the orgasm scene from the 1989 film *When Harry met Sally*. While she asks the audience to *forget the movie for a moment*, the fact remains that it is the title of the book, and a Christian is encouraged to pursue life as if it were an orgasm. Houston expressively and deliberately used a title from a movie that depicted a *fake orgasm* scene, but then rhetorically attempted to detract from the movie by asking readers to concentrate instead on the meaning of the word *orgasm*, which she defined as *height, summit, zenith*.

> 'I'll have what she's having!' Yes? No? Or absolutely! In the scene I referred to earlier from the movie *When Harry met Sally*, Sally fakes an orgasm. The word orgasm means 'height, summit, zenith'. Now forget the movie for a moment. Shouldn't who we are in Christ reach the summit, zenith, the utmost heights in life? I think so! When it comes to life, let's not settle for a fake experience; let's go for the genuine article. There are so many things capable of containing this wonderful journey, so let's look at some of them and break the containment that limits so many. (Houston, 2008: 30)

The relevance of the scene to the point Houston is making is tenuous, but it illustrates Hillsong's practice of using attention-grabbing titles drawn from popular culture in the production and promotion of their artifacts.

The framing of this aspect of the consumerist discourse is that it is natural (not sinful) to *want what others have* and that Christians ought to be living a lifestyle worthy of the envy of others:

> Our goal should be to have stories of powerful testimony, where a woman may look at another woman who is skilful in managing a home, a marriage, a business, or whatever, and ponder, 'How does she do it?' In her heart she may silently say, 'I want what she's got'. Then one day (somewhere in this equation of friendship), the pondering one will actually ask, 'What makes you tick? I want what you've got.' (ibid., 50–51)
>
> We have countless friends and colleagues whose winning experience proves you can have it all. A little God-wisdom, a little sensitivity, some clever planning, respect for the seasonal ebb and flow of life, and a sense of determination has them enjoying God, church, passion, kids, family, friends, and others. The cat and the dog get fed, the in-laws are happy, and hopefully the garden is a good testimony. (ibid., 58)

In relation to human desires, wanting somebody else's lifestyle is natural and normal (as demonstrated by the two excerpts above), rather than something to be avoided and denigrated. While *wanting* is an extremely common consumerist discourse, its use in church artifacts suggests a deliberate strategy which plays upon human desires for the ideal life that enhances the appeal toward the Hillsong brand of religion. Hillsong promotes aspiration to the *ideal life* where you can *have it all*, and where prosperity and success are compatible with spirituality. Because this brand of church promotes *winning experiences*, individuals who represent such success become positive role models for aspirational desires and actions.

Exploiting this notion further, offering what is *appealing* to the market becomes part of the de facto practice under the marketing discourse. Messages, products, and communication produced, therefore, deflect any negative connotations that are *un-market friendly*. An intriguing finding that demonstrates this point explicitly is found in Hillsong's 2006 album, *Mighty to Save*. On the last page of the CD cover of this album, a Bible verse from 2 Chronicles 7:14 is quoted. What is noteworthy is that this verse, as printed on the cover, is an incomplete reference to the verse. The complete version from the New International Version is stated as follows, and the words italicized are the missing components from the Hillsong cover: "If my people, who are called by my name, will humble themselves and pray and seek my face *and turn from their wicked ways*, then will I hear from heaven and will forgive their sin and will heal their land" (2 Chronicles 7:14).

Hillsong's selective quotation still made sense in the *edited* verse, but the abbreviated version attempts to make prominent God's call for salvation without the overtly negative prerequisite of repentance, or the connotation of people as *wicked*. By use of a selective quotation, the church omits overtly negative constructions, and instead reconstructs God and salvation only in a positive light. Salvation, therefore, is *recontextualized* into an organizational construction that is consistent with the interests of the church.

Conclusion

Hillsong Church is a branded church embedded in the marketing discourse in order to perpetuate its own brand of religion. Marketing produces practices, such as the sale of products and services, building and managing the brand, as well as drawing upon familiar and attractive consumerist discourses in creating appeal to the brand. These practices, while being part and parcel of the marketing of consumer products and brands, are not commonly and traditionally associated with a *non-business* context, such as a church. In other words, Hillsong knows how to market itself in ways which are deemed attractive to its target market. This is the self-reinforcing logic of marketing, for if the market is ignored or neglected, organizations that are unable to cater to specific needs will suffer. Markets are also dynamic by nature; therefore, the scripting of ideas, products, and messages in relation to the current market appeal will change and cause mega churches to be mindful of these changes and adapt accordingly.

This is not to say that the church does not promote Christianity; however, marketing is a discourse that can exert its dominance and ideology through transforming religious organizations, such as mega churches into businesses. This discourse actually affects religion as demonstrated through the ways in which Hillsong successfully employs marketplace discourses and deploys strategies to make it more marketable and generate more business. Through the use of popular music that speaks to individual agency, branding practices that lead to market expansion, as well as drawing upon familiar, consumerist discourses, the church organizes itself in such a way that is relevant for today's *religious consumers*. By engaging in marketing, an organization automatically inherits the ideologies and strategies that embrace the market model, which is to achieve results. With this emphasis on achieving results, it is no surprise that mega churches, given their fixation on size, employ marketing techniques and embrace its philosophy. One might argue that it is the mega church's engagement with marketing that explains its size, which is considered necessary to sustain its ongoing business. To grow in size, a church needs not to only attract new customers, but also to maintain existing ones. Marketing provides the "activities and processes" to do so which inherently focuses on the customer (Firat & Dholakia, 1982).

The market is not simply a process that facilitates exchanges, but an all-encompassing social principle (Mautner, 2010) that leaves its imprint on the language of the church. Language choice is not ad hoc; this mega church selected the language and discourses of the market in producing artifacts that so centrally refers to the individual and associated consumerist ideologies. Regardless of whether the function is to inform, convert sinners, empower, or simply to entertain, the church draws upon and mirrors the market mode signifier. It appears that religion cannot escape the hegemony of the market. This hegemony has influenced mega churches to behave as if they are operating in a marketplace, thus being concerned with branding strategies and market-friendly product offerings. While this case study is a demonstration of successful religious marketing, what it also exemplifies is that there appears to be no field, product, or ideology (not even God) that is exempt from this dominant discourse and the hegemonic influence of the market. This, however, is not the only premise that this chapter aims to illuminate. Marketing is not based on mere language use, nor is it simply a set of strategies to communicate, or even to sell. Its practice and ideology are capable of substantively reforming, reordering, and restructuring contents and practices. Therefore, highlighting marketing's function in a non-business entity is not a question of applicability or simply as a use of a *medium*, but it ought to be used as a critique of why it is so pervasive that even salvation does not appear to stand in its way. In the process of transporting the marketing discourse to the realm of religion (or any context for that matter), the practice and substance of religion change (ibid.). Business practices are not *neutral*; they are girded by an underlying and unshakeable principle of making profits. And as long as mega churches continue to openly embrace and engage with the marketing discourse, it cannot be presumed that the original and timeless teachings of the Gospel do not get tainted in the process. As Riches and Wagner (2012: 20) point out, "these mega churches understand that the medium is still the message and that the message is most effective when it is a brand." Marketing *is* the medium; the message *is* the Gospel and *not* a brand. This business of religion is booming, but whether it is ultimately and authentically the *good news* that is being so successfully marketed, is left to the individual believer to discern.

Notes

1. An *emic* approach (sometimes referred to as *insider* or *bottom-up*) has as its starting point, the perspectives, descriptions, and words of research participants who are on the inside of a religious or cultural group. In taking an *emic* approach, a researcher allows the participants and data to *speak* so as to bring out common themes, patterns, and concepts from within. An *etic* approach (sometimes referred to as *outsider* or *top-down*) uses as its starting point, theories, hypothesis, perspectives, and concepts from outside of the setting being studied.
2. See http://www.capitolchristianmusicgroup.com/. Retrieved on August 25, 2014.
3. In Biblical Greek, this word refers to a service or ministry of the priests, relative to the prayers and sacrifices offered to God. The singing of hymns and spiritual songs are part of the worship offered to God.
4. See http://www.bmcferrell.com/work/pastor-brian-houston. Retrieved on August 25, 2014.
5. See http://www.chrisperrydesign.com.au/index.html. Retrieved on August 25, 2014.
6. See http://mumbrella.com.au/hillsong-australias-most-powerful-brand-104506. Retrieved on August 25, 2014.
7. See http://creativestudiodc.ogilvy.com/brand-storytelling-3-tips-to-building-a-better-brand-story/. Retrieved on August 25, 2014.
8. See http://hillsongcollected.com, August 25, 2014.
9. See http://new.hillsongcollected.com/creative/digital-storytelling-your-content-defines-you. Retrieved on August 25, 2014.
10. See www.hillsong.com. Retrieved on August 25, 2014.
11. See http://new.hillsongcollected.com/creative/our-church-has-50-how-many-does-yours-have. Retrieved on August 25, 2014.

Bibliography

Australian Broadcasting Corporation (Producer). 2005a. *Interview with Brian Houston* [Documentary program]. Retrieved from www.abc.net.au/austory/content/2005/s1427560.htm on May 1, 2008.

Australian Broadcasting Corporation (Producer). 2005b. *Interview with Bobbie Houston* [Documentary program]. Retrieved from www.abc.net.au/austory/content/2005/s1427576.htm on May 1, 2008.
Australian Broadcasting Corporation (Producer). 2005c. *The Life of Brian* [Documentary program]. Retrieved from www.abc.net.au/austory/content/2005/s1428533.htm on May 1, 2008.
Balmer, J.M.T. & S.A. Greyser. 2003. *Revealing the Corporation: Perspectives on Identity, Image, Reputation, Corporate Branding and Corporate-Level Marketing*. London: Routledge.
———. 2006. "Corporate Marketing: Integrating Corporate Identity, Corporate Branding, Corporate Communications, Corporate Image and Corporate Reputation," *European Journal of Marketing*, 40(7/8): 730–741.
Baudrillard, J. 1995. *Simulacra and Simulation* (S.F. Glaser, Trans.). Ann Arbor: University of Michigan Press. (Original work published 1981).
Baudrillard, J. 1998. *The Consumer Society: Myths & Structures* (C. Turner, Trans.). London: Sage. (Original work published 1970).
Bauman, Z. 1998. "Postmodern Religion?" In P. Heelas, D. Martin, & P. Morris (eds), *Religion, Modernity and Postmodernity* (pp. 55–78). Oxford: Blackwell.
Bouma, G. 2006. *Australian Soul: Religion and Spirituality in the Twenty-First Century*. Melbourne: Cambridge University Press.
Brownlie, D., M. Saren, R. Wensley, & R.Whittington. 1994. "The New Marketing Myopia: Critical Perspectives on Theory and Research in Marketing," *European Journal of Marketing*, 28(3): 6–12.
Clark, A. 2004. "Interview with Hillsong Founder Brian Houston." *Christian Today*, Retrieved from http://www.christiantoday.com/article/interview.with.hillsong.founder.brian.houston/1257.htm on May 6, 2009.
Einstein, M. 2008. *Brands of Faith: Marketing Religion in a Commercial Age*. Oxon: Routledge.
Fairclough, N. 1989. *Language and Power*. London: Longman.
———. 1994. "Conversationalization of Public Discourse and the Authority of the Consumer." In R. Keat, N. Whiteley, & N. Abercrombie (eds), *The Authority of the Consumer* (pp. 252–268). London: Routledge.
Ferguson, A. 2006. "God's Business." *Business Review Weekly*, June 29–July 5, pp. 42–46.
Firat, F. & N. Dholakia. 1982. 'Consumption Choices at the Macro Level', *Journal of Macromarketing*, 2(Autumn): 6–15.
Gabrielsson, A. 2001. "Emotions and Strong Experiences with Music." In P.N. Juslin & J.A. Sloboda (eds), *Music and Emotion: Theory and Research* (pp. 431–449). Oxford: Oxford University Press.
Gibbs, S. 2004. "Hillsong Farewells a Lost Sheep Pioneer." *Sydney Morning Herald*, November 13. Retrieved from www.smh.com.au. on May 7, 2009.
Grant, D.C.H., C. Oswick, & L. Putnam. 2004. *The Sage Handbook of Organizational Discourse*. London: SAGE.
Hackley, C. 2003. "'We Are all Customers Now...' Rhetorical Strategy and Ideological Control in Marketing Management Texts," *Journal of Management Studies*, 40(5): 1325–1351.
Hammond, S. 2006. *BE Brands: Creative Brand Revolution*. Sydney: Wiley.
Houston, Bobbie. 2001. *Heaven is in This House*. Castle Hill: Maximised Leadership.
———. 2008. *I'll Have What She's Having*. Nashville, TN: Thomas Nelson.
Houston, Brian. 1999. *You Need More Money*. Castle Hill: Maximised Leadership.
———. 2008. *For This I Was Born: Aligning Your Vision to God's Cause*. Nashville, TN: Thomas Nelson.

Kapferer, J.N. 2002. "Corporate Brand and Organizational Identity." In B. Moingeon & G. Soenen (eds), *Corporate and Organizational Identities: Integrating Strategy, Marketing, Communication and Organizational Perspectives* (pp. 175–193). New York: Routledge.
Keat, R.N., Whiteley, & N. Abercrombie 1994. *The Authority of the Consumer*. London: Routledge.
Kitiarsa, P. 2010. "Toward a Sociology of Religious Commodification." In B.S. Turner (ed.), *The Sociology of Religion* (pp. 563–583). Chichester, West Sussex: Wiley-Blackwell.
Kornberger, M. 2010. *Brand Society: How Brands Transform Management and Lifestyle*. New York: Cambridge University Press.
Leitch, S. & J. Motion 2007. "Retooling the Corporate Brand: A Foucaldian Perspective on Normalisation and Differentiation," *Journal of Brand Management*, 15(1): 71–80.
Lyon, D. 2000. *Jesus in Disneyland*. Cambridge: Polity Press.
Marcus, C. 2008. "Brands Leave Their Mark." *Sydney Morning Herald*, September 15. Retrieved from www.smh.com.au on October 1, 2008.
Marriner, C. 2009. "Next Stop Secular Europe, says Hillsong Founder." *Sydney Morning Herald*, May 25. Retrieved from www.smh.com.au on May 25, 2012.
Mautner, G. 2010. *Language and the Market Society*. New York: Routledge.
McIntyre, E.H. 2007. "Brand of Choice: Why Hillsong Music is Winning Sales and Souls." *Australian Religion Studies Review*, 20(2): 175–194.
Morgan, G. 2003. "Marketing and Critique: Prospects and Problems." In M. Alvesson and H. Willmott (eds), *Studying Management Critically* (pp. 111–131). London: SAGE Publications.
Mottner, S. & J.B. Ford. 2010. "'Editorial: International Journal of Nonprofit and Voluntary Sector Marketing': Special Issue on Marketing and Religion," *International Journal of Nonprofit and Voluntary Sector Marketing*, 15(4): 301–304.
O'Shaughnessy, J. & N.J. O'Shaughnessy. 2007. "Reply to Criticisms of Marketing, the Consumer Society and Hedonism," *European Journal of Marketing*, 41(1/2): 7–16.
Ostwalt, C. 2003. *Secular Steeples: Popular Culture and the Religious Imagination*. Harrisburg: Trinity Press International.
Pass, D. 2007. "The Heart of Worship: The Leitourgic Mode and Christian Sanctification in Contemporary Worship Music." In R. Woods & B. Walrath (eds), *The Message in the Music: Studying Contemporary Praise & Worship* (pp. 106–126). Nashville, TN: Abingdon Press.
Payne, T. & G. Cheng. 2007. "The Surprising Face of Hillsong." *The Briefing*. Retrieved from www.matthiasmedia.com.au/briefing/libray/3883 on August 23, 2010.
Raiter, M. 2008. "The Slow Death of Congregational Singing," *The Briefing*, 355(April): 11–14.
Riches, T. 2010. "The Evolving Theological Emphasis of Hillsong Worship (1996–2007)" *Australasian Pentecostal Studies*, 13: 87–133.
Riches, T. & T. Wagner 2012. "The Evolution of Hillsong Music." *Australian Journal of Communication*, 39(1): 17–36.
Rickard, N.S. 2004. "Intense Emotional Responses to Music: A Test of the Physiological Arousal Hypothesis." *Psychology of Music*, 32(4): 371–388.
Schultz, M., Y.M. Antorini, & F.F. Csaba. 2005. *Corporate Branding: Purpose/People/Process*. Copenhagen: Copenhagen Business School Press.
Skålén, P., M. Fougère, & M. Fellesson. 2008. *Marketing Discourse: A Critical Perspective*. Oxon: Routledge.
Slater, D. 1997. *Consumer Culture and Modernity*. Cambridge: Polity Press.

Strasser, S. 2003. *Commodifying Everything*. London: Routledge.
Twitchell, J.B. 2004. *Branded Nation: The Marketing of Megachurch, College Inc., and Museumworld*. New York: Simon & Schuster.
Woods, R., B.Walrath, & D. Badzinski. 2007. "We Have Come into His House: Kerygma, Koinonia, Leitourgia—Contemporary Worship Music that Models the Purpose of the Church." In R. Woods & B. Walrath (eds), *The Message in the Music: Studying Contemporary Praise & Worship* (pp. 92–105). Nashville, TN: Abingdon Press.
Zwartz, B. 2006. "We've Got to Have Faith." *Sydney Morning Herald*, April 14. Retrieved from www.smh.com.au on August 23, 2010.

6

Populist Movement to Mega Church: El Shaddai in Manila, Philippines*

Katharine L. Wiegele

Introduction

In this chapter, I attempt to uncover the socio-cultural, political, and economic contexts of El Shaddai, a populist movement with loose affiliation to the Catholic Church. I used firsthand observation, interviews, surveys, and analysis of El Shaddai media texts to collect my data.

El Shaddai is a popular Catholic Charismatic movement founded and based in Manila, Philippines.[1] It began in 1984 as a non-denominational Christian radio program, and within a few years described itself as a Catholic lay group, in keeping with the affiliation of its founder and the majority of its followers. Within 15 years, the group had become a substantial movement with a followership in millions.[2] The group has chapters in nearly every province in the Philippines and in over 35 countries, with overseas participation comprising around 30 percent of the total followership. The group is most known for its massive outdoor Saturday night rallies in Manila which attract a half million to a million followers each week. These *prayer and healing rallies*, which feature emotional preaching by *Brother Mike Velarde*, the group's charismatic founder and *servant–leader*, are broadcast on television and radio throughout the country, while tapes of Velarde's sermons circulate widely among Filipino overseas workers. Velarde is a businessman turned preacher, without any formal religious training. His evocative and entertaining preaching style, his populist persona and message, and the belief that he can channel miracles to the faithful, however, allow him to attract

---

*This chapter is an adaptation from a previously published book. It is reprinted with the kind permission of the publishers of "Mediated Spaces of Religious Community in Manila, Philippines." In M. Bailey and G. Redden (eds), *Mediating Faiths* (pp. 217–229). Farnham: Ashgate. Copyright © 2010.

crowds and monetary collections that are the envy of clergymen (Wiegele, 2005). Followers in Manila, elsewhere in the Philippines, and in Filipino communities overseas have formed local El Shaddai chapters in which they gather for smaller prayer meetings. The El Shaddai congregation and Velarde himself have been influential in national politics during successive presidencies, beginning with the term of Fidel Ramos (1992–1998). While members do not vote as a block, Brother Mike's endorsement is highly sought-after, and he often voices his opinions publicly on matters of national importance. He even seriously explored running for president of the country in 2010, but eventually decided against it.

El Shaddai is officially recognized by the Philippine Roman Catholic Church as a Catholic lay movement, but it appeals to many of the same desires that popular Protestant groups in Manila do. As in other Charismatic and Pentecostal Movements worldwide, El Shaddai religiosity emphasizes the workings of the Holy Spirit (for example, faith healing, miracles, and emotional worship experiences) over doctrine (Poewe, 1994: 2). El Shaddai can be classified as belonging to a specific wing of Charismatics called the *prosperity movement,* also called *neo-Pentecostal* owing to its origins in Pentecostalism, its acceptance of material prosperity, and its appeal across social classes and religious denominations (Coleman, 2000). Like other prosperity groups, El Shaddai's theology not only accepts material prosperity, but also emphasizes healing, the personal elicitation of miracles through *seed faith,* and what others have called "positive confession" or "name it and claim it" (ibid.). Seed faith has, at its heart, the principle that giving tithes with faith will result in miracles or even a *100-fold return.* Members practice positive confession in part through *prayer requests* (written requests for miracles) with the belief that specific statements can claim God's generosity in the present. In this context, life events are continuously interpreted as miracles, and those who have received miracles are encouraged to testify publicly at El Shaddai rallies and prayer meetings.

Velarde's prosperity gospel affirms people's desire for upward mobility and teaches that paradise is to be achieved now, not postponed until after death. Furthermore, suffering and poverty are not in themselves virtuous, in contrast to mainstream Filipino Catholic norms that emphasize *taking up the cross*—the idea that there is spiritual value in suffering and hardship. Like the American Preacher Pat Robertson, creator of the television show 700 Club, Velarde teaches that suffering can be alleviated by faithfully following God's principles, one of which is tithing. According to my own nonrandom survey of 259 people at several El Shaddai rallies in 1996, approximately 80 percent of El Shaddai members were below the national poverty level, a statistic similar to national poverty levels at that time. Elsewhere, I have described how the aspirations expressed in Velarde's prosperity theology seemed to fit in with the attempts of national government to focus energies on development and material well-being, especially during the decade or so immediately following the 1986 EDSA People Power Revolution (*Asiaweek*, 1996). In addition, the vacuum of power created by the end of the Marcos dictatorship, the ultimate disappointment with the subsequent leadership's effectiveness in dealing with poverty, corruption, land reform, and human rights abuses, and the weakening of the communist insurgency in the 1990s and 2000s provided the sociopolitical context for the emergence of *Brother Mike*, whose populist message emphasized not only prosperity, but self-reliance and hope also. El Shaddai reframes deterministic class-based cultural models implied in development, liberation theologies, leftist, and other progressive discourses—discourses that define the average El Shaddai member as one of the oppressed. Using Brother Mike's story as a model (one of transformation from illness and destitution to health and wealth through active faith and the resultant miracles), members emphasize individual faith and action, and reject structural or historical understandings of inequality, as well as those that accept suffering as a natural aspect of spirituality. In doing so, they redefine themselves (Wiegele, 2005).[3]

El Shaddai's Catholic affiliation confers some legitimacy within this predominantly Catholic country. Although El Shaddai operates as if it were an independent church, local chapters are linked with local Catholic parishes, and the movement has a clergy member as a spiritual advisor. The link to the Catholic Church is further seen in two practices: mass is said at El Shaddai rallies and a portion of the weekly collections goes to the Catholic Church. However, in local neighborhoods, El Shaddai healers merge ritual elements of Roman Catholicism, prosperity theology, Charismatic Christianity, and local shamanic traditions to produce a revitalized spiritual arena in which the so-called *authentic healing power* has shifted to El Shaddai contexts. These ritual innovations and experiential elements, as well as Velarde's personal charisma, offer power and credence to the prosperity theology.[4]

Becoming *Live*

As mentioned, the El Shaddai Movement began as a radio program whose listening audience soon organically evolved into a rally audience, as people gathered outside the radio station for thanksgiving for the blessings and miracles received. This gathering then became a regular weekly occurrence, and eventually developed into mass rallies. The radio (and later TV) programming expanded greatly to become hallmarks of the movement.

Many El Shaddai followers' first exposure to the group is through radio or TV. DWXI, El Shaddai's radio station, is one of the more popular AM band radio stations in Metro Manila. The group also buys airtime from other radio stations throughout the Philippines, as well as in other countries, and airtime on TV stations throughout the Philippines. El Shaddai produces and distributes *Bagong Liwanag* magazine (and an English version, *The Miracle Newsletter*) for free throughout the Philippines and internationally. The predominance of radio and television in El Shaddai religiosity differentiates it from mainstream Catholic experience and helps to create a new form of religious space, new understandings of religious community, and a more personalized relationship with God. From its inception until now, the community is, to a large extent, a mass-mediated community. Despite the fact that El Shaddai outdoor rallies and other events are now also experienced *live*, mass media actually produce this *live-ness*. The boundaries between these two communities (radio and live rally) are blurred both conceptually and spatially.

Going to an El Shaddai mass rally on a Saturday in Manila involves merging the world of the mass media community with the anonymous, but physically manifest, congregation of El Shaddai devotees in the field of the Philippine International Cultural Center (PICC), the huge open field El Shaddai ministries have rented for its rallies. The description as follows, adapted from my field notes, provides an experiential account of this process.

> I am the last person to arrive at Eddie's dwelling—a two-room section of a house in a cramped semi-squatter area in the heart of Manila. Eddie's wife, Celia, and their two children, are still preparing for the El Shaddai rally, as their neighbor Josie and two other young women wait on the couch. The TV in front of them is on, competing for attention amidst the bustle of the rally preparations.

The TV is tuned to the live broadcast coming from the stage at the rally site. The rally has not actually begun yet, but on TV we can see the activity on the stage. A series of individuals give short, impassioned testimonies of miracles they have received, a choir from a provincial chapter sings religious songs, and an emcee mediates each transition with introductions, announcements, short prayers, and pep talks about the exciting rally, or 'Family Appointment with Yahweh El Shaddai,' that will begin in several hours. As the cameras pan the crowds, we see the commotion of hundreds of thousands of followers getting settled in the open-air field for the evening. Peddlers sell plastic mats, food, and other necessary supplies. Ushers keep people from sitting in the roped-off aisles, and hand out envelopes for 'prayer requests' and tithes. On the fringes, people wait in line to use portable toilets. As the emcee on stage pauses to lead a short prayer, Josie and the others present in the living room fall silent and listen, concluding the prayer with an 'amen' spoken out loud, in unison with the emcee. Josie joins in, momentarily, as the choir sings the popular song, "We will serve the Lord." Josie's friend, Nhelin, sits beside her on the couch and writes her 'prayer request.'

When Eddie's family is ready to go, he lowers the volume of the TV, and we join hands in a circle for a binding prayer with each other. Then Eddie turns off the TV. Although the house is less than two kilometers away from PICC field, it will take us over an hour to navigate our way via public transportation to our final destination: a spot on the rocky lawn, close enough to see the stage area, but far away enough to be able to sit comfortably, with enough fresh air.

Celia flips on the radio as we begin the journey, tuned to DWXI, where the rally is being broadcast live. We leave the house, and then the 'interior' of Sinag by walking through the many iskinita, or narrow corridors between houses and buildings—the dark urban footpaths that wind around and between the two- and three-story buildings. Neighbors greet us as we pass through the densely populated neighborhood where according to the local priest; at least 85 percent of the residents live below the national poverty level. One neighbor greets us with "See you there, sister!" even though she knows she'll never find us in the crowds at the rally. A young man, half-mockingly, hums the first line of the El Shaddai theme song.

After fifteen minutes waiting by a major thoroughfare, a jeepney (public jeep) finally stops for us, and the eight of us get on. As we sit in the cramped jeepney, we listen to a woman's humorous testimony coming from the radio. She is talking about her husband, exaggerating his former bad qualities, and then testifying to his transformation. My companions laugh and say 'Amen! Praise God!' as we imagine those in the crowd at the rally are doing the same.

Forty-five minutes and two jeepney transfers later, we arrive outside the Harrison Plaza shopping mall. By now, all of the passengers are hot, grimy, and a little light-headed from the humidity, heat and air pollution. Here we pile out and walk three blocks on the side of the street to a designated spot outside Rizal Baseball Stadium, where enterprising jeepney drivers have formed a new jeepney route. These jeeps go from here, to the PICC grounds, and back to Harrison Plaza, all day long, every Saturday. This particular route has expanded in recent years to accommodate the hundreds of thousands of travelers going this way to the El Shaddai rally.

As we wait in line, along with at least a hundred other people, for space on the next available public jeep, radios of various volumes and levels of clarity can be heard throughout the crowd, all tuned to the live broadcast from PICC. There is a feeling of camaraderie amongst the people waiting in line. People greet each other as El Shaddai followers—with the titles 'Brother' and 'Sister.'

Everyone inside the jeepney is going to the rally and a more powerful 'boom box' blasts the live transmission. Within ten minutes we are inside the PICC grounds, slowing to avoid hordes of pedestrians. We are dropped off near one of the parking areas and walk the rest of the way.

Outside the PICC grounds, El Shaddai activity extends as far as the highway—a good 20 minute walk from the stage. On Saturdays (the day of the rally), the area of the city surrounding PICC becomes, in effect, El Shaddai space. Not only are decorated and bannered jeeps, taxis, cars, tricycles, bicycles, busses, and mobile vending stalls blocking movement and traffic, but pedestrians and vendors adorned with markers of El Shaddai membership—El Shaddai handkerchiefs, portable chairs, T-shirts, candles, hats, and blasting radios—seem to flow from every corner en masse toward the PICC grounds. Those passersby stalled in traffic on the highway can sometimes gaze at vending stalls with El Shaddai religious items, which include wall calendars, banners, El Shaddai cassette tapes, and ritual items for the day's rally, such as eggs or flowers. El Shaddai participants get a small kick out of inconveniencing the unconverted through these huge weekend traffic jams. To them, it is a form of evangelism.

As the crowds get thicker and the back of the grandstand area is in sight, we no longer need our radio—we can hear the live transmissions from countless radios around us, of people who have decided to sit down here on the fringes. Some people can't even see the grandstand at all because their view is blocked by another building in the PICC compound. Nonetheless, when Brother Mike begins speaking in several hours, these people will listen to the live radio and face the grandstand while going through all the same motions as everyone else, actively participating in the rally

As we head toward the grandstand, the sounds of portable radios are gradually replaced by the sounds coming from the loudspeakers near the stage. Soon we can actually see the emcee on the stage as we squint in the brightly lit area. We are now part of the 'live' rally. Huge stands with camera and audio equipment block the view of the stage as we get closer. The area directly in front of the stage is blocked off and reserved for the 'very sick'—those with terminal illnesses or deformities—so that they can receive the strongest healing power coming from Brother Mike on stage. There is a feeling of excitement, of being part of history, as a video camera's gaze passes over us and simultaneously transmits our image to people across the country. Josie told me once that she loves going to the rally at PICC, as opposed to the smaller rally in her local chapter, "because it's live!" Were it not for the cameras, the simultaneous broadcast, and the instant playback (after the event is over), this 'live' feeling would not exist. In the floodlights and in the camera's gaze, we have come out of the 'interior' into the spotlight. For a few hours this evening we are, it seems, significant, and in a sense de-marginalized.

As the crowds of people leave the area and journey home after the rally around midnight, many radios will be tuned to the playback, a repeat broadcast of the event that just occurred. (Wiegele, field notes, 2004)

Radio and TV broadcasts of rallies are often a person's first contact with El Shaddai. DWXI announces the upcoming rally all week long, orienting followers to the stage where Brother Mike gives his *healing message*. The journey that followers undertake each week, from areas of Manila or from far-flung provinces, is oriented toward Brother Mike, who becomes, in effect, a locus of miracles. Yet the ritual sphere of the rally extends beyond its immediate locale because radio and TV are played constantly, before and after the event. Since the broadcast is live, one begins experiencing the event even while still at home. Listeners, at times, *tune in* electronically to the rally as audience—members far from the stage listen to radios and watch oversized film screens on the perimeters of the massive rally lawn. Many watch or listen to rallies without even attending them, but go through the motions, the songs, and the prayers as if experiencing it *live*. Within the PICC grounds, radios serve as links with Brother Mike at the center. The mass-mediated community is gradually transformed into the more immediate, physical community of the rally. While leaving the rally, the opposite occurs. The rally community is transformed once again into the media audience.

Within the rally context itself, mass media help to create a *live* feeling. The rally becomes *live* when participants enter a zone they understand to be mediated to others who are watching or listening via TV or radio. This brightly lit, colorful sphere presents a larger-than-life, amplified reality that doesn't stop with the self, but flows outward. This feeling is enhanced by Velarde on stage who is aware of this outward flow, as he directly addresses people listening from home. "There is a woman in Naga City listening right now who is in need of a miracle. She has been suffering from cataracts for several years. Woman, you will be healed, and you will see your son graduating from high school next year!" (Inevitably a person fitting this description will surface later to publicly tell a miraculous story of healing.) Many followers, I interviewed, testified to having been healed through radio or television, from blessings Velarde gave either during a live rally broadcast or during another one of his radio programs. Some hold up objects to the radio or television to be blessed, as is done at rallies or use the radio or the TV to keep evil spirits away from the house, for example, spirits that bring drugs into the neighborhood or cause discord within families.

Ritual Space, Community, and the Holy Spirit

By expanding the boundaries of ritual space through the airwaves, El Shaddai creates a direct individual experience of sacredness, ritual blessing, and the Holy Spirit in the home within a very personal sphere. El Shaddai prayer and counseling sessions on the radio and the implication that blessing can travel through the airwaves allow for a personal relationship with God that is not mediated through traditional Catholic channels, such as priests, saints, the Virgin Mary, the Eucharist, statues, crucifixes, or the Catholic mass. Velarde told me that the calling of his ministry was to *free people from the bondage of religion*. He said that religion built walls that blocked one's relationship with the Holy Spirit. By *religion*, he meant *tradition* or, more specifically, conventional Catholic traditions (such as the mediators mentioned above) that divert people's attention away from meaningful relationships with the Holy Spirit. At the same time, he still supports the sacraments and the practice of attending mass on Sunday, and regards the El Shaddai Movement as a Catholic movement.

Furthermore, by locating the channels of sacredness and blessings in radio and TV airwaves, and in open-air rallies, Velarde has avoided constructing a physical structure—a church. Mass media has allowed the group an independent existence as a mass-mediated congregation that transcends specific geographical, social, and institutional boundaries and contexts (Babb, 1995: 17) without requiring a denominational separation. El Shaddai's coexistence with the Catholic Church, then, has been unproblematic (on this level) because, from its inception, it has occupied a wholly different sort of religious space.

By claiming privilege in the realm of spiritual mediation, El Shaddai in effect relegates the church to the position of repositories of tradition. Velarde acknowledges the need for certain *traditions*, such as the sacraments, but says the church and its clergy are bogged down with intellectualism and ritual. Velarde himself is fond of pointing out that he is *just a businessman* and never formally studied religion. While Catholic priests' connections with God are *man-made* (the result of studying), Velarde's connection is *spiritual* (the result of a more authentic connection with God). When God healed him of heart disease, he wrote that he became "a channel of God's grace and power to heal," and "a channel of countless miracles by appointment and prayer request" (Velarde, 1992a: 3). "This is no longer the work of man," Velarde told me personally. "We are just willing vessels. Like me. I have a covenant with God that no man can ever understand." Furthermore, Velarde speaks in Tagalog[5] with a provincial accent, giving the impression that he has a *common man* or even lower class background. In contrast, Catholic priests, who may speak English and schooled Tagalog, are often seen by my informants as connected to an intellectual or elite class.

Velarde also uses El Shaddai in-house publications to establish contact between himself, his readers, and God. In *El Shaddai The Almighty God,* one of El Shaddai's free publications, Velarde writes:

> Do you need a miracle? Would you want me to pray with you? Wherever you may be, this Newsletter can serve as a contact point of our faith for God's miracle power to operate—if you only believe and accept Jesus Christ as Lord and Savior! (Ibid., 5).
>
> I'm excited! I know something good is going to happen to you. Are you ready? Okay, let's do it. Put your hands on this page as our point of contact, as if I am with you. (Did I not tell you that wherever I go, even simply through this El Shaddai Miracle Newsletter, Jesus is with me?) (Velarde, 1992b: 4)

Recorded voice tapes of Brother Mike Velarde, circulated among Filipino migrants and overseas workers, function in the same way as do his live radio programs. *Alay Pagmamahal* (Love Offering), for example, is a live radio program that airs several times a week on DWXI in which Velarde leads prayers, interprets the Bible, and takes calls from listeners asking to be counseled, *prayed over*, and blessed. Here he is addressing the general listening audience, as well as the followers in and around his office building who have gathered to listen.[6] (The program is translated here from Tagalog, with the exception of the words in quotation marks, which were spoken by Velarde originally in English.) Prior to the following excerpt, he has already asked the listeners to stand up, raise their hands, and bow their heads:

> Put those hands on top of the head of the one beside you .... "wherever you may be." The hands you lifted earlier were blessed by the Lord. Don't worry, the hands of Brother Mike and your hands have no difference. "If only I had a million hands, I'd put them on your heads, but there is no way." Your hands have been blessed by the Lord, so offer them to Him. Put your hand on top of the head of the one beside you. Bow and I will pray for your requests. "It's just impossible for me to touch your foreheads." ... Ask now while those hands are laid on you whatever you wish to receive from the Lord. And I believe the hands laid on your heads are the Lord's hands more than the hands of Brother Mike. All those healed are because of the Lord's miraculous and wondrous hands ....
>
> Place yourself in the presence of the Lord. "Just continue to meditate right now. It's healing time." If you have brought oil or if you have [bottles of] oil in your houses, get them out. ... Lift them up and we will pray over them. ... rub the oil on the forehead of the one beside you in the name of Jesus our Savior. And on their palms. We're together and one now. The Lord is rubbing your foreheads. Lift the oil and we'll pray. This seldom happens in our program—the Lord's spirit is moving now. He knows all your needs. If you have no doubts, I believe everyone here right now is receiving an extraordinary strength and miracle in their lives.

This program segment powerfully creates a moment of simultaneous, shared ritual experience and an explicit awareness of a real-time gathering that is yet imagined and geographically dispersed (and which goes well beyond the passive *imagined community* of nation or ethnicity described by Benedict Anderson) (Anderson, 1983). "We're together and one now," he reminds them. "If only I had *a million* hands, I'd put them on your heads."

In addition, sacredness and the ability to heal move from conventional ritual space to Velarde's hands, which become God's hands and which then become each and every individual's hands. "... I believe the hands laid on your heads are the Lord's hands more than the hands of Brother Mike," he says. As with the newsletter, the blessing and the Holy Spirit also seems to move from him, through the radio, into each person's home, into each person's own hands, and, in this case, into the healing oil. One's body and one's home become sacred, and ordinary individuals are empowered to bless and heal. Through the radio, he is able to bring *the Lord's hands* to people, and yet his own hands are still there to mediate this process.

Velarde's mobilization of this common ritual form (laying-on-of-hands) in radio and print media releases it from its more typical religio-social contexts. The classless, populist nature of El Shaddai religiosity is a point lost neither on *Brother Mike* nor his followers, who repeatedly mentioned the absence of social distinctions as a significant difference between El Shaddai events (where, followers told me, "[A]n engineer stands next to a maid.") and *ordinary Catholic* rites in church. One of Velarde's favorite stories is of an illiterate man who became an El Shaddai preacher. The invisibility of social difference (between each other and with Brother Mike) creates a feeling of *communitas* (spirit of community) that participants have told me is transforming and empowering.

Furthermore, the mediated space of the airwaves and the open air of the rally are seen by followers as conducive to the free movement of the Holy Spirit. The Holy Spirit is at the rally, they say, in part because of the open space. Informants consistently associated the rally with God as spiritually manifested and the church with *just tradition*, devoid of the efficacious presence of the Holy Spirit. As one El Shaddai member said, "At church, God is near. At the rally, He is actually there." They say they can *feel* God at the rally, in the open space—as energy, as heat running through their veins, as rain water on their skin (when it's not raining), or as wind (when there's no wind blowing). Moreover, they say the feeling of God's presence follows them into their everyday lives, whereas going to *church* (that is, in a Catholic Church) is seen as limited in space and time: "you go in, you go out" or "after one hour, it's over."

It is understandable that El Shaddai followers enjoy the rallies in the open space at PICC, on the coast, and that they *feel God* there. One emerges from cramped, tunnel-like streets and neighborhoods to a rare, wide, open space with a view of the sunset, and on the horizon, a partial view of the Makati skyline. The fresh air, sea breeze, open space, and stars signify a different, liberating sort of existential state to many of those who come to spread blankets on the PICC grounds.

In this space, El Shaddai members get a perspective not only of the city, but of themselves and their own critical mass. They are able to express the force of this mass to outsiders by disrupting the city and its imposed *order* and by occupying, even reclaiming, public spaces. They create massive traffic jams at unusual times and take over the clean, posh segments of the city. In the interior barrios, El Shaddai's mass is dispersed and unseen, but a rally crowd is a totality that can be seen and felt. As part of this collectivity that is simultaneously broadcast on national TV, El Shaddai members are in a sense demarginalized.[7] Seeing El Shaddai's impressive assembly, especially from atop the steps of the Film Center building (part of the PICC compound) or through the TV cameras above the stage, gives participants a sense of significance, even empowerment. This view of *the numbers* is, in part, what makes El Shaddai seem awesome to outsiders as well.

In *coming out* from the barrios, El Shaddai members also enter a space where mediation with the elites and the power brokers of Philippine society seems possible. People in the rally audience are courted by politicians and candidates who *perform* for them on stage, address them directly, and banter with Brother Mike. In El Shaddai/PICC space, formerly invisible people now exist, at least on some limited level, for the nation—they are on the national political map and in the national consciousness. Not only do politicians, candidates for political office, high officials of the church, prominent businessmen, etc., regularly visit them giving them a sense of importance, but these visits also reach a national audience through mass media. It is thus not surprising, either, that El Shaddai followers from other provinces in the country make long trips to be part of these national rallies. Even for those who see hypocrisy in the words and actions of their visitors, the visits are important to them because, as some participants have put it, "These politicians *need our prayers*." In other words, "They need *us*." Furthermore, just by being at the rally, these politicians will receive the Word of God and be blessed. This, they say, can only be for the good.

A Mega Worship Center

The evolving relationship between El Shaddai and the Philippine Roman Catholic Church (PRCC) has not been without controversy, as mentioned. Brother Mike has been summoned several times by the Catholic Bishops

Conference of the Philippines (CBCP), and has been involved with the CBCP in an ongoing dialogue about specific El Shaddai practices, Catholic orthodoxy, and the PRCC's role within El Shaddai, ritually, theologically, and administratively, which continues to unfold today (Wiegele, 2005). Despite their differences, my research indicates that the PRCC as well as El Shaddai have walked a mutually beneficial fine line. El Shaddai has defined itself in opposition to Catholic tradition, as well as with legitimacy from its Catholic affiliation. The church has been able to retain a revitalized segment of its congregation that it might otherwise have lost to Pentecostal denominations, and it has gained a renewed spiritual relevancy in Philippine society.

Interestingly on August 20, 2009, Velarde opened the *El Shaddai International House of Prayer*, a US$20 billion worship structure with a floor area of one hectare, in the Velarde-owned Amvel City, San Dionisio, Paranaque City (within metropolitan Manila). The structure is said to have a seating capacity of 15,000 with a standing-room capacity of 25,000, and an overflow capacity of 200,000. It claims to be the biggest place of worship in Asia. The then Philippine president, Gloria Macapagal-Arroyo, among other VIPs, attended the inauguration. Joro Archbishop Angel Lagdameo, the outgoing president of the CBCP, was the main celebrant of the concelebrated mass for the inauguration. He said, "This is my first time to address a people equivalent to six cathedrals" (Esguerra, 2009). A news article on the CBCP official news website, the CBCP News, stated "… after 25 years, the charismatic group [whose] membership has tremendously grown to 7 million, found its home in Amvel City" (2009). And the church was there to help it celebrate.

What are the implications of El Shaddai owing its state-of-the-art worship center? Will this institutionalize the movement and take away its *live space* mediation of the faith? Will it affect its Catholic ties? Future studies will hopefully take a closer look at the ongoing dynamics of this mega movement.

Conclusion

Early Methodism's sense of freedom of the supernatural from established religious hierarchies and the notion that the supernatural is accessible to ordinary individuals in everyday life are echoed in today's *Pentecostalisms* (Martin, 2002). The emphasis on religious autonomy, individual freedom, and personal choice is part of the modern message of Pentecostalism. This autonomous religious self is chosen rather than inherited, in a marketplace of religious options (Martin, 1990). The El Shaddai option, like other Pentecostal options in the Philippines and elsewhere, displays these distinctly modern social forms of autonomy, achievement, entrepreneurship, and personal spiritual empowerment (Wiegele, 2006: 495–520). El Shaddai followers, like their Pentecostal counterparts, redefine who they are through their deliberate religious choices, which in turn may help them find their footing in the modern world.

Congregation, sacredness, and community have been transformed and expanded in El Shaddai contexts to create forms of religious experience that are very different from those of the mainstream church. Most notable are the ways El Shaddai followers see their relationships with God and with others in the religious community, their experience of ritual, their emphasis on the spiritual manifestations of God, and their orientation toward Velarde as a conduit to God. By using mass media and open-air rallies, Velarde also puts El Shaddai ministries in a strategically favorable position with the Church institution, allowing El Shaddai to remain both independent from the church and under the wing of the church at the same time. This gives El Shaddai a perceived distance from Catholic orthodoxy, while allowing it to capitalize on the sense of legitimacy that comes from its Catholic identity. Likewise, the fact that El Shaddai religious practice occurs mainly outside Catholic structures, it makes it easier for church officials to overlook or downplay unorthodox practices. El Shaddai members' use of religious programming, combined with their participation in mass rallies, extends the sacred and ritual sphere beyond the immediate locale into the home and the body, blurring the boundaries between mass-mediated religious experience and more temporal forms of religious practice. The emergence of the mega worship complex has altered El Shaddai's *religious space*, and time will tell whether this will affect the dynamics of the movement as well.

Notes

1. El Shaddai DWXI Prayer Partners Foundation International, Inc.
2. El Shaddai estimates of its own *followership* have been based on crowd estimates at mass rallies and other events, prayer requests and tithes, prayer group attendance, chapter

membership, radio listenership surveys, and official membership. *Followership* numbers around five million (or even 9–10 million at one point in time), according to El Shaddai officials, were also confirmed through presidential election results. Given the nature of El Shaddai participation and the fact that official registration of members is not stressed by the group, many participants/followers are not *official* members. Therefore, official membership numbers are much smaller: 252,463 as of September 19, 2005 (Personal interview at El Shaddai headquarters, Makati City, September 2005).

3. For a fuller discussion, see Wiegele, 2005. Indeed, resisting class identification is itself part of a class-based discourse, as the dominant discourse is deployed in its very resistance.
4. The prosperity gospel's emphasis on worldly, over eternal, concerns has been a major point of contention with mainstream Filipino Roman Catholics and clergy. Velarde has also been criticized for preying on the needs and desires of a class of Filipinos for whom survival itself is often a struggle. In response, Velarde has begun a variety of social services for members. Furthermore, far from just giving members a way to elicit miracles, Brother Mike's prosperity message and seed faith principle offer members an opportunity for transformations of the self.
5. Tagalog is the basis of Filipino, the national language of the Philippines.
6. This program was aired on February 13, 1996.
7. El Shaddai is considered, within the Philippines, to be a movement of and for the *masa* or the masses (the common person), a group that is often marginalized from politics and economic growth and opportunities, in a country with widespread poverty and large income disparity.

Bibliography

Anderson, Benedict. 1983. *Imagined Communities: Reflections on the Origin and Spread of Nationalism*. London: Verso.
Asiaweek, 1996. "The Prophet of Profit: El Shaddai's Mike Velarde Brings Religion Down to Earth." *Asiaweek*, September 20, 2013.
Babb, Lawrence A. 1995. "Introduction." In Lawrence A. Babb and Susan S. Wadley (eds), *Media and the Transformation of Religion in South Asia*. Philadelphia: University of Pennsylvania Press.
Coleman, Simon. 2000. *The Globalisation of Charismatic Christianity: Spreading the Gospel of Prosperity*. Cambridge: Cambridge University Press.
CBCP News. 2009. "El Shaddai P1-B Church Opens Today." Retrieved from http://newsinfo.inquirer.net/inquirerheadlines/nation/view/20090820-221130/P1-B-church-of-El-Shaddai-opens-Thursday on August 22, 2014.
Esguerra, Christian V. 2009. "Velarde opens El Shaddai Church." *Philippines Daily Inquirer*, Retrieved from http://www.inquirer.net/specialreports/inquirerpolitics/view.php?db=1&article=20090821-221325 on August 22, 2014.
Martin, D. 1990. *Tongues of Fire: the Explosion of Protestantism in Latin America*. Oxford: Blackwell.
———. 2002. *Pentecostalism: The World their Parish*. Oxford: Blackwell.
Poewe, Karla. 1994. *Charismatic Christianity as Global Culture*. Columbia, SC: University of South Carolina Press.

Velarde, Mariano "Mike" Z. 1992a. *El Shaddai the Almighty God*, Vol. I. Makati, Philippines: El Shaddai Miracle Publications.

———. 1992b. *El Shaddai the Almighty God*, Vol. II. Makati, Philippines: El Shaddai Miracle Publications.

Wiegele, Katharine L. 2005. *Investing in Miracles: El Shaddai and the Transformation of Popular Catholicism in the Philippines*. Honolulu, Hawaii, USA: University of Hawaii Press.

———. 2006. "Catholics Rich in Spirit: El Shaddai's Modern Engagements," *Philippine Studies*, 54(4): 495–520.

7
Nurturing Globalized Faith Seekers: Mega Churches in Andhra Pradesh, India

Y.A. Sudhakar Reddy

Introduction

In this chapter, I will describe the characteristics of three mega churches in the Indian state of Andhra Pradesh: Calvary Temple in Hyderabad, Holy Ghost Fire Ministries in Visakhapatnam, and Bible Mission in Gooty. I will begin by giving a thumbnail sketch of *union* churches (denominational mainline churches) in India, as there have been attempts in the past to bring all churches under one body. I will also describe briefly, the move towards the indigenization of the Indian church. I will then proceed to argue that whereas globalization brought about the mega church phenomenon to India, it is the strong folk culture ethos of the religious setting that sustains the ongoing life of mega churches in India.

Church is used in two ways in Christian theology: First, as an artifact in the sense of it being *ecclesia visibilis*, that is, a physical construct where the people of God meet and worship; second, as a *mentifact* with *ecclesia invisibilis*, that is, a mental construct in which Christian faith seekers look and work for the kingdom of God (Smith, 1892: 453–454). The early church believed in the commandment of Christ to make disciples of the nations. In the course of worldwide church history, many sects and denominations have developed; although it is fair to say that mainly, the church is founded on four basic sacramental activities: Baptism (repentance and faith), teaching the apostolic doctrine, communion, public worship and prayer. It must be noted, however, that the first sacrament, baptism, is a much contested issue in Indian Christianity as the majority of Christian converts are from Scheduled Castes (SC). Once, a convert from SC is baptized, the mainline churches give a certificate of baptism which then goes on record that he or she is an *Indian Christian*. This record may jeopardize the convert's future employment prospects as converted Christians from SCs are treated as Backward Classes (BCs). Only the Hindu SCs are recognized and granted all government benefits. Mega churches, by and large, get around this sensitive issue by not insisting on baptism as a prerequisite for membership in their churches. Converts in mega churches, therefore, benefit from their dual status as SCs and Christians. This is one reason why crowds, especially young adults, are attracted to mega churches in India.

As missionary work started growing in India during the first half of the 19th century, there arose conflicts between the various mission organizations in terms of territory of service. To resolve these issues, attempts were made by the mainline churches to form a church union.

Church Union

It was during one of the early eastward travels of the Judeo-Christian diaspora that Christianity came to India. According to Indian church tradition, St Thomas, one of the 12 apostles of Jesus Christ, brought Christianity to India in the 1st century. The Syrian Christians of Malabar, in Kerala, today trace their spiritual roots to the Apostle Thomas. During the 16th century, Catholicism was introduced to the Indian subcontinent. It was only after the advent of the Europeans in the 1790s[1] that Protestant missions of different denominations began their work in India.

Until the late 20th century, churches in India had been dependent on the West, both for administrative and fiscal resources (Firth, 2008: 233). The churches were established through the modern missionary movement from Europe and America (and in late 20th century from Australia). The Roman Catholic Church formulated one ecclesiastical system for the whole country; but this uniformity was not possible for Protestant missions in India because the sending missions were independent organizations, bound more or less rigidly to their denominational roots in the West with differing views in theology and church polity (Rouse & Neill, 1954). Each foreign mission propagated its own type of teaching, and consequently developed its own style of organization. As a result, a great number of separate Christian communities came into existence in India, such as the Lutheran, Anglican, Methodist, and Presbyterian. Even among Christians of the same denominational type, there were various theologies and structures due to missions originating from different countries.[2]

Starting in 1855, decennial conferences were held intermittently for the whole of India to resolve issues connected with the provincial governance of mission fields.[3] It was at one of these conferences, held in Madras, in 1902 that the principle known as *comity* was agreed upon; comity meant that each mission was permitted to occupy certain territories and that other mission entities should abstain from entering and working in those territories.[4] However, the principle of comity neither applied to the larger towns, nor could it be fully implemented in places where more than one mission already existed. Furthermore, the Roman Catholic Church was not party to this agreement, and the Baptist, Pentecostal, and Assemblies of God (AoG) denominations also declined participation (Richter, 1908: 227–229).

The Church of South India's (CSI's) inauguration, on September 27, 1947, was a significant event in the Church Union Movement because after centuries of historic divisions, Episcopal and non-Episcopal Churches were brought together in a united Episcopal Church (Firth, 2008). Thus, four different church traditions—Anglican (Episcopal), Congregational, Presbyterian, and Methodist—became the CSI.[5]

The bishops of various denominations assembled in the Council and resolved a four-point articulation of Anglican identity to enforce the principle of comity in 1888. This came to be known as the *Lambeth Quadrilateral*, which became the foundation for the CSI. The four basic principles agreed upon were:

1. The Holy Scriptures of the Old and New Testament as containing all things necessary to salvation and as the supreme and decisive standard of faith;
2. The two creeds (the Apostles' Creed and the Nicene Creed) as witnessing to and safeguarding this faith;
3. The two Sacraments of Baptism and the Lord's Supper; and
4. The ordained ministry with the historic episcopate.

However, despite the commitment of the four churches to this union, serious divisions still occurred—brought about mainly by the churches' foreign mission agencies (ibid., 244). Several efforts were made during the period prior to 1947 to divest the CSI of its denominational links with churches in the West, but none of these efforts was successful (Latourette, 1937–1945).

From Western to Indigenous Church

During the 19th century, there developed among Indian Christians a concern for self-reliance and independence. There was a leaning among early converts in South India (from 1820s to 1910s) to seek Indian ways of expressing their Christian devotion because they realized that the Western forms of worship were inappropriate to the Indian cultural norms and practices. For example, in the Telugu-speaking state of Andhra Pradesh, Purushottam Choudhury (1803–1890), a Brahmin convert baptized at Cuttack, composed Indian devotional songs which were used in many churches (Devadoss, 1946). He also published a book of poems, the *Gospel Trumpet*, in 1827. Another Brahmin convert, Pulipaka Jagannadham (1826–1896), a pastor in Visakhapatnam, and Gollapalli Nathaniel (1839–1914), an Evangelist in the Godavari Delta, composed Indian worship songs which were highly renowned for their contribution toward the indigenization of Indian Christian worship (Devadoss, 1946: 76–82).[6]

The growth of nationalism in the subcontinent, between the final quarter of the 19th century and the first half of the 20th century, also influenced Indian Christians to turn toward the indigenization of their faith, despite Indian Christians being an insignificant minority (Firth, 2008: 249). The majority of the converts to Catholicism and Protestantism in Andhra Pradesh were from marginalized communities[7] and, to a lesser extent, from Brahmin and dominant peasant castes, such as *Reddy*, *Kapu*, and *Kamma*. It was during the period of the nation's struggle for independence from Britain that several Bhakti poets of distinction emerged: For example, Narayan Vaman Tilak (1861–1919), who composed songs in Marathi language, and K.T. Paul (1915), who composed songs in Tamil language (Popley, 1938). In the Tinnevelly and Dornakal dioceses of the CSI, certain parts of the Anglican liturgical order of service were set to Indian music (White, 1957). Some lyrical settings (using the CSI liturgy) with *Carnatic* music[8] were produced in Tinnevelly, Jaffna, and Andhra Pradesh.[9]

Other modifications were made in Christian *jatras* and harvest festivals, and occasionally to a Hindu festival, such as *Deepavali* (Divali). Jatras are basically village annual ritual festivals celebrated in honor of village deities, wherein all the village folk participate as a congregation. The chief feature of jatras is that the deity is taken in a procession to make the devotees feel that the deity has come in person to bless them. In the Christian jatras, images of Christ and other saints, as well the cross, were taken in the procession. New rituals were also devised incorporating Indian concepts during the early morning Easter services held in cemeteries at the Gossner Evangelical Lutheran Church (Pickett, 1938: 251–253) and the Christian Home festival.[10] The latter was designed on the basis of Gospel narratives of Mary and other women visiting the tomb of Christ before sunrise on Easter Sunday. A sepulcher-like structure was erected in the premises of the church, and womenfolk enacted the narrative with a procession carrying candle lights. Even today, this festival is followed in the churches of the Medak Diocese of CSI in Andhra Pradesh.

Apart from these indigenization efforts, there were also attempts made in the early 20th century by certain converts to live like sages (*sannyasis*). A Marathi brahmin convert, Narayan Vaman Tilak (1862–1919), spent the last 20 months of his life this way after resigning from his position at the American Marathi Mission (Winslow, 1923). He believed that *sannayasis* would be a more natural and attractive way to bring out the Christian message to the Hindus. He planned to form, what he called, *God's durbas*—a loosely knit fellowship of believers who would pledge themselves to follow Christ as their guru in an Indian way, whether baptized or not (ibid., 123–126). Tilak's action was a striking attempt to use one of the traditional forms of Hindu spirituality for Christian purposes. Similarly, B.C. Sircar, a Bengali who had worked in the Young Men's Christian Association (YMCA), practiced yoga in his later years and set up a Christian shrine at Puri, one of the sacred places of Hinduism (Latourette, 1937–1945: 211).

The indigenization of worship also became a matter of concern for the early converts during this period. Christian worship, the converts discovered, is essentially a corporate exercise, something foreign to Hinduism. The early converts favored congregational worship, which became more church-centered than mission-centered. The mission-centered mindset was construed on the basis of the Lord's commandment: "[G]o ye to the utmost parts of the world to make gentiles as disciples" (Matthew 28:19).

While Evangelism was the foundation of the mission-centered mindset, the church-centered mindset sought to establish churches and cater to the needs of converts within the faith. As a result, a good deal of attention was given by the mainline churches to constitutional and administrative matters, which included the formation of councils and committees to administer the church activities. The converts realized that ultimately the church consists of communities of faithful men and women living by the *word* and the *sacraments* as local manifestations of the body of Christ. In order to achieve this, administrative and fiscal decisions were made at the level of local councils and committees to ensure effective functioning.

With the advent of the Baptist denomination in 1800 in India,[11] the localization of the church gained further momentum in Evangelical Protestantism because Baptists traditionally practiced congregational church governance. *Autonomy* (self-rule) of the local church is a Baptist distinctive; therefore, no bishop, pastor, pope, conference of churches, or civil government had any say over the religious affairs of Baptist congregations. Baptists recognize two ministerial offices: pastors and deacons. In Andhra Pradesh, the Baptists are organized as the *samavesham* of Telugu Baptist Churches (STBC), with the following objectives:

1. To promote fellowship among the churches;
2. To affirm commonly held beliefs;
3. To provide counsel and assistance to local churches; and
4. To establish a structure through which churches could cooperate in their broader ministries, such as theological education, publications, and mission work (Shurden, n.d.).

The self-rule of congregation in Baptist churches also led to *free verse preaching* directly from the Bible, rather than from the liturgical, calendar-driven Bible lessons. The preachers displayed skills of oratory and homiletical abilities in their preaching, which stood out from the rest of the union, denominational churches. This observation is crucial because most pastors of contemporary mega churches in India have been influenced by Baptist missions, especially in terms of their preaching style and organizational practices.

In the 1920s, Pentecostalism emerged within Evangelical Protestantism as a strong movement in India. Pentecostal Christians, like their other Evangelical counterparts, believe in the inerrancy of Scripture and the necessity of accepting Christ as personal *lord* and *savior*. However, Pentecostalism is distinguished by its belief in baptism with the Holy Spirit as an experience that is separate from mere conversion. This two-stage belief results in empowerment of the believer, which includes spiritual gifts such as speaking in tongues and divine healing. Some of the larger Pentecostal organizations in India are: The Church of God in India, the AoG, the Indian Pentecostal Church of God (IPC), Sharon Fellowship, and The Pentecostal Mission (formerly Ceylon Pentecostal Mission). There are numerous other groups that are either independent or affiliated to the aforementioned Pentecostal groups. With strong support from churches and organizations in the USA, Europe, and Australia, these groups have been able to build solid churches with their presence seen and felt in almost every state of India (Poloma & Green, 2010: 64–65).

However, in the early 20th century, these Pentecostal missions felt the need to be more indigenous, resisting inflows of foreign funds. For example, in 1924, K.E. Abraham, a pastor who had worked closely with Robert F. Cook for several years, decided that he no longer wanted mission work to be financed with foreign funds. He broke away from Cook's leadership and established a separate church. Thus, Abraham was one of the pioneers of the IPC, along with many other men. The AoG, with early work in Calcutta and Kerala, also grew rapidly and by 1970s, it established reputable Bible Schools throughout India.

However, it must be noted that many of the Pentecostal groups in India were more Charismatic in theology and did not conform to the foundational teachings accepted by the mainline Pentecostal churches.[12] For example, the Charismatic movement, a group within mainstream congregations adopted beliefs and practices similar to Pentecostals.[13] Among Protestants, the Charismatic Movement began around 1960. Among Roman Catholics, it originated around 1967. Charismatic Christians believe that the gifts of the Holy Spirit, as described in the New Testament, are available to contemporary Christians through the infilling or baptism of the Holy Spirit, with-or-without the laying on of hands. These spiritual gifts are believed to be manifested in the form of signs, miracles, and wonders, including, but not limited to, speaking in tongues, interpretation of tongues, prophecy, healing, and discernment of spirits. From the Charismatic groups, the mega church founders adopted the practices of healing and baptism with the Holy Spirit,[14] which virtually liberated the congregation from the fear of losing their status and identity (according to the Fifth and Ninth Schedules of the Indian Constitution as discussed in the introduction).

Having become indigenous in the 1940s, the churches in India emerged into a phase of conflict, both within and without to hold back their congregations. Politics became manifest because individuals could not get access to power through councils and synods; and, as a result, congregations began to split on the basis of caste and regional locations. For example, the CSI congregation was dominated by a caste of Dalits known as *Malas*, whereas the Baptist congregation was dominated by another caste of Dalits known as *Madigas*. This sense of caste was so culturally rooted that even in the general Christian councils, these differences were overtly expressed. However, when it came to the sharing of public resources made available by the government as a constitutional right, both the groups jointly craved for the status of SC (Rao, 2010).[15] The converted Christians from SCs are considered under the *BC-C* category, where the ruling does not promise a profitable share of public resources.[16] In the years 1955, 1980, and 2004, several representations for these two caste groups were made by the leaders of the Christian community to consider Dalit Christians as SCs, that is, at par with the SC converts who convert to Buddhism and Sikhism. The Dalit Christian leaders argued that caste and religion are two separate entities in India and religion has to be seen as faith, whereas caste is a matter of social identity.

Globalization: Its Impact on the Formation of Mega Churches

Global interdependence is not a new phenomenon, but it has certainly been more prevalent in recent decades. Broadly speaking, globalization means that decisions made by individuals and their agencies in one part of the world may influence people, companies, and governments in other parts of the world—sometimes positively and often negatively. Thus, globalization is the process by which political, cultural, and economic boundaries are superseded, and the world is more and more like a village in which cultures are interconnected (McLuhan, 1962). Globalization is associated with the rise of world financial markets and free trade zones, resulting in the global exchange of goods and services which in turn breeds transnational corporations. The concept of *post-Fordism* (which will be explained) is intrinsic to the process of globalization.

Harvey (1989), a neo-Marxist, analyzed capitalism and proposed the following phases in capitalist development:

1. Capitalism started with *primitive accumulation* and entered, through it, into industrialization.
2. During most of the 20th century, industrialization passed through the era of Fordism (named after the American automobile manufacturer, Henry Ford): industrial mass production of standardized goods in an automated assembly line, which emphasized the *dehumanization of the workforce* (autonomy taken from workers, and transferred to machinery and management).
3. In response to the crisis in capitalism during the early 1970s (markets saturated with goods, tax revenues down, and inflation out of control), *flexible accumulation* emerged, which is broadly analogous with *post-Fordism*. The term flexible accumulation depicts manufacturers' ability to rapidly change product lines in order to manufacture small batches for niche markets, using a smaller number of adaptable multiskilled workers, information technology, and computerized production systems. It also reflects manufacturers' propensity to deploy advertising and other strategies in order to continually generate shifts in demand for new and trendy products.

As a result of post-Fordism and globalization, arguably, culture and mass media have become more and more important in society as lives revolve around the consumption of symbols, while image and space have replaced narrative and history, as organizing principles of cultural production. According to Lash (1990: 4–5), global society is "confined to the realm of culture"; it is a cultural paradigm, a "regime of signification" in which "only cultural objects are produced" (ibid.). Lash claims that whereas "cultural modernization is a process of cultural differentiation... cultural globalization is a process of cultural de-differentiation" (ibid., 5).

The term de-differentiation is important to my thesis in this chapter. According to Lash (1990:5–15), the concept of *difference* is a modernist perception revealed through the writings of Weber and Secher (1962), who dichotomized social spaces as sacred or secular, fane or profane, public or private. Within *difference*, religion was conceived as a cultural regime confined to the sacred. However, *de-difference* interrupts the special divide in cultural behavior as sacred or secular; de-difference is structured as a process of cultural signification that privileges the image, rather than words and texts. Figural signification is interested in the (sensuous) impact rather than the (discursive) meaning of texts, and it "operates through the spectator's immersion, the relatively unmediated investment of his/her desire in the cultural object" (Lash, 1990:175). Hence, in the context of mega churches, the interior architectural structures and worship services that make use of light, sound, and video effects are immensely appealing to church goers, presumably drawing them closer to the message and mission of the church. Most of the church members in the three mega churches in Andhra Pradesh come from middle-class backgrounds, and since many of them are employed by *high-tech* software companies, they are familiar with digital culture. They, therefore, accept these media technologies used by the church as a *spatial* continuum between the secular and the sacred. Also, public and private spaces have become points of discourse in the mega churches, with pastors addressing the issues of private and public with ease—claiming their authority as *men of God*.

However, there is a downside to globalization. As noted by Harvey (1989), economic forces have become increasingly obdurate and weaker groups are often marginalized. This has resulted in:

1. Inequality;
2. Financial crises;
3. Reshaping cultural identity;
4. Breakdown of community and family ties; and
5. Increasing global crime.

Unsurprisingly, many people are frightened by visible signs of globalization, such as the closure and/or privatization of government undertakings and corporations, resulting in large-scale retrenchment of the workforce, relocation of personnel in private companies, instability in financial markets, and worldwide enforcement of cultural changes through effective marketing of cultural products (Lash, 1990). This fear is associated with a lack of faith in the possibility of ordinary citizens being able to influence and alter the course of globalization, and hence the emergence of *imagined communities* (Anderson, 1983; Bauman, 1992: XX–XXI) which cut across the frontiers of class and caste. To sum up: The developments, as have been outlined, have brought forth changes in social organization and in religion, gradually replacing the social stratification of the pre-modern and modern social order in India. As such, social structures based on production relations, and caste and class (the *varna-jati* paradigm)[17] have increasingly become irrelevant. Caste has remained an identity marker at the domestic level for the purposes of rites of passage, such as birth, puberty, marriage, and death, but this is largely symbolic.

A further impact of globalization has been the trend for urban centers in India to emerge as mega cities, combining the spaces of urban and rural; the latter is referred to as *rurbanization*, wherein a large number of rural people have migrated to the urban centers seeking work, resulting in a tremendous increase in the labor supply, and growth of colonies and residential areas (Lefebvre, 2003). The term *rurban* was coined in the early 1970s, by French Philosopher Henri Lefebvre, to describe areas that combined intensive agricultural spaces with sub-urban living and industrial sites (ibid.). To cater to the needs of new immigrants, churches with Charismatic leadership began to emerge in cities, such as Hyderabad, Vishakhapatnam, and Vijayawada. Gradually, the membership of these churches grew to more than 4,000 members, which entitled them to be called *mega churches* (some church leaders even claim that their membership is 55,000.[18]

To facilitate effective ministries for all, pastors in these three mega churches in Andhra Pradesh conduct at least four worship services every Sunday in addition to services during the week. The leaders of mega churches have designated themselves as *pastors* or *brothers*, and have acquired honorary doctorate degrees to use as prefixes to their names. Most of the mega church leaders hail from Charismatic Church backgrounds, and some are recent converts from the Hindu religion. Most of them do not have any formal theological training, but are recognized as *men of God* with special powers of healing and miracles. They all started their career as Evangelists or itinerant preachers before establishing their mega-church ministries. Leadership in these churches is based on individual creativity, efficiency, and ability to control the congregation effectively through prayers and healing practices. The congregation's acceptance of an individual as a *man of God* is what differentiates the mega church from the other churches, and this belief is the innate strength of the mega church. Respect and reverence for the leaders by the congregation eliminates all denominational and structural control. The individualization of leadership in mega churches which negates homogenization has brought forth variations in gospel ministries, worship orders, and liturgy, as explained as follows.

Globalized Faith Seekers: What Sustains Them?

Despite the compelling evidence that globalization led to the emergence of mega churches, it is my contention that other influences are more significant to their sustenance in India. Certainly, the post-capitalist world has introduced homogenization in cultural products and practices (Jennings, 2010) through the popularization and diffusion of a wide array of cultural symbols, customs, ideas, and values (Barker, 2008). O' Connor (2006) describes homogenization as "the process by which local cultures are transformed or absorbed by a dominant outside culture." However, since *oracy* (oral communication) is the driving force of culture and expressive traditions in India's everyday life, Indian culture has by and large resisted, if not modified, the influences of homogenization (Reddy, 2001:293–213). Religion is not simply a set of beliefs, but a symbolic system that bestows identity and meaning through territorial rites of passage and life cycle ceremonies to its members—not only in this mundane world, but even in the world to come "whose builder and maker is God" (Hebrews 11:10).

The fieldwork for this study on mega churches in the state of Andhra Pradesh yielded some interesting insights. For example, the Calvary Temple in the city of Hyderabad has reached *mega church* status in less than a decade, and it seems that the key to this amazing growth is its ability to minister to the needs of its congregation. On the other hand, the Holy Ghost Fire Ministries in Vishakhapatnam, which is more than two decades old and has only acquired the status of *mega church* recently, has put its emphasis on Evangelical ministry. Both founders of these churches started their career as pastors, rather than preachers. These facts are noteworthy because mega churches combine both pastoral as well as Evangelical pursuits, unlike the mainline churches where these two objectives are separated.

The Bible Mission Church, in Gooty, is a mega church of a different kind. The founder of the Bible Mission, the late Pastor Devadossiah, lived and worked in such a way that he influenced his intimate followers profoundly. After Devadossiah's demise, his followers started missions in different regions, and Gooty is one of them. Unlike the two other mega churches in Andhra Pradesh, the Gooty Mission is located in a remote place and caters to the rural masses, which shows that mega churches are not restricted to urban centers. The phenomenal success surrounding the Gooty Mission is perhaps due to folk religious beliefs, which are strongly held in India.

Folk religion is full of versions and variations, and it makes sense in the context of India's social composition and hierarchies (social castes/classes). Christianity, in my opinion, is not a monolithic religion governed purely by *textual* sources, such as liturgy. It is also based on *lived experiences*, where the followers appropriate Christ and his doctrine in everyday life through the narratives of the faith. Hence, the narratives contained in the Bible are ably used by several mega church pastors as a means to help the congregation to *live out* the story of Christ.

The following are the characteristic features of folk religion in the Indian context:

1. India is primarily an oral-based nation, and its ethos of Indian folk religion basically lies in *oracy* (communication by word of mouth). This is distinguished from the worship in mainline churches which strictly follow the liturgical order (biblical lessons are fixed well in advance). In mega churches, pastors and preachers base their messages on metaphysical (cosmic) temporality in imparting messages: Every message is regarded as an inspiration or revelation from God. This is analogous to the narrative of Moses when he came down from Mount Sinai after receiving the Ten Commandments, and the Israelites observed him closely (Exodus 34:29–35).

2. Since Indian folk religion exists primarily in oracy, the concept of time and space within the narrative (preaching/message) becomes *cyclical*, and hence the *stories* oscillate between the past and the present, with a few marked references by the narrator. Therefore, the congregation relates to the narrative and applies it to everyday life. The themes of the messages/stories in mega churches are structured

on Biblical personalities, lives of men of God, and faith expositions as revealed from the founders of churches and their own life experiences. To connect the past and the present lived experiences of the aforementioned, the pastors of the mega churches mostly entitle the themes of their messages as *abundant life, successful life,* the road to success, and *victorious life*. Thus, every message is instructional, promise-filled, and relevant to the everyday life of the listener.

3. The cyclical nature of oral narratives is achieved by a structural formulation in the very plot itself by the pastors of mega churches. For example, the message on *redemption from sin*, by Pastor Stephen Paul, always connects a Biblical event, such as David's adultery and the repercussions thereof, as one narrative plot structure; this is then connected with a recent life experience of a known personality as the second plot structure. The third structure is when the pastor connects the first two parts to the listeners' realm. All these subplots are accompanied with suitable verses from the Bible, together with tales, proverbs, and jokes at appropriate places during the message—just as a folk story teller does.

4. The Christian folk narrative performance is a *collective* enterprise, connecting the congregation with its pastor. For instance, Pastor Satish Kumar of Calvary Temple strongly believes that the family is the basic unit of the church, and therefore the well-being of family life is his core concern. One of the requirements for Calvary Temple members is that they have to declare their assets and properties, and make an agreement in the presence of the pastor and elders as to how the family assets will be divided amongst family members. This, according to Satish Kumar, reduces family conflicts, and also reduces the risk of the church being dragged into family conflicts. Likewise, caste, kin groups (families having same surnames), and denominational identities are not at all encouraged in the church so as to eliminate *power politics* within the church. Mega church pastors work hard to provide a sense of community and oneness in the church home.

It is interesting to note that members of the three mega churches are mostly young adults and young couples. More than 70 percent of the members are between the ages of 25 and 45.

5. Since folk religion is collectivist, it is in a sense *anonymous*. Pastors of the mega churches often add the disclaimer in their preaching that

what they share is not *their* thoughts, but the words of the Spirit of God. The preacher communicates directly (face-to-face) with the listeners, so that even during the Sunday worship services, family issues, such as, conflict in the home can be addressed as examples in the sermons. By these means, anonymity of the families who have conflicts and crisis is observed, yet practical resolutions are sought through the scriptures. The pastor, as the *servant of God*, claims that all the preaching and decisions are derived from God.

6. The anonymity, as already described, makes folk religion operate beyond a person's own lifetime as a *traditional* narrative. *Traditional*, here, is both intrinsic and extrinsic. Intrinsically, tradition refers to the group which looks at its own tradition as if it is in continuity with the past, and therefore authenticates itself by repeating the traditions. Extrinsically, tradition means the groups of communities which look at their interrelationships as means of mutual coexistence (Ben-Amos, 1982). This dual character of tradition is essential to understand how a narrative (preaching/message) adapts itself to present circumstances, and yet is considered traditional. For example, the mega church at Gooty in Anantapur District strongly believes in miracles—especially, deliverance from sickness, demonic possessions, and visions. The pastor allows space for the members to share testimonies of that kind. During the recent platinum jubilee celebrations of the church, from January 27–29, 2013, the church commemorated its tradition and looked back to how the church was founded. However, the pastor announced that the actual dates for the celebration were given by God to a female lay member of the church through a vision. When the church members heard of this vision, many of them were moved to contribute gifts to the church in the form of food grains, vegetables, sheep, goats, and money for distribution to the poor as part of the celebration.

Mega churches in India, therefore, are creating a culture-sensitive niche for their faith seekers, keeping in tune with the principles of *de-difference* by reaffirming their identities and preserving their valued ways of life based on spiritual experience and prosperity against, what are taken to be, the pernicious effects of foreign and global influences. My case studies of the three mega churches reveal that churchgoers of mega churches are looking for de-difference in the worship order and their reception of theology, in the form of simple and comforting messages, during the worship services. Thus, in keeping with the concept of de-difference, the secular, and the sacred intersect with each other. The behaviors that were specialized for a specific function lose their specialization and become simplified or generalized to cater to the needs of all people.

Features of Mega Churches

To add to our understanding of the unique place that mega churches have in India, I elaborate on six features of the mega churches in Andhra Pradesh.

First, the architecture of the mega churches is redefined from *permanent*, gothic physical structures to postmodern, large, makeshift convention shelters. The Calvary Temple in Hyderabad is one such example. The founder of the church, Brother Satish Kumar, recently built a church that can accommodate more than 17,000 people in one sitting. Even more remarkably, this structure was completed in 52 days, thereby emulating Nehemiah's feat (from the Old Testament) in building the walls of Jerusalem in 52 days. Bro Kumar reasoned: "Why can't a servant of God who has faith in the same God [as Nehemiah] not build Calvary Temple in the same way?"[19] However, it should be noted that Bro Kumar received considerable help from his congregation in building the new church—with physical labor, such as masonry, electrical, plumbing works, and financial help. The seating in the church is designed in a semicircle fashion, like an indoor auditorium, and the entire building is air-conditioned (this is a novelty because very few churches in India have air-conditioning). Pastor Stephen Paul is planning to construct a prayer stadium on the lines of an indoor sports stadium in Vishakhapatnam with seating arrangement for several thousand people. It will also be used for convocations, training programs, and revival prayer meetings. In 2003, Bro Adbhuta Kumar, of Bible Mission in Gooty constructed a massive concrete structure on his 61 acre piece of land, which can accommodate more than 10,000 people. However, in this church every one sits on the carpeted floor (a commonplace thing to do in India); there are no pews. The Gooty Church resembles a traditional structure with a cross on the tower.

Second, the leadership in mega churches has replaced the traditional institutional setup (a clergy-driven bureaucracy supported by an elected synod) with Spirit-embodied persons, such as Charismatic leaders, to whom special powers are attributed. Mega churches have trained the volunteers from within the congregation to act as employees, with little or no remuneration. For example, Bro Satish Kumar has three types of volunteers to serve the church:

1. Calvary Army, who are full time employees
2. Calvary Soldiers, who are semi-employed voluntary workers; and
3. Calvary Amateurs (enthusiasts) from the regular congregation (unpaid).

Thus, the congregation is transformed into voluntary unpaid *co-workers* in the ministry of the Lord. The creation of this largely non-specialized service sector by the mega churches is critical for their survival.

Third, mega churches have become *communal shelters* or *imagined communities* to their congregations (faith seekers) due to the aforementioned fears of losing employment, identity, and the like. Most of the faith seekers who attend the mega churches in Hyderabad and Vishakhapatnam are settlers who have migrated from different parts of Andhra Pradesh in search of employment. They hail from the middle or lower middle class and since most are in the service sector, their job security is subject to the vagaries of the global market. Caste distinctions, which are still dominant in traditional denominational churches, are obscured in the mega churches because converts from different castes take shelter in these churches for their spiritual needs and comfort. In traditional churches, face-to-face communication and recognition is essential between the pastor and the members of the church because the pastor makes regular visits to the homes of members during rites of passage. In the mega churches, it is the church *volunteers* who visit the houses of members of the church and deliver cakes or other presents on occasions, such as, birthdays, marriages, and other important ceremonies. Volunteers also use SMS and email for greeting and informing members of special announcements. As mentioned, most of the churchgoers of mega churches are young (below the age of 40)—in contrast to traditional churches.

Fourth, the preaching in mega churches by Charismatic leaders/pastors is geared toward seeking an authority powerful enough to relieve the congregation of their fears through faith healing, fasting prayers, and special prayers, using all forms of modern electronic gadgetry. In these mega churches, the involvement of family members (of the leaders) is common. For example, in the Calvary Temple, Satish Kumar is supported by his brother, who is a convert from the Hindu faith and comes from a peasant community. In the case of Bro Stephen Paul, his spouse runs the church in his absence, and she is also regarded as a powerful preacher. Bro Stephen's young son, who is hardly seven years old, is already giving brief sermons, and his eight-year-old daughter participates in singing. Pastor Adbhuta Kumar of Gooty is strongly supported by his spouse in all matters of the church ministry; four of his very young daughters also support him in the church activities. All three mega churches use televangelism, and their programs are telecast in all major Telugu Christian channels every alternate day. The preaching in the churches on Sunday worship lasts for almost an hour and the *altar call* lasts for half an hour. The altar call is an effective device used by these leaders to establish the congregation's relationship with the Lord and with the church. Every worship service includes testimonies from the congregation on healing or gaining prosperity in order to strengthen and encourage the whole church. Conversely, in the denominational churches, the preaching time is limited to 20–30 minutes, and there is no provision for altar call or testimonies. The sermons in India's mega churches, in general, have the structure of: sin–repentance–salvation–prosperity (in this world and the world to come). Thus, the mega church preachers give the impression that the spiritual needs of the congregation are paramount in ministry. Every message, somehow or other, touches on Christian *eschatology* (the doctrine of future hope) and prepares the congregation for this *blessed hope*.

Fifth, having no other anchors, except the affections of their members, *imagined communities* are reinforced by the respective church leaders through occasional, spectacular outbursts of *togetherness*, which take the form of festivals, revival meetings, Holy Spirit anointing meetings, in addition to the multiple worship services on Sundays. Almost every month, these leaders conduct revival meetings in different parts of the state and announce these activities through their TV programs. They also conduct separate prayer meetings for youth/students in preparation for school examinations. Counseling meetings are conducted for young couples on family relations, and special healing meetings are arranged for the dramatic casting out of demonic spirits. Testimonies from the healed are organized simultaneously. All of these symbolic actions of public display at religious gatherings help to enlarge and sustain the membership of the church community; they focus primarily on one purpose: To bring together all the heterogeneous groups as one congregation.

Sixth, these mega churches reach out to people beyond their local congregations through a *cafeteria* mode of ministry: By selling their products, such as recorded sermons, songs, testimonies, calendars, and anointed sacred objects, and by conducting sermons and online worship services in the rented secular spaces, such as function centers and hotels. For example, even though Bro P.J. Stephen Paul runs his church from Vishakhapatnam, he conducts regular Sunday evening services at a marriage hall in Secunderabad (600 kilometers from the main church in Vishakhapatnam) through an online telecast of his messages, while a Secunderabad-based pastor conducts the worship service.

Conclusion

In this chapter, I have argued that even though globalization is responsible for the formation of these three mega churches in Andhra Pradesh, it is the impact of the folk religious ethos that is the driving force to sustain their rural and *rurban* scenarios. I have asserted that Christian folk religion is the source of cultural variation, difference, and de-difference in the formation and operation of these mega churches. Unlike the Western paradigm, folk religion seems to play a more fundamental role in the private realm and everyday life in India, thus eroding the difference between private and public life, and mega churches have cleverly adopted and incorporated this phenomenon through preaching and worship.

Sadly, for at least two centuries, efforts to unite the mainline churches by forming different councils and assemblies have failed miserably, and the churches remain segmented on denominational and doctrinal aspects. The advent of globalization has given vent to postmodern social formations cutting across the denominational and doctrinal divide in church life—paving the way for the formation of mega churches in India with strong local (folk) cultural roots. Thus, the phenomenon of the *glocal* (global plus local) has emerged as the sustaining force for these mega churches and their faith seekers. What remains is further research to see whether these phenomena are prevalent elsewhere in India and beyond.

Notes

1. For example, the Baptist Mission started in AD 1792, and the London Mission started its work in AD 1799.
2. There were, for example, English Congregationalist missions and American Congregationalist missions, English, American, and Canadian Baptists, and among the Lutherans, a large number of missions from different countries and different synods or missionary societies in the same country; all Lutherans, but each independent of the others started their work in the colonies.
3. In 1855, representatives of six missions and their European churches from Bengal met in Calcutta. Since then, conferences of missionaries working in particular provinces have been held, and later a series of decennial conferences for the whole of India took place at Allahabad in 1872. (Latourette, 1937–1945: VI, 129).
4. The principle has been recognized earlier in some parts, but not in others. Previous decennial conferences had discussed the matter, but were unable to secure general agreement. Even in Madras, total agreement was not reached; but the conference was able to set up a Court of Arbitration to deal with cases where one mission trespassed on the territory of another (Richter, 1908: 229).
5. The Anglican Church was established through the work of the Church Missionary Society and the Society for the Propagation of the Gospel, both closely linked with the Church of England. The congregational churches were established through the missionary activities of the London Missionary Society with missionaries from Great Britain and Australia, and the American Board of Commissioners of Foreign Missions. The Presbyterian Churches established the Church of Scotland Mission, the Dutch Reformed Church in America, and the Basel Mission in Switzerland and Germany. They also had connections with the Presbyterian Churches in England and Australia. The Methodist Church was established by the Methodist Missionary Society of the Methodist Church in Great Britain (Firth, 2008: 239–240).
6. Krishnarao Sangle of Ahmednagar composed Marathi lyrics in Indian meter and set to Indian *ragas* (melodic modes used in Indian classical music): A collection of them, called *Gayanamrit*, was published in 1867.
7. SCs, such as *Mala* (engaged in scavenging, especially the disposal of the dead and agricultural works) and *Madiga* (carrying leather works, scavenging specially disposal of the carcass, and currently engaged in agricultural pursuits), are the marginalized communities in Andhra Pradesh, and during pre-independence times they were considered as outcastes and forced to live outside the village as *untouchables* due to purity and pollution norms.
8. Carnatic music is a system of music commonly associated with the southern part of the Indian subcontinent. The main emphasis of Carnatic music is on vocal music, and most compositions are written to be sung. Even when played on instruments, they are meant to be performed in *gayaki* (singing) style. It is one of two main sub-genres of

Indian classical music that evolved from ancient Hindu traditions, the other subgenre being Hindustani music, which emerged as a distinct form because of Persian and Islamic influences in North India. Carnatic music is mainly sung through compositions, especially the *kriti* (or *kirtanam*)—a form developed between the 14th and 19th centuries by composers, such as Purandara Dasa, Tyagaraja, Muthuswami Dikshitar, and Syama Sastri of Carnatic music. All these compositions form part of the Bhakti (devotional) literature, as they are sung in worship and praise of deities.

9. The early converts hoped that such experiments would go on, until not merely hymns and metrical versions of Psalms and portions of services assigned to the people, but a complete Indian liturgical chant for the whole service, perhaps along the line of the *kirtan* or the intonation of poetry.
10. The ceremony with lights in the Christian Home Festival historically belongs to the Easter Vigil.
11. Baptists are Christians who comprise a group of denominations and churches that subscribe to a doctrine, that baptism should be performed only for professing believers (believer's baptism, as opposed to infant baptism), and that it must be done by immersion (as opposed to sprinkling). Other tenets of Baptist Churches include: Salvation through faith alone, scripture alone as the rule of faith and practice, and the autonomy of the local congregation.
12. The Pentecostal Movement experienced a great explosion in growth with the arrival of a number of foreign missionaries. Most significant among them was Robert F. Cook from the USA. He arrived in North India and established a few mission posts there.
13. While Pentecostals and Charismatic groups share these beliefs, there are differences. Many in the Charismatic Movement deliberately distanced themselves from Pentecostalism for cultural and theological reasons. Foremost among theological reasons is the tendency of many Pentecostals to insist that speaking in tongues is always the initial physical sign of receiving Spirit baptism. Although specific teachings will vary from group to group, Charismatics generally believe that the baptism with the Holy Spirit occurs at the time of new birth and prefer to call subsequent encounters with the Holy Spirit by other names, such as *being filled* (Menzies & Menzies, 2000: 39). In contrast to Pentecostals, Charismatics tend to accept a range of supernatural experiences (such as prophecy, miracles, healing, or "physical manifestations of an altered state of consciousness") as evidence of having been baptized or filled with the Holy Spirit (ibid.). Pentecostals are also distinguished from the Charismatic Movement on the basis of style. Also, Pentecostals have traditionally placed a high value on evangelization and missionary work. Charismatics, on the other hand, have tended to see their movement as a force for revitalization and renewal within their own church traditions.
14. In some cases, the Holy Spirit baptism replaces water baptism; however, the practices differ in different groups.
15. I am indebted to Rev Dr B. Prabhaker Rao, the pastor of the United Church, BHEL Township, Hyderabad, for his valuable information on this topic as well as on comity.
16. According to the Indian Constitution, the percentage of government jobs to be reserved for SCs is 15 percent, for STs is 7.5 percent, and OBCs is 27 percent. In the state government, the OBC category only gets 3 percent of the quota of government jobs. For instance, an SC Christian is considered as BC (C) category (Backward Community–C) in Andhra Pradesh. (We have four categories in Backward Castes, and they are grouped as A-B-C and D.) A person belonging to BC community does not enjoy the same benefits as that of a SC person. If a Dalit (a *neolog* for oppressed class) gets converted

into a Christian, he or she loses all benefits as an SC. Therefore, currently there is a movement being carried out by the Dalit Christians to press the government to retain their status as SCs.
17. Indian society is organized on the basis of varna-jati paradigm; *varna* is a ritual ranking based on purity and pollution norms, where as *jati* (caste) is based on occupation (actual position). Varna is hierarchical in nature, and hence vertical in graphic depiction where as jati is horizontal within each varna.
18. See http://calvarytemple.in/about-us.html. Retrieved on August 22, 2014.
19. See http://www.aradanatv.com/home.html. Retrieved on January 30, 2013.

Bibliography

Anderson, Benedict. 1983. *Imagined Communities: Reflections on the Origin and Spread of Nationalism*. London: Verso.
Appasamy, A.J. 1958. *Sundar Singh*. Cambridge: Lutterworth Press.
Appasamy, P. 1923. *The Centenary History of the C.M.S. in Tinnevelly*. Palamcottah: Palamcottah Press.
Barker, Chris. 2008. *Cultural Studies: Theory and Practice*. New Delhi: SAGE Publications.
Baudrillard, Jean. 1998. *The Consumer Society: Myths and Structures*. (C. Turner, Trans.) New Delhi: SAGE Publications. (Original work published 1970).
Bauman, Zygmunt. 1992. *Intimations of Postmodernity*. London: Routledge.
Ben-Amos, Dan. 1982. *Folklore in Context: Essays*. New Delhi/Madras: South Asian Publishers.
Benjamin, Walter. 1985. *The Work of Art in the Age of Mechanical Reproduction, Illuminations: Essays and Reflections*. New York: Schoken Books.
Bertens, Hans. 1995. *The Idea of the Postmodern: A History*. London: Routledge.
Devadoss, D. 1946. *The Life of Poet: H.A. Krishna Pillay*. Madras: NMS Press.
Featherstone, Mike. 1995. *Consumer Culture and Postmodernism*. London: SAGE Publications.
Firth, Cyril Bruce. 2008. *An Introduction to Indian Church History*. Serampore: ISPCK.
Harvey, David. 1989. *The Condition of Postmodernity: An Enquiry into the Origins of Cultural Change*. Cambridge, MA: Blackwell.
Hewat, E.G.K. 1950. *Christ and Western India*. Bombay: J. Kellock.
Hough, J. 1839–1845. *A History of Christianity in India*. (4 Vols) London: Seeley and Burnside.
James, Jonathan D. 2010. *McDonaldisation, Masala McGospel and Om Economics: Televangelism in Contemporary India*. New Delhi: SAGE Publications.
Jennings, Justin. 2010. *Globalizations and the Ancient World*. London: Cambridge University Press.
Lash, Scott. 1990. *Sociology of Postmodernity*. London: Routledge.
Latourette, K.S. 1937–1945. *A History of the Expansion of Christianity*, Vol. 7. New York: HarperCollins.
Lefebvre, Henri. 2003. *The Urban Revolution* (Revised ed.). Minneapolis: University of Minnesota Press.
Leidner, R. 1993. *Fast Food, Fast Talk, Service and the Routinization of Everyday Life*. California: California Press.
Lyotard, Jean-Francois. 1984. *The Postmodern Condition*. Manchester: Manchester University Press.

McLuhan, Marshall. 1962. *The Gutenberg Galaxy: The Making of Typographic Man.* Toronto: University of Toronto Press.
Menzies, William W. & Robert P. Menzies. 2000. *Spirit and Power: Foundations of Pentecostal Experience.* Michigan: Zondervan.
O' Connor, David E. 2006. *Encyclopedia of the Global Economy: A Guide For Students and Researchers.* New Delhi: Academic Foundation.
Parker, A. 1951. *Sadhu Sundar Singh: Called of God.* Madras: C.L.S.
Pickett, J.W. 1938. *Christ's Way to India's Heart.* London: Livingstone Press.
Pike, Kenneth. 1954. *Language in Relation to a Unified Theory of the Structure of Human Behaviour.* Glendale: California Summer Institute of Linguistics.
Poloma, Margaret M., & John C. Green. 2010. *The Assemblies of God: Godly Love and the Revitalization of American Pentecostalism.* New York: New York University Press.
Popley, H.A. 1938. *K.T. Paul, Christian Leader.* Calcutta: Y.M.C.A.
Rao, Prabhaker Bandari. 2010. *The Missiological Motifs of the Miracles of Jesus Christ.* New Delhi: ISPCK.
Reddy, Sudhakar Y.A. 2001. "Ritual Performances and Theoretical Validity to Folklore: The Case of Andhra Pradesh." In B.Ramakrishna Reddy (ed.), *Dravidian Folk and Tribal Lore* (pp. 293–313). Kuppam: Dravidian University.
Richter, J. 1908. *A History of Missions in India.* Edinburgh: Oliphant.
Ritzer, George. 1996. *The McDonaldizsation of Society.* Thousand Oaks, CA: Pine Forge Press.
Rouse, Ruth & Stephen Charles Neill. 1954. *A History of the Ecumenical Movement 1517-1948.* Philadelphia: Westminster Press.
Sandkler, B. 1954. *Church of South India.* Cambridge: Lutterworth Press.
Schillar, H.I. 1976. *Communications and Cultural Domination.* New York: Sharpe.
Shurden, Walter B. (n.d.). "Turning Points in Baptist History." Retrieved from http://www.centerforbaptiststudies.org/pamphlets/style/turningpoints.htm on April 16, 2013.
Smith, Philip. 2001. *Cultural Theory: An Introduction.* Massachusetts: Blackwell.
Smith, William. 1892. *Dictionary of the Bible.* Cambridge: Riverside Press.
Thompson, Stith. 1977. *The Folktale.* Berkeley: University of California Press.
Tilak, Lakshmibai. 1950. *I Follow After.* (E.J. Inkster, Trans.) New Delhi: Oxford University Press. (Original work in Marathi, *Smriti Chitra*, published between 1934 and 1937).
Weber, Max & H.P. Secher. 1962. *Basic Concepts in Sociology.* New York: Citadel Press.
White, Emmons E. 1957. *Appreciating India's Music: An Introduction to the Music of India, with suggestions for its use in the churches of India.* Serampore: CLS Press.
Winslow, J.C. 1923. *Narayana Vaman Tilak.* Calcutta: Y.M.C.A.

SECTION IV

Mega Churches in Latin America

8

Concentrations of Faith: Mega Churches in Brazil

Dennis A. Smith and Leonildo S. Campos

This chapter will compare traditional Protestant, Pentecostal, neo-Pentecostal, and Roman Catholic mega churches in Brazil. Most have a Charismatic emphasis; all demonstrate sophisticated media and marketing strategies—including the purchase of their own media outlets—and adept use of emerging social media. All have been active in Brazilian politics, pursuing particular policy agendas. We will also demonstrate how tending to such massive flocks—both those that attend services and those serve virtually—has led to the emergence of a new kind of pastor/religious entrepreneur.

The Latin American Religious Context

Early Protestant mission efforts in the 19th century coincided with Latin American political and military movements that led to the creation of the region's nation states. As Latin America moved beyond the colonial era, Protestants demonstrated a decidedly modern approach to religious practice, while Roman Catholicism positioned itself as the defender of conservative religious tradition and declining European empires. Throughout the colonial era, Catholicism, the religion of both Portuguese and Spanish royalty had great cultural and economic power, and had been charged with cultivating religious identity, sustaining the political and economic status quo, and defining the differences between the colonizer and colonized.

As the colonial era came to an end and nation states were formed, the emerging Latin American political and economic elites were deeply influenced by European liberalism—they promoted less-regulated markets, representative democracy, and the concept of the separation of church and state. They were also influenced by the philosophical school of positivism, postulated by Auguste Comte and John Stuart Mill, and therefore believed that education, science, and technology offered the key to a promising future. In this context, the new Protestant missions have become the de facto allies of the elites of Latin America. Many missionaries from the USA built schools and hospitals, and came to be noted for their practicality and entrepreneurial spirit. Such initiatives offered liberal politicians living examples of their revolutionary ideologies.

The Protestant missionary impulse was also rooted in their understanding of themselves as the children of the Enlightenment and in their disdain for the Catholicism practiced in Latin America. Not only did they see Catholicism as being locked in medieval obscurantism, they also felt it had become highly unorthodox due to the syncretic influences of African and indigenous spiritualities.

At the level of popular religious imagination, Catholicism and Protestantism approached worship and personal piety very differently: Catholic worship focused on the mystery of the Eucharist; daily religious practice included devotion to the saints, praying the rosary, and observing— or at least being conscious of—the liturgy of the hours as a way to keep track of time throughout the day. Furthermore, the liturgical calendar divided the year into a regular cycle of religious festivals, including patron saint days for each community. Protestant worship focused on the sermon—a reasoned discourse on a religious text. Many Protestant Churches tended to be austere spaces, eschewing liturgical vestments, the liturgical calendar, and even candles because they were considered too Catholic. Many Protestant communities celebrated the Eucharist only quarterly, some only annually. Daily religious practices included personal and family prayer, devotional Bible reading, and bearing testimony to one's faith before the community. Despite Protestantism's privileged ideological position in Latin America's new political universe, their numbers were few and Roman Catholicism continued to be the religion of the masses.

In 20th-century Brazil, liberalism's promise of progress gave way to the reality of conflict and profound social polarization. In time, the failures of liberalism—and of government in general—gave birth to deep popular distrust in public institutions. In a harsh economic environment marked by mass migration to the cities, many new urban residents embarked on a search for consolation, meaning, and transcendence.

Concentrations of Faith 171

Public expressions of religiosity and spirituality have grown rapidly in recent decades. At the same time, Brazil has witnessed the consolidation of a market economy and consumer society, driven by the rapid growth of the mass media. In this context, both traditional and emerging media have become powerful tools for promoting not only consumer culture, but also political ideologies and religious belief systems.

One new development in recent decades has been the appearance of the Brazilian mega church. In his pioneering research at the Hartford Institute for Religion Research, Scott Thumma has identified several criteria that characterize mega churches in the USA: At least 2,000 in regular attendance, a senior minister with an authoritative preaching and administrative style, a non-denominational emphasis and extensive offerings of small groups, recreational activities, and volunteer service opportunities to combat anonymity in the ranks. Thumma has chosen not to include Roman Catholic parishes in his study.[1] This chapter will argue that Thumma's study does not fit into the Brazilian context, and therefore different criteria may apply for Brazil.

The Boom in Brazilian Protestantism

In popular Brazilian parlance, the word *Evangelical* is used to refer to a broad swath of religious groups ranging from traditional Protestant denominations, such as Presbyterians and Lutherans who trace their roots to 16th-century Europe, to Pentecostal denominations that arrived from Sweden and the USA early in the 20th century, and even to indigenous Brazilian neo-Pentecostal Churches that began to thrive in the 1980s.

Brazil's Evangelical mission churches trace their history to the arrival of the first US Presbyterian missionary, Rev Ashbel Green Simonton, in Rio de Janeiro, in 1859. Other US-based denominational mission agencies, including Methodists and Baptists who arrived after the Civil War, also initiated mission efforts in Brazil in the 19th century. In addition, hundreds of thousands of European immigrants, including many German Lutherans and Dutch Calvinists, arrived in Brazil in the 19th century. Many of these immigrants maintained their traditional religious affiliations in their new Brazilian homeland and have used their churches as spaces for preserving their European languages and culture.

According to the Instituto Brasileiro de Geografia e Estadística (IBGE), the 2010 Census registered a total Brazilian population of 195 million people. According to the 1970 Census, only 5.2 percent of Brazilians identified themselves as Evangelicals, suggesting that at that time Evangelicals still hovered on the margins of Brazil's traditionally Roman Catholic society. By 2010, that number had exploded to 22.2 percent, more than 42 million people. The 2010 Census found that 18.18 percent of these were *mission Evangelicals* (including both mission and immigrant churches), 60.01 percent were *Pentecostals*, and 21.81 percent were *unspecified Evangelicals* (IBGE, 2012). The comparative size and growth of Evangelicals is seen in Figure 8.1. Census figures also reveal that the Roman Catholic population fell dramatically from 91.8 percent in 1970 to 64.6 percent in 2010 (ibid.).

Focusing on the decade from 2000 to 2010, census data reveals that the ranks of Evangelicals grew by 4,408 persons per day. Overall population growth in Brazil during the decade was 5,721 persons per day. Of the newly self-identified Evangelicals that emerged during the

Figure 8.1:
Comparative Size of Evangelical Groups, 2000–2010

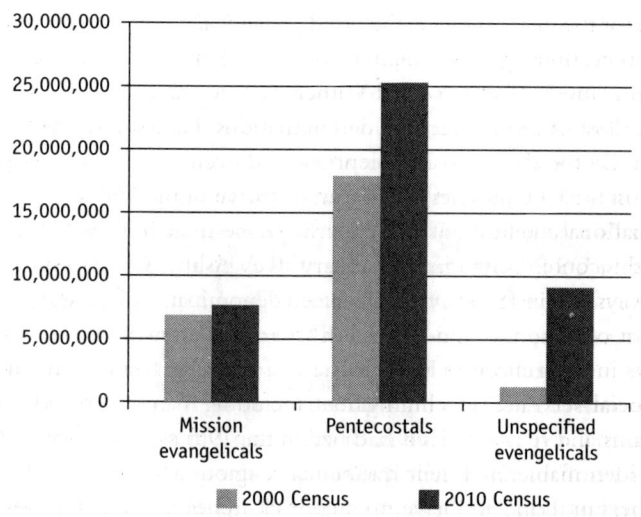

Source: Authors.

decade, 2,124 per day joined Pentecostal Churches. The largest group of Pentecostals, the Assemblies of God (AoG), added an average of 1,067 new faithful followers each day. But the greatest gains during the decade were registered by *unspecified Evangelicals*, with a figure of 2,177 per day. During this same period, *mission* Evangelicals grew by only 204 new members each day, while Roman Catholics lost 465 members daily. This suggests a seismic shift in Brazil's religious landscape, where a growing number of people are abandoning both Roman Catholicism and specific denominational affiliations for a generic Evangelical religious identity.

One reason for the recent rapid growth of Protestantism has been the accelerating urbanization of Brazilian society in the 20th century. IBGE studies point out that 64 percent of Brazilians lived in rural communities in 1950; by 2010, that number had fallen to 16 percent nationally, and in the highly industrialized states of Rio de Janeiro and São Paulo, to less than 5 percent. The rapid concentration of masses of people in emerging urban centers created a level of social dislocation that made changing religions a viable option for many new urban dwellers, an alternative that would have been much less attractive in their traditional rural settings. In many cases, small Pentecostal Churches offered desperately needed social networks to people who, by moving to the city, felt cut loose from the family structures and traditional social mores, characteristic of rural communities. Another reason for the surge in Evangelicals has been the dramatic growth of Brazil's communication infrastructure in the second half of the 20th century. Until this time, most of Brazil's vast territory was only sparsely populated; even today, most of the population lives within 300 kilometers of the Atlantic Ocean. By the 1970s, roads, telephone lines, and electric cables began to crisscross the national territory. Television networks began to build a common national identity out of a patchwork of regional cultures.

In this context, emerging Charismatic religious groups began to explore new ways of living out religious faith in Brazilian culture. Faith healers, adept at offering the hope of health and prosperity, began to draw large crowds in marginal areas of major cities, areas marked by violence, limited social services, and high unemployment. While Evangelical radio programs and religious films had been contributing to the consolidation of an identifiable Evangelical subculture since the 1930s, Brazilian TV preachers in the 1980s began to change the public image of Evangelicals by developing a sophisticated and politically influential network of media outlets. They produced quality programming rooted in popular music, Charismatic preaching, and dramatic testimonies. Evangelical music, known as *música gospel*, came on its own as a multimillion dollar enterprise. By the end of the 20th century, new information technologies, such as the Internet and web-based social media accelerated this process. Using this powerful toolkit, religious entrepreneurs—both Roman Catholic and Evangelical—were able to tailor their messages to broadly diverse target audiences, ranging from the urban poor to middle-class youth and young urban professionals. Some Evangelical TV preachers designed their messages to directly challenge deeply ingrained religious practices related to folk Catholicism and Afro-Brazilian religions.

In an increasingly urban population, religious change became less difficult. The 2010 Census demonstrates the growing fragmentation of religious affiliation in Brazil, as shown in Table 8.1.

Anecdotal evidence suggests that in the midst of an increasingly diverse religious landscape, Brazilian religious identity has become both more fluid and more nuanced. It is not unusual for Roman Catholics to attend neo-Pentecostal mega churches, nor is it unheard of for Evangelicals, in moments of personal crisis, to consult Spiritist leaders for advice and counsel.

Historically, traditional church leaders had the power to silence or marginalize Charismatic Christian groups and other religious minorities. Mega church pastors and other new religious actors on the Brazilian stage now compete with traditional church leaders, both Evangelical and Roman Catholic, for cultural and political power.

Table 8.1:
Religious Affiliation in Brazil, 2000 versus 2010

Religious Affiliation	2000 Census	2010 Census
Roman Catholic	73.6 %	64.6 %
Evangelical	15.4 %	22.2 %
Afro-Brazilian	0.3 %	0.3 %
Spiritism	1.3 %	2.0 %
No religious affiliation	7.4 %	8.0 %
Other religious groups	1.8 %	2.8 %
No response	0.2 %	0.1 %

Source: Authors.

Traditional Evangelicals Meet the Mega Church

Mega churches in Brazil are usually associated with the populist religious movements, typically associated with TV preachers and mass religious rallies. Presbyterians, on the other hand, with their emphasis on a highly educated leadership, formal worship styles, and thoughtful preaching tend to attract the middle classes. Their two flagship churches are the Presbyterian Cathedral in Rio de Janeiro (1862) and the First Presbyterian Church of São Paulo (1865), also known as the Evangelical Cathedral of São Paulo. Curiously, the word *cathedral* means a church that holds the seat of a bishop—but Presbyterians do not have bishops. The appropriation of the word *cathedral* suggests the long struggle of Brazilian Evangelicals to establish themselves as credible actors on the religious landscape, to the extent of embracing a term from Roman Catholicism which is alien to their church polity.

Both churches are built in the heart of their respective cities, a strategy designed to lend visibility, status, and credibility to these distinctively non-Catholic places of worship. Both churches have the tall-steeple Gothic architecture associated with downtown Protestant Churches around the world, not the theater-style auditoriums typical of contemporary Charismatic Churches. Maintaining such buildings on prime commercial real estate represents a drain on denominational resources, but Brazilian Presbyterians have felt that preserving such a visible presence in the heart of Rio and São Paulo is worth the cost.

Mega churches tend to presuppose mega temples, but neither of these Presbyterian temples seats a thousand people. However, both churches stream their worship services online,[2] offer multiple activities throughout the week targeted to women, men, and young people, and run extensive social service programs. Mega churches also tend to have Charismatic, entrepreneurial preachers who carefully cultivate a populist appeal. While some Presbyterian preachers have sought to embody such Charismatic leadership, most tend to focus their energy on erudition, pastoral care, and navigating the intricacies of denominational politics.

Some traditional Evangelicals have actively pursued the mega church model, usually borrowing heavily from the neo-Pentecostal play book: mass religious rallies promising miracles and prosperity, worship held in an auditorium setting—not a traditional church building—and organizing the burgeoning faithful into closely monitored cell groups to encourage disciplined participation. For example, in 1993, Central Independent Presbyterian Church of Londrina, Paraná, bought a downtown warehouse and converted it into an auditorium called *Space of Hope*, where the church holds weekly Charismatic worship services that include contemporary music and preaching, enthusiastic audience participation, and liturgical dance. For years, this congregation embraced a strong Charismatic element. Other members of the congregation continue to meet at their downtown sanctuary for traditional Sunday worship. This is one of the few traditional Evangelical congregations that has been able to accommodate this level of diversity, perhaps due to the fact that the Independent Presbyterian Church of Brazil had specifically embarked on a process of internal dialog with their Charismatic members in the 1990s (Silveira Lima, 1996: 191). The Londrina Church, now with more than 2,800 members, has organized cell groups throughout the city, operates an online radio station, and offers traditional social services, such as food distribution and a psychological counseling center.[3]

Pentecostal Mega Churches

Pentecostalism's roots in Brazil dates back to the beginning of the 20th century. In 1907, Luis Francescon, an Italian immigrant to Chicago, was introduced to the Pentecostal revival that was sweeping across the USA. He moved to Argentina in 1909, then on to Brazil in 1910. His evangelistic efforts in an Italian working-class neighborhood in São Paulo led to the creation of Brazil's oldest Pentecostal denomination, the *Congregação Cristã no Brasil* (CCB).[4] Today, according to the 2010 Census, CCB is Brazil's second largest Pentecostal denomination with 2.3 million members, exceeded only by the AoG with a membership of 12.3 million. The AoG trace their heritage to the missionary efforts of Gunnar Vingren and Daniel Berg. In 1910, these two Swedish Baptists, also having experienced a Pentecostal rebirth in Chicago, felt called to bring this message to Pará, a northern state at the mouth of the Amazon River.

For decades, Pentecostals were a marginal group within the Evangelical community, concentrating on poor and working class neighborhoods.

Pentecostals emphasize the *baptism of the Holy Spirit*, a post-conversion religious experience that energizes the believer. Part of the drawing power of the Pentecostals is their emphasis on the body. Instead of the passive worship often practiced by traditional churches, Pentecostals encourage enthusiastic audience participation ranging from lively music, the clapping of hands to literally dancing in the aisles. Pentecostals also directly address such concrete needs as physical illness and emotional distress—divine healing offers relief from physical infirmity and *glossolalia* (speaking in tongues) offers the release provided by emotional catharsis.

Brazilian Pentecostalism entered a new phase in 1953 when Harold Williams and Raymond Boatright, missionaries of the Foursquare Gospel Church, came to São Paulo. This Pentecostal denomination was founded in Los Angeles, in 1927, by the pioneering media Evangelist and faith healer Aimee Semple McPherson. Williams and Boatright brought to Brazil McPherson's sense of dramatic religious spectacle. They began their ministry by holding a series of healing services at the Independent Presbyterian Church, located in São Paulo's Cambuci neighborhood. Word quickly spread that the faith healers had arrived and the church, that held only 200 people, filled to standing room only. Local newspapers picked up the story, and soon thousands were coming to Cambuci seeking healing. In the following months, 90 percent of the members of the Cambuci Church abandoned their own denominations, and, under Williams and Boatright, set up the interdenominational *Cruzada Nacional de Evangelização*. They imported tents from the USA (until then only used by circuses in Brazil) and began to spread their healing ministry to vacant lots throughout the country.

One of the faith healers who worked with the *Cruzada Nacional de Evangelização* was Manoel de Mello (1929–1990). De Mello transformed his *A Voz do Brasil para Cristo* radio ministry from a modest endeavor that held tent meetings in São Paulo into *O Brasil para Cristo*, a new Pentecostal denomination. In July 1979, de Mello inaugurated an 11,000 square meter auditorium that seated 9,000, considered to be the largest Evangelical temple of its time. With an ecumenical flourish highly atypical of Brazilian Pentecostals, de Mello welcomed both the cardinal archbishop of São Paulo and the general secretary of the World Council of Churches to the inauguration. De Mello demonstrated his skills in self-promotion early in his career: On March 13, 1960, he held a rally in São Paulo's central plaza (*Praça da Sé*) celebrating the dismissal of a lawsuit that accused him of being a *curandeiro*, one who offers illegal medical treatment. De Mello did not shy away from taking a public stand on controversial issues. On October 12, 1982, during Brazil's military dictatorship, he held a rally at the Pacaembu football stadium challenging Roman Catholicism's privileged relationship with the Brazilian state by protesting President Figueiredo's decision to declare a national holiday in honor of Our Lady of Aparecida, Brazil's patron saint.

Another Pentecostal mega church pioneer is David Martins de Miranda, also a faith healer and radio broadcaster. Miranda, a farmer's son from the southern state of Paraná, immigrated to São Paulo, underwent a dramatic conversion and began the *Igreja Pentecostal Deus é Amor* in 1962. By 1980, he had purchased dozens of radio stations and converted a ramshackle, São Paulo warehouse, into a 20,000 square meter auditorium. In 2004, he inaugurated the dramatic *Temple of the Glory of God*, a project said to cost $30 million and seat 60,000. The 2010 Census identified 845,000 members of this denomination spread among 11,000 congregations, many of them tiny, store-front operations. Each local pastor is obligated, under threat of loss of salary, to bring annual pilgrimages to the mother church. Miranda uses radio and Internet, but not television, to provide regular teaching to his churches and to help them feel part of the great outpouring of the Spirit taking place at the temple in São Paulo. Curiously, Miranda exhorts his followers to neither own nor watch television.[5]

The AoG includes dozens of mega church congregations that have membership and regular attendance numbering in thousands. The older congregations meet in traditional-style temples but when they rebuild to accommodate burgeoning growth, they invariably build theater-style auditoriums equipped with modern communication technology conducive to live webcasting and sophisticated staging.

Bitter internal rivalries have led to the creation of a number of different AoG *conventions*. The depth of these rivalries is illustrated by the presidential election held by the largest AoG group, the *Convenção Geral das Assembléias de Deus no Brasil* (CGADB), in April 2013. Twenty-four thousand pastors gathered in Brasilia, the nation's capital, for the election. The incumbent, Pastor Jose Wellington, now in his late 70s, has held this prized office for 20 years. His opponent, Pastor Samuel Câmara, is the minister of the mother church—founded by Vingren and Berg—in Belém, Pará. Câmara had already announced his candidacy in 2011, the year of the AoG centennial; being pastor of the Belém Church made him a serious candidate. In an apparent attempt to undercut Câmara's advantage, Wellington staged

Concentrations of Faith   179

a massive AoG centennial celebration in Belém, in 2011, without inviting Câmara or his congregation to the festivities. In what the local press described as a close race, Wellington was reelected with 54 percent of the vote.[6] Shortly, thereafter, the newly reelected CGADB Board voted to sack Câmara and his followers out of their AoG wing.[7]

A notable characteristic of the AoG in recent decades has been their active involvement in electoral politics. When Brazil emerged from decades of military rule in 1986, Evangelicals chose to participate aggressively in the drafting of a new constitution—a task assigned to the Chamber of Deputies elected that year. As Pentecostal and neo-Pentecostal denominations began to build mega churches in most major Brazilian cities, denominational leaders quickly understood the political benefits of having auditoriums filled weekly with thousands of followers. Mega church pastors campaigned aggressively from the pulpit for specific candidates, and the faithful proved to be a disciplined enough voting block to give Evangelicals true political power: 34 Evangelicals were elected to the 487-seat chamber. Specifically, the Evangelical legislators sought to write the new constitution legal protections for themselves as a religious minority, and block further concessions to the Catholic hierarchy.

The AoG developed a significant presence in the Chamber of Deputies (the federal legislative body in Brazil). They elected 24 candidates in 2002, dropped to 12 deputies in 2006 due to allegations of corruption and influence-peddling, but rallied to field 22 successful candidates in 2010. The rivalries existing within the AoG also manifested themselves in the political realm. In the 2010 Chamber of Deputies race in Pernambuco state, Jose Wellington's wing of the AoG fielded Adalto Santos as their candidate, while a rival AoG wing supported the candidacy of Pastor Cleiton Collins. Although both were elected—Collins with 137,157 votes and Santos with 120,174—and although both belonged to the same political party, local church members experienced the race as a heated competition between the two AoG groups (Smith & Campos, 2012: 211–217).[8]

Most Evangelical legislators have proved to be ineffective politicians. Many have been Pentecostal pastors whose self-image have been defined by their notion of their charisma and vocation. When they arrived at the Chamber of Deputies, they found themselves to be small (and naïve) fishes in a quite large and mercenary pond. Furthermore, few had any experience in public service or any real sense of how government works. Sociologist of Religion, Saulo Baptista studied the background, discourse, and performance in the office of AoG legislators, between 1999 and 2006, and found that the traditional Evangelical discourse rooted in sobriety, honesty, and reliability was no match for the clientelism, corruption, and authoritarianism that characterized national Brazilian politics (Baptista, 2009: 66).

Neo-Pentecostal Mega Churches

To the Charismatic gifts of baptism in the Spirit, divine healing, and *glossolalia* celebrated by classic Pentecostals, neo-Pentecostals add an emphasis on more exotic spiritual gifts, such as exorcism, in addition to their embrace of prosperity theology. Neo-Pentecostal churches tend to abandon traditional denominational structures for a more entrepreneurial model centered on the charisma and marketing prowess of the founder.

The emphasis on prosperity as a concrete sign of God's blessing is well suited to a rapidly urbanizing population struggling to build a sense of self-esteem in a market economy that lifts up the capacity to purchase goods and services as a key indicator of personal worth. The preacher/religious entrepreneur who is able to amass a considerable fortune points to his success as a sign of God's special blessing. On January 17, 2013, *Fortune*, the business magazine, posted on its website a story on *The Richest Pastors in Brazil* (Antunes, 2013). A review of the religious entrepreneurs highlighted in the story will allow us to survey key trends in neo-Pentecostal mega churches:

1. *Bishop* Edir Macedo, founder of Brazil's flagship neo-Pentecostal denomination, the *Igreja Universal do Reino de Deus* (IURD), is said to be worth at least $950 million. His empire includes *TV Record*, one of Brazil's major commercial TV networks, dozens of radio stations, a major daily newspaper, music labels, and a private jet. In Brazil, the IURD has 1.8 million members, 10,000 pastors, and 5,000 churches. IURD claims to be present in 200 countries. The IURD has built dozens of mega churches throughout Brazil, each with a capacity of more than 5,000. Daily worship in these temples is broadcast live on local TV, calling the public to experience their

services live—where cash donations are encouraged—to receive full spiritual benefit. Macedo's most recent mega project is to build in São Paulo, a 76,000 square meter reproduction of Solomon's Temple complete with a gold, bejeweled Ark of the Covenant budgeted at $200 million.[9] Macedo became a recognized player in Brazilian politics after successfully backing the presidential campaigns of Luis Inácio Lula da Silva in 2002 and 2006.[10]

2. *Apostle* Valdemiro Santiago, a former Macedo protégé, split with the IURD in 1998 to form his own denomination, the *Igreja Mundial do Poder de Deus* (IMPD). This IURD rival claims 900,000 members and 4,000 churches; his website lists affiliates in 21 different countries.[11] Business magazines in Brazil estimate Santiago's net worth at $220 million. One study shows that the IURD lost 30 percent of its members between 2003 and 2009, many of them to the IMPD. (Neri, 2011: 60). Santiago is one of the few Afro-Brazilians to have established a successful career as a mega church television preacher. He is said to pay $5 million per month for 22 hours of airtime on *Rede Bandeirantes*, another national commercial TV network. On January 1, 2012, more than a million people attended the inauguration of his new 40,000 square meter temple near São Paulo's major international airport. Traffic was tied up for hours.

3. *Pastor* Silas Malafaia, leader of the Victory in Christ wing of the AoG, headquartered in Rio de Janeiro, ranks third in the Fortune list with an estimated net worth of $150 million. His presence on this list illustrates how fluid the lines can be between Pentecostals and neo-Pentecostals. Both groups are emerging actors on the religious landscape, both are rooted in Charismatic expressions of the Christian faith, both have proved adept at establishing a presence in the commercial media, and both pursue explicit public policy objectives. Also known as a rival to Macedo, Malafaia is a religion advisor to *O Globo*, Brazil's biggest media conglomerate. *O Globo* competes aggressively with Macedo's *TV Record*. Malafaia is a major player in the multimillion dollar Evangelical music industry, and is also an outspoken opponent to abortion and same-sex marriage. Malafaia organizes the annual March for Jesus in Rio de Janeiro, a giant Evangelical street party and political rally that according to *O Globo*, attracted 500,000 people in 2013.[12] Magali do Nascimento

Cunha, a scholar specializing in media, religion, and culture, notes that Malafaia used the 2013 march to attack President Rousseff's appointment the week before, pending confirmation by the Senate, of constitutional lawyer Luis Roberto Barroso to Brazil's highest court. Barroso is considered to be a progressive; conservatives fear that if confirmed to the court, he may not oppose abortion and same-sex marriage. Malafaia entered the political fray by proclaiming to March for Jesus participants his energetic opposition to Barroso's nomination, insisting that his followers are not second-class citizens and would use their power to influence politics, the arts, science, and commerce (Cunha, 2013).

4. *Missionary* Romildo Ribeiro Soares, known as R.R. Soares, is Macedo's brother-in-law, and he founded the *Igreja Internacional da Graça de Deus* (IIGD) after breaking with Macedo, in 1980. His estimated net worth is $125 million. Soares may be the least adventurous of the mega church television preachers; his worship services seldom stray from the traditional AoG model. Soares has become one of the most familiar faces on Brazilian TV; he appears Monday through Saturday evenings on *Rede Bandeirantes*.[13]

5. *Apostle* Estevam and *Bishop* Sonia Hernandes have focused on young urban professionals as their target constituency. Prior to his church career, Estevam worked as a marketing executive for IBM. They founded the *Igreja Apostólica Renascer em Cristo*, in 1986, in São Paulo, and were early movers in the gospel music industry. In the 1990s, they established a reputation for organizing high-energy worship services with quality contemporary music, and quickly became a desirable venue for young people. In 1993, Estevam was the first to organize a March for Jesus in Brazil. Their combined net worth is said to be $65 million. The Hernandes' have also faced their share of scandals, having been arrested for money laundering in the USA and pending prosecution in Brazil for the collapse of the ceiling of one of their temples, a disaster that caused nine deaths.[14]

Neo-Pentecostalism has grown so quickly and become so pervasive that Christian groups in Brazil and all of Latin America—from Roman Catholics to Pentecostals to Presbyterians—have been influenced by both its style and substance.

As illustrated in the aforementioned list, neo-Pentecostal leaders often assume titles to affirm their religious authority. Since their churches tend to be new enterprises organized by Charismatic individuals, they do not conform to the structures proffered by traditional ecclesiology. Their leaders tend to adopt titles revealed to them by divine revelation such as—Apostle, Bishop, and Missionary—all terms of authority rooted in the Bible and Christian tradition.

Peruvian Pentecostal researcher Bernardo Campos notes that Latin American Charismatics began to import this new leadership model from the USA in the 1980s. *Apostles* are considered to be a contemporary expression of the messianic and apostolic traditions that imbued the early Christian church with authority and dynamism. Campos observes that many Charismatic Churches interpret their recent growth as a confirmation that more traditional churches have missed the boat by not putting into practice the power inherent in the Apostolic Movement (Campos, 2004: 20–23). Members of the Apostolic Movement throughout the world have formed an active network, act as one another's spiritual confidants and sponsors, speak regularly at one another's public campaigns, and consider themselves to be part of a *new Apostolic reformation*.[15]

By combining their major media presence with daily religious services offered in huge auditoriums, the Charismatic mega churches break dramatically with the parish system of church organization still used by Roman Catholics. Under the parish system, residents in a particular neighborhood know that their religious needs will be attended to by the priest named to that parish. This system presupposes that a church organized in parishes—even if that church is no longer the established religion of the land—benefits from the inherent cultural authority granted by history and tradition. Evangelicals organized around a different principle when they arrived in the 19th century, understanding their churches to be—in the spirit of the times—voluntary religious associations of individuals. Still, participation in such churches tends to be limited to those living relatively near the church building. Rolando Pérez observes that the new media-based religious enterprises function parallel to community-based congregations, becoming, effectively, *deterritorialized* churches. He suggests that this emerging system makes the local congregation, but one of many public spaces where the faithful can celebrate their faith (Pérez, 1997: 21).

The emerging cultural and political power of the Charismatic mega churches is also illustrated by, what Magalí do Nascimiento Cunha calls, the *explosion* of *gospel culture* in Brazil. From ringtones to t-shirts, karaoke soundtracks to massive live concerts, local radio stations to national TV networks, scandalously corrupt politicians to valiant role models for fighting gang violence, the Charismatic mega church movement has become a major creator of content and meaning in Brazilian culture. Charismatic mega churches break with the traditional Evangelical emphasis on sobriety and austerity by affirming the value of consumption in a consumer society. Also, by becoming makers of meaning and owners of major media outlets, the mega churches have become subjects—no longer just objects—of public opinion while simultaneously becoming a defined, powerful segment of the national market (Cunha, 2007).

Roman Catholics and Mega Churches

Throughout most of Brazil's history, to be Brazilian was to be Roman Catholic. The folk Catholicism that established deep roots in colonial times promoted devotion to the saints and to the Virgin, as well as dependence on the pastoral initiative of lay leaders. Till date, ordained Catholic clergy has never been able to attend to the pastoral needs of the millions of faithful spread out over Brazil's eight million square kilometers. Nevertheless, despite heavy membership losses in recent decades, Brazil continues to be the world's largest Catholic country.

Mass expressions of Catholic religious fervor have always been part of the Brazilian experience. As in many Latin American countries, folk Catholicism is expressed in a vibrant pilgrimage tradition: For example, 10 million pilgrims a year visit the Shrine of Our Lady of Aparecida. But for most of history, such exercises have been an expression of personal and family devotion, not always tied to a deep individual commitment to the institutional church.

The Catholic Charismatic Renewal Movement began in 1967 as an outpouring of the Spirit at a student retreat at Duquesne University in the USA. It has now grown into a global movement coordinated through International Catholic Charismatic Renewal Services in the Vatican.

Although the movement is clearly an authentic expression of Charismatic religious experience, its growth in Latin America in recent decades has provided the Catholic hierarchy with a timely and strategic pastoral tool with which to staunch the massive hemorrhaging of the faithful to Pentecostal and neo-Pentecostal Churches. Catholics on the ground experience the Charismatic Renewal Movement as Pentecostalism plus Mary and devotion to the Saints, grounded in thoughtful theological reflection and the (sometimes stultifying) institutional framework provided by the local bishop—with the devotional energy and religious souvenirs typical of pilgrimages thrown in for good measure.

Ordained as a Salesian priest in 1964, Monsignor Jonas Abib became part of the Charismatic Renewal Movement, in 1971. In 1978, he began a media ministry called *Comunidade Canção Nova*. With a team of like-minded young people, Abib developed liturgical and devotional materials to sustain a new evangelistic emphasis within Catholicism, understanding that many Catholics lacked the experience of personal conversion—and baptism in the Holy Spirit—that had energized the Pentecostal and neo-Pentecostal competition. Abib and his team focused on creating an environment—both liturgical and physical—where people could have a personal encounter with Christ and with the Spirit. They call *cultural* Catholics to a personal, vital, and traditional faith within the Roman fold.

In the early stages, *Canção Nova* (New Song) focused on radio broadcasting, as well as recording and marketing music. Abib was the singing priest who provided Brazil's nascent Charismatic Movement with the songs to sustain it. Building on Catholicism's pilgrimage tradition and having garnered the support of the Catholic hierarchy, Abib developed a huge training complex in Cachoeira Paulista, São Paulo. The complex includes a church that seats 10,000 and a convention center for 70,000. Not surprisingly, the charisma of this community is explicitly evangelistic and catechetical in nature. The community claims to hold about 18 conferences and receive up to 550,000 people per year. *Canção Nova* also offers its followers web-based live radio and TV, and an extensive library of print materials, recorded music, podcasts, and videos.[16]

Not all bishops sympathize with the style and substance of the Charismatic movement, and in Roman Catholicism, the local bishop has the authority to block such activities within his diocese or force them underground. To sidestep this problem, Abib carefully cultivated a personal relationship first with Pope John Paul II and then with Benedict XVI. In 2008, Benedict rewarded Abib by giving special Papal status to the *Canção Nova* community, giving them global access beyond the authority of local bishops. This new status is proudly touted on their websites, and *Canção Nova* is working to build a worldwide network of affiliated Charismatic communities.[17]

Abib's work must also be seen as an attempt by the hierarchy to defuse Liberation Theology and the effervescent mass Catholic Movement personified by the Base Ecclesial Communities that began to spread rapidly in the 1980s—a movement that in its essence questioned the authority of the hierarchy, while simultaneously calling them to a level of social engagement and political advocacy far beyond the comfort levels of Popes John Paul II and Benedict XVI. Anecdotal evidence suggests that a large number of base community leaders, frustrated by endless battles with church authorities, moved either into secular political militancy or leadership positions in Pentecostal congregations.

The superstar of the Catholic Charismatic Movement is Father Marcelo Rossi. He projects raw charisma, a tender passion, and just a touch of the sexual energy of a young Elvis Presley. He approaches the faithful with a nonchalance and spontaneity that generates enthusiastic audience response. His CDs and DVDs have sold millions of copies—he has even produced exercise videos—and his charismatic persona has been actively promoted by the *O Globo* media empire. His *Theotokos Mother of God Sanctuary*—still under construction—is located in the southern part of São Paulo and covers 30,000 square meters. The amphitheater seats 30,000 under a sloping, wing-like roof with space for an additional 80,000 on-lookers outside, who follow the singing masses on huge video screens.[18]

Rossi seems to be less focused on catechesis and the Charismatic experience than Abib, and more focused on getting the faithful reconnected with the mass as the central experience of the Roman Catholic religious practice. Rossi's masses also include an emphasis on divine healing. Rossi has understood that the success of neo-Pentecostal preachers who offer blessed objects—ranging from anointing oil to roses to symbolic plastic swords of the Spirit—is rooted in the Roman Catholic folk tradition of venerating sacred relics. Rossi closes his mass having everyone wave pre-blessed white monogrammed handkerchiefs—purchased ahead of time. These linen handkerchiefs allow the faithful to continue their connection with the sacred beyond the moment of the mass.

Sociologist Brenda Carranza, in her analysis of Rossi's meteoric rise to fame, notes that his success has been the product of the careful cultivation of his public persona in the commercial and religious media, as well as the persistence in Brazilian society of what she terms as *conservative utopia* (Carranza, 2011: 82). His rise, she notes, coincides with the consolidation of the consumer society, the growing cult to youthfulness in the media, and the renewed emphasis on the corporality of the religious experience embraced by both Evangelical and Roman Catholic Charismatics (ibid.).

Conclusion

The religious map, as already described, has led to the emergence of a new kind of religious leader. Three to four years of pastoral and theological training does not prepare one to become a religious entrepreneur, adept at designing and implementing mass marketing strategies, preparing simple, repetitive messages easily interwoven with dynamic images, negotiating effectively with diverse actors ranging from the commercial media to political parties, staging high-energy religious spectacles, and organizing highly motivated teams of volunteers. While some Bible institutes are now offering courses on how to project an effective image on camera, most of the new religious entrepreneurs learn their craft on the job.

On the other hand, most traditional pastors are not trained to understand how the media have become the spaces where modern societies create meaning. They have very little understanding of how to effectively engage existing structures of cultural and political power, and how to advocate on behalf of the silenced, the *invisibilized*, and excluded.

Another clear trend emerging is the increasingly fluid and complex nature of Brazilian religious affiliations. If one were to reduce the religious experience to a commercial transaction of symbolic goods, then these new religious emporia would seem to be making great strides in consolidating their market share and supplanting traditional symbolic goods with newer, shinier models that bring greater personal satisfaction to the consuming public. The increased cultural and political power enjoyed by the new religious entrepreneurs would seem to strengthen their hands.

What is not yet clear, however, is whether these new groups actually strengthen and deepen religious faith, or, on the contrary, strengthen the impulse toward individualism and secularism. Evidence suggests that a sizeable number of Brazilians move from traditional religious groups to Charismatic groups, and then continue on to abandon institutional religion altogether. This is one way to interpret the massive growth of unaffiliated Evangelicals, described in the 2010 Census. One must also take into account the growing number of individuals who have felt used or abused by the phenomena of *religious spectacle*—especially those who have brought to the altar their desperate need for health or prosperity. Nor is it clear whether traditional religious groups will be able to reinvent themselves in such a way that they might be able to draw unaffiliated Evangelicals back into the fold.

Notes

1. For extensive resources on mega churches, see the Hartford Institute for Religion Research. Researcher Scott Thumma and colleagues provide access to a variety of articles and books drawing mostly, but not exclusively on the US Protestant context (http://hirr.hartsem.edu). These criteria are drawn from the *definitions* section. http://hirr.hartsem.edu/megachurch/definition.html. Retrieved on May 7, 2013.
2. See www.catedralonline.com.br to monitor webcasts of worship at the São Paulo Church and www.catedralrio.org.br/multimidia/culto-ao-vivo for Rio de Janeiro. Retrieved on May 7, 2013.
3. To capture the feel of the Londrina Church, visit their website: www.ipilon.org.br. This clip illustrates traditional worship http://www.youtube.com/watch?v=88DSioRgxzQ and this one contemporary worship http://www.youtube.com/watch?v=QL9otn428C4. Retrieved on May 9, 2013.
4. The CCB is among the most traditional of Brazil's Pentecostal denominations. This is clearly illustrated by their webpage http://www.cristanobrasil.com/index.php?ccb=index, by far the most staid and least personality-driven of any of the major Pentecostal denominations. Retrieved on May 26, 2013.
5. See www.ipda.com.br for a visual tour of Miranda's ministry. The website also includes links to Miranda's radio stations, known collectively as The Voice of Liberation. For links to Miranda's radio outlets in 17 countries and 23 Brazilian cities, see http://www.ipda.com.br/nova/vozlibertacao/vozdalibertacao.html (In Latin America, the word *liberation* is often used as a synonym for *exorcism*). Retrieved on May 24, 2013.
6. For coverage of the election, see http://noticias.gospelmais.com.br/cgadb-pr-jose-wellington-reeleito-presidente-assembleia-deus-52642.html. Retrieved on May 27, 2013.
7. Wellington and his colleagues accused Câmara and his colleagues of breaking the decorum of the Brasilia Assembly. See http://noticias.gospelmais.com.br/cgadb-expulsa-pastor-samuel-camara-ditaduras-54355.html. Retrieved on May 12, 2013.
8. Among the main wings of the AoG are those led by the following four ministers: Pastor Jose Wellington (http://www.pastorjosewellington.com.br/), Pastor Silas Malafaia (http://www.vitoriaemcristo.org/_gutenweb/_site/gw-inicial/), Pastor Samuel Câmara

(http://www.adbelem.org.br/), and Pastor Abner Ferreira (http://www.portaluniversogospel.com.br/pastor-anuncia-projeto-de-evangelismo-digital/). They are bitter rivals for the public spotlight and for bragging rights to being the authentic heirs of the AoG tradition in Brazil. Retrieved on May 26, 2013.

9. See the dramatic presentation of the temple at http://www.otemplodesalomao.com/. The webpage includes a tab that takes the viewer to a live webcam tracing construction progress. Retrieved on May 31, 2013.

10. With a nice touch, the IURD website senses the default language of one's computer and automatically connects to either English, Spanish, or Portuguese content: See http://www.universal.org/. Also worthy of note is that the website refers simply to "The Universal Church," an interesting exercise in branding since *universal* is a synonym for *catholic*. Retrieved on August 22, 2014.

11. The IMPD website immediately connects to a webcast showing Santiago ministering to the needs of his faithful. See http://www.impd.org.br/portal/. Retrieved on May 27, 2013.

12. The 2013 event was held on Saturday, May 25. Malafaia, sporting jeans and the commemorative t-shirt sold for the occasion, is the only minister quoted in this story carried on *O Globo's* national evening news broadcast: See http://g1.globo.com/jornal-nacional/noticia/2013/05/marcha-para-jesus-reune-cerca-de-500-mil-pessoas-no-rio.html. Retrieved on May 27, 2013.

13. After years on *Rede Bandeirantes*, Soares is working to build his own TV network, *Nossa TV*. His webpage promotes his books, as well as DVDs. See http://www.ongrace.com/portal/. Retrieved on May 27, 2013.

14. Compare the modern, clean feel of *Renascer's* website https://foursquare.com/v/igreja-apost%C3%B3lica-renascer-em-cristo-bras%C3%ADlia-distrito-federal/4f973ac5e4b01cb74ec2260f with the high-energy impact of their gospel music site http://www.renascerpraise.com.br/. Also note that Estevam (http://www.apostoloestevam.com.br/2012/index.html)—sporting a black t-shirt and looking like an aging rocker—and Sonia (http://www.bispasonia.com.br/)—confidently smiling against a white and pink background—both have individual websites in addition to the denominational site. Retrieved on August 22, 2014.

15. One of the founders of the New Apostolic Reformation is C. Peter Wagner, a former missionary to South America. In this op-ed piece, Wagner argues that the Apostolic Movement is a serious and legitimate expression of emerging leadership in the Christian church: See http://www.charismanews.com/opinion/31851-the-new-apostolic-reformation-is-not-a-cult. Retrieved on May 30, 2013.

16. The *Canção Nova* website, http://www.cancaonova.com/, bears witness to the community's evangelistic fervor and traditional flavor. Programs are warm and earnest, but tend to lack the slickness and production values of the best of their neo-Pentecostal competition. On the other hand, *Canção Nova* clearly enjoys the authority imbued by the support of the Pope and the local Roman Catholic hierarchy. Retrieved on May 31, 2013.

17. See, for example, http://comunidade.cancaonova.com/cancao-nova-celebra-3-anos-de-reconhecimento-pontificio/. Retrieved on May 31, 2013.

18. Rossi's website, http://www.padremarcelorossi.com.br, is the only one visited in this study that required the viewer to register a name, e-mail address, and phone number within Brazil before granting access to recorded videos and music. One interesting touch in Rossi's video masses is the invitation to web viewers, unable to receive the elements of the Eucharist, to participate in spirit through song.

Bibliography

Antunes, A. 2013. "The Richest Pastors in Brazil." *Fortune.* Retrieved from http://www.forbes.com/sites/andersonantunes/2013/01/17/the-richest-pastors-in-brazil/ on May 27, 2013.

Baptista, S. 2009. *Pentecostais e neopentecostais na política brasileir–Um estudo sobre cultura política, Estado e atores coletivos religiosos no Brasil.* São Paulo/Belo Horizonte: AnnaBlume e Instituto Metodista Isabela Hendrix.

Campos, B. 2004. "El Post Pentecostalismo: Renovación del Liderazgo y Hermenéutica del Espíritu," *Cyberjournal for Pentecostal-Charismatic Research.* Retrieved from http://www.pctii.org/cyberj/cyberj13/bernado.html on May 29, 2013.

Carranza, B. 2011. *Catholicismo midiático.* Aparecida: Editora Idéias e Letras.

Cunha, M. 2007. *A Explosão Gospel: Un olhar das ciências humanas sobre o cenário evangélico no Brasil.* Rio de Janeiro, Mauad X: Instituto Mysterium.

———. 2013. "Marcha para Jesus no Rio gana conotação mais política." *Mídia, Religião e Política.* Retrieved from http://midiareligiaopolitica.blogspot.com.ar/2013/05/marcha-para-jesus-no-rio-ganha.html on May 27, 2013.

IBGE. 2012. *Censo Demográfico 2010–Características Gerais da População, Religião e Pessoas com Deficiência.* Rio de Janeiro: Instituto Brasileiro da Geografia e Estatística.

Neri, M. 2011. *Novo Mapa das Religiões.* Rio de Janeiro, Brazil: Fundação Getulio Vargas.

Pérez, Rolando .1997. "La iglesia y su misión en la opinión pública." *Iglesias, medios y estrategias de evangelización.* Buenos Aires: Asociación Mundial para la Comunicación Cristiana-América Latina.

Silveira Lima, Eber. 1996. "The Independent Presbyterian Church of Brazil and Pentecostalism: A Pastoral Approach to Conflict." In B.F. Gutiérrez and D.A. Smith (eds), *The Power of the Spirit: The Pentecostal Challenge to Historic Churches in Latin America* (p. 191). Pennsylvania: Skipjack Press.

Smith, D.A. & L.S. Campos. 2012. "God's Politicians: Pentecostals, Media and Politics in Guatemala and Brazil." In P.N. Thomas and P. Lee (eds), *Global and Local Televangelism* (pp. 211–217). Hampshire: Palgrave Macmillan.

9

Evangelical Representations in the Public Sphere: The Peruvian Case

Rolando Pérez

This chapter[1] seeks to understand the contemporary public practices of Evangelicals, mainly Charismatic and neo-Pentecostal groups—many classed as mega churches[2]—through the assumptions and perceptions of their leaders, who are leading collective forays into the public sphere. I will analyze how public participation shapes and re-signifies the religious identity of Evangelicals, especially with regard to the changes in institutionalized religion. In this sense, I will discuss what kind of negotiation or resistance is taking place in the relationship between the public empowerment of religion and institutional religious authority, as the dynamics of *sacrality* and secularity are seen in the public and the private spheres.

In particular, the chapter addresses issues pertaining to how mediated religion facilitates the creation of new meanings, forms, and approaches of public engagement. It is particularly relevant because the public participation of conservative Evangelical groups—linked to the Charismatic and neo-Pentecostal sector—is spurring the development of new leaderships, representations, and relationships beyond the boundaries of institutionalized religion. In this way, it is also relevant to observe what kind of negotiations (or resistance) is happening in the relationship between religious public empowering and institutional religious authority.

Evangelical Presence in a Pluralistic Latin America

Since the mid 1980s, the Latin American political and religious landscape has changed drastically. The statistical information allows us to picture quantitatively the shifts of the Latin American religious map.[3] Frances Hagopian asserts, "[S]elf-identified Protestants now comprise roughly one-fifth of the population of the region, about one in ten Latin Americans identify with no religion at all, and only about 70 percent of the population is nominally Roman Catholic" (Hagopian, 2009: 2).

Several studies (Bastian, 2001; Freston, 2008; Levine, 2009; Parker, 2009) turned their focus toward the contemporary process of religious pluralism and plurality[4] that characterize the religious beliefs and practices in Latin America. It entails—as Levine observes—not only a multiplicity of voices speaking *in the name of religion*, but also conflicted voices within specific religious denominations and confessions (Levine, 2009). In Freston's words, "a plurality of voices can be heard within both the Catholic and Protestant camps: different organizations, groups, and programs, often with autonomous resources and international funding" (Freston, 2008: 210).

The new religious discourses and practices show us that this continent is passing "from being a 'Catholic continent' to being an increasingly religious pluralist region"[5] (Parker, 2009: 31).

Levine describes the characteristics of this new religious face:

> The contrast with the traditional face of religion reflects a net of related changes. Where there was monopoly, there is now pluralism; where a limited number of spaces were once officially reserved for religious practice (with a limited number of authorized practitioners), there is now a rich profusion of churches, chapels, and mass media programming, not to mention campaigns and crusades that carry the message to hitherto 'profane' spaces... Instead of limited number of voices 'authorized' to speak in the name of religion, there is now a plurality of voices, not only from among distinct denominations but within churches as well. (2009: 406)

This internal pluralism within religious confessions or denominations is not necessarily new. What is new is that this pluralism, within and among religion, is affecting the political life and other public processes related to the Latin American democratic transitions and the rearticulations of civil society (Romero, 2009).

Hence, the contemporary religious face is characterized by "pluralism instead of monopoly, a plurality of voices, not only from among distinct denominations but within churches" (Levine, 2009: 406).

This religious scenario is relevant because other religious groups are competing to gain symbolic power, political and social recognition, moral authority, and public legitimacy. One of the prominent non-Catholic groups that is gaining public power is the Evangelical Church.

Today, although Catholicism still remains the only officially recognized religion, Evangelical Churches are becoming more socially and culturally embedded. This phenomenon is producing, on the one hand, new dynamics among religious actors as well as reconfigurations of the relations between the religious practices and the ordinary structures of power and identity in the contemporary society. On the other hand, the democratic transition is generating new processes that have led to the public empowering of non-Catholic groups.

The decline of institutionalized Catholicism's authority has been paralleled by the increase in other religious expressions in which Evangelical groups have gained public visibility. As Parker points out, "in the last three or four decades the alternative to Catholicism has come not mainly from the growth of nonbelievers and atheists but from the expansion of Evangelicals, in particular Pentecostals" (2009: 131).

More precisely, the public emergence of Evangelicals is producing, within the Catholic Church, an intense debate about the strategies to avoid the increase of catholic migration toward Evangelical congregations. José Luis Pérez Guadalupe, an influential Catholic thinker, has suggested that in the Peruvian context, the Catholic Church should take into account the Evangelical Church's evangelization strategies to recover the trust of its believers:

> We [Catholics] have to go out and reach the people, like Evangelicals do. They have got rid of its sect image. Formerly, people were born as Latin American, Third World citizen, mestizos and Catholic. But, not now ... Today there is a gap between one´s birth identity and sacramental identity. After 500 years of becoming accustomed to people to come to us, we have taken it for granted and now we do not know how to reach them. Twenty years ago there were no Evangelical temples in middle and upper class areas; today, there are. They have people in every social class, with every kind of professional background, as well as in politics and management. They have become diversified and have changed that image of 'poor people' who let others brainwash them. (Pérez-Guadalupe, 2007: 3)

The public emergence and cultural empowerment of Evangelicals has generated a crucial debate about the new configurations of religious actors, discourses, and representations. In his remarkable book, *Is Latin American turning Protestant?: The Politics of Evangelical Growth*, Stoll (1990) provoked an important debate around the public irruption of Evangelicals.

His investigation aroused great interest regarding the political and social implications of political participation of Protestants and Catholics in Brazil and Chile. At that time, Stoll revealed that Protestants were far more likely than Catholics to participate in religious organizations, where civic skills may develop along political engagement.

The contemporary scenario shows that Evangelicals are playing a significant role beyond the religious domestic sphere: "They open public life to hitherto excluded groups and silent voices, and together represent the creation of a series of spaces of public life" (Levine, 2006: 406).

Sources and Trends in the Evangelical Public Representations

Evangelical groups, networks, and congregations linked to the mega churches in Peru are re-elaborating their religious discourse and their representations in the public sphere.

This Evangelical public involvement is characterized by diverse kinds of public engagements and efforts that occur beyond the traditional political spaces. Most of these groups are participating and interacting within diverse public spaces, such as civil society-based movements, inter-faith networks, and official commissions named by governmental institutions.

It shows that many emergent movements linked to these Evangelical groups are rethinking their biblical assumptions on public participation and political engagement, as well as their active role in the social change process. In the past, many conservative Evangelical leaders and lay believers criticized and refused individual participation and collective involvement in the political processes because they assumed the public realm to be incompatible with spiritual matters.

Now, however, contemporary Evangelical public engagement reveals that the public sphere is considered an appropriate field to gain political power and public influence, as well as an avenue to change society according to their (conservative) theological and ideological views.

The theological conception that supports the public involvement of these groups is based on the Bible's mandate for the restoration of society. Based on this principle, the leaders conceive public participation as a strategic way to have influence in different public spaces in order to restore and reconstruct the nation, and to develop it upon the base of Biblical principles and Evangelical morality.

Bernardo Campos and Oscar Amat y León contend that this kind of Evangelical perspective on public engagement is based on the idea of getting "power to reign instead of power to govern which means that the conservative evangelical sectors enter into politics based on a theocratic vision of power" (Campos & Amat y Leon, 2007: 25). This worldview is closely connected to the American Reconstructionist perspective[6] that proposes a theocratic view of political participation.

Hence, the idea of the restoration of society is an important aspect in the pastoral agenda of leaders of this sector because they view society as a space where Christian values are not taught and lived rightly. As David Cauracuri, president of Peruvian Fraternity of Evangelical Pastors, asserts: "There is a social crisis in our country; there is no message of hope, with principles, with values. We think we are the ones who have to lift up this message" (David Cauracuri, personal interview, May 19, 2009).

Another important motivation for participating in the public sphere is related to the particular interpretation of the biblical command that Christians are responsible for establishing godly authority in all aspects of the life, thus entailing efforts to gain a privileged position in influential spaces of the public sphere. Most of the Charismatic and neo-Pentecostal leaders mention that they are working in the public because they believe God has commanded them to be in the world not as the tail, but as the head.[7] As Soria, leader of Union of Peruvian Evangelical Christian Churches, contends:

> Two months ago I began to share the vision of a culture of truth as a principle of the Kingdom applicable to all of society... I think that our leaders have the tools to prepare the church people, instruct them in these principles and share them with the society so they can be 'the head, not the tail' (Eliazar Soria, personal interview, May 20, 2009).

In the same way, Daniel Vega, vice president of Peruvian Fraternity of Evangelical Pastors, asserts:

> In politics, if you know how to handle power, you can get things done in a positive way, but also in a negative way. But, power resides with the

majority. That's why we have to be the head and not the tail, because if you are the head, you have the bull by the horns. On the other hand, when one becomes part of the power establishment, you have a quota of power (Daniel Vega, personal interview, May 27, 2009).

This conception implies a kind of appropriation of important aspects of American Reconstructionism[8] (Amat y León, 2004; Campos, 2009; Freston, 2001) which assume that "Christians have a moral imperative or 'cultural mandate' to extend their religious dominion over the earth" (Pottenger, 2007: 77).

However, unlike the American experience, this Reconstructionist model has some particular characteristics. First, the Peruvian case reveals that the public representation of this movement is more engaged with the public platforms. In order to attain political power and have a privileged and legitimized place in the public sphere, they have built alliances not only with conservative organizations within the Evangelical community, but also with civil society-based networks.

Second, the Peruvian Reconstructionist model has incorporated secularized issues in their public agenda. Unlike the past, they are talking not just about *conservative religious concerns*, such as, abortion, homosexuality, family crisis, or religious discrimination. Rather, they are raising their voice on politically controversial issues, such as, domestic violence, political corruption, and even structural poverty. As David Cauracuri, president of Peruvian Fraternity of Evangelical Pastors, argues:

> When we give a message against corruption, or against injustice or against inequality, these ethical principles lead us to (keep others from) running over our principles and it does not make any difference who is in the government. We cannot be silent (David Cauracuri, personal interview, May 19, 2009).

Another relevant aspect that characterizes this tendency is related to a re-signification of conversion and salvation that goes far beyond the individualistic view, traditionally expressed in public Evangelical discourse, as noted by Stoll and Levine:

> The key premise is the Evangelical belief in the power of moral transformation, of individuals being regenerated or 'born again.' To change society you have to start by changing the hearts of individuals, Evangelicals leaders argue. Change enough individuals, they believe, and you will change

society .... paying to 'raise up a nation' is an attempt to turn a gospel of personal empowerment into a language for building confidence of fair play among diverse social groups. (1995: 12)

We observe that contemporary Evangelical leaders in this sector are talking now about evangelization more in terms of influence rather than conversion. As Robert Barriger, senior pastor of *Path of Life Church*, sees it:

... some people use influence for good, and others for evil. Now we are trying to influence the influential for positive change. In this sense, we need to enter into dialogue and conversation with decision-makers (Robert Barriger, personal interview, June 4, 2009).

In the same way, Miguel Bardales, coordinator of Thanksgiving Ministry, asserts:

The self-esteem of evangelicals is changing. People believe that we can do anything. If we have been able to preach to the whole country, we can keep doing that. It is like a wave of optimism, an improvement of our image....I am very excited that everything we are as evangelicals, connects immediately with the sensibilities of the population... We can preach to the whole country; we can talk with government ministers, mayors or ambassadors (Miguel Bardales, personal interview, May 29, 2009).

However, this strategic change does not imply a denial of the traditional *conversionist* approach; rather, in this case, the concept of conversion is being re-signified. In doing so, when these Evangelical groups talk about public influence, in essence, they are talking about the conversion of structures and cultural spaces, as well as mentalities.

It is important to note that some Evangelical leaders of this sector base their conception of public participation on the theological understanding of the so-called *spiritual territorialization* (Freston, 2001), by which they believe that it is important not only to influence the mentality of political leaders, but also to fight against the spirits that are contributing both to the demoralization of society and obstructing the prosperity and progress of the nation.

Finally, we must point out that even though these new Evangelical leaders agree that they share an exclusive calling to restore—spiritually— the nation, they express different understandings and views of the practical implications in the current Peruvian context.

I observe three worldviews among these leaders. On the one hand, many believe that the restoration of the nation will be possible if Christian Evangelicals participate actively in governmental spaces, and take control of social and political power. As Márquez, coordinator of Evangelical Public Workers and Servants Networks, points out:

> I think that we have moved from seeing Evangelicals as only needing to pray for authorities so that they might stay on the straight and narrow, to thinking that we can be those authorities and keep all of society on the straight and narrow. This is a huge step. (Márquez, personal interview, May 26, 2009)

On the other hand, other leaders believe that the most important role of Christian believers is related to the *shepherding* of political and social leaders. This view is based on the idea that the restoration of the nation will come through the spiritual change of these leaders. Finally, another group is working with the logic of promoting religious ritualization within governmental spaces. Based on this view, many leaders are deploying efforts to organize public rituals, such as *Evangelical Te-Deums*[9] with the participation of political leaders or prayer services in state institutions. Such actions grow out of their understanding that: "reduces the solution of political problems to ritualism; complex power relations embedded in political systems are ignored in favor of expressive solutions related to territorial spirits" (Freston, 2001: 315).

Institutional Religious Authority in the Public Sphere

The emergence of diverse forms of Evangelical public representation constitutes, on the one hand, a new re-configuration of institutional representation. For many years, Peruvian Evangelical leaders understood the historical National Evangelical Council of Peru (CONEP) to be the unique and official voice of the Peruvian Evangelical community. Today, even though Evangelical leaders agree that CONEP played an historical leadership role, they hold that the Evangelical sector now is more plural and diverse. They attribute a certain level of authority or legitimacy to traditional organizations. But, at the same time, they are building other ways of representation that are connected to more fluid interaction with diverse agents in the public sphere.

One can observe, here, a process marked by intense competition to gain power in the public sphere. In this context, shifting loyalties and commitments is part of intense processes of negotiation among Evangelical actors who are trying to obtain public legitimacy.

In this context, even though historical Evangelical organizations might not agree with the motivations of the new Evangelical movements, they are setting up alliances with them because they recognize their connections with political mediators, such as, politicians, governmental organizations and political parties, and with public *legitimators*, such as, the media, journalists, and opinion leaders. On the other side, the new movements avoid breaking their ties with historical organizations because they have recognized that historical institutions, such as CONEP still play the roles both of legitimator within the Evangelical community and interlocutor with many state institutions.

Hence, the current landscape of Evangelical public representation reveals that Evangelical institutional authority is not concentrated in one institution alone, as occurred traditionally. What is important to observe is that these multiple Evangelical public voices are legitimated not only as a function of their interaction with traditional interdenominational *ministries*, or support of an influential institution, or network within the larger Evangelical community, but also through their outward interactions within state, media networks, and civil society.

This case shows, as Freston (2001: 293) observes, that they can be empowered in the public sphere "without the help of doctrine or tradition, assuming public roles based on their dynamic profile as private religions of salvation. Private success underlies their public role, whether as substitutes-in-waiting for the old publicly dominant religion or, more modestly, as recipients of largesse from the state."

In this way, it is interesting to observe that while traditional denominations and organizations linked to the CONEP try to maintain an organizational dynamic based on a certain kind of vertical and formal authority, the Charismatic- and neo-Pentecostal-based movements are building their legitimacy based both on an organizational structure and doctrinal flexibility, as well as a more pragmatic political strategy.

These two views of ecclesiastical structure have repercussions in the relations that they build in the public sphere. Non-traditionalists more rapidly stake out a presence in the public spaces through the media, civil society networks, and secularized public events because in their understanding, it is important to seize the opportunity to have greater public presence and power.

Using this tactic they have, for instance, obtained the official support of the Peruvian government to establish the religious service called *Evangelical Te Deum*. As mentioned above, for five consecutive years, as part of Peru's Independence Day celebrations, President Alan García, the first lady, state ministers, the chief of the Military Political Command, members of the Congress, and other political leaders attend on 30 July, each year, the *Service of Thanksgiving for Peru*. This liturgical event has been organized by the *Thanksgiving Ministry*, promoted by leaders of diverse Evangelical denominations, and mostly linked to Charismatic and neo-Pentecostal mega churches and ministries.

This liturgical event demonstrates how an emerging sector of Evangelical leaders has been able to surpass the authority of traditional leaders, since they are acquiring power in the public sphere and building more fluid relationships with public figures that have been legitimated by the media and entities that have political power. It also plays an important mediating role restoring "the dominance of symbol ...and sentiment, all wrapped in ... authority and transcendence" (Smith, 2001: 8).

Here, it is important to recognize the emergence of a new organization beyond the large interdenominational institutions. Miguel Bardales, coordinator of the *Thanksgiving Ministry*, asserts that they act as individuals, rather than as representatives of their respective denominations or of the large Peruvian Evangelical movement:

> My responsibility is to teach, to sow principles. I do not represent any evangelical institutions. My approach to the public sphere is not to fight for the interests of the evangelical church .... Ten years ago, never in my life would I have dared to express an opinion without the support of an organization. (2009)

Even though the institutional legitimacy of the non-traditional Evangelical Movement still lies in the authority of a Charismatic leader, they have configured what Berger (1967) calls *plausibility structures* which contribute to the continuity of religious socialization and the maintenance of their world view in the new space and time, beyond the domestic sphere (Cornwall, 1987).

In this case, it is important to notice how public interaction and engagement produces intense processes of negotiation and transactions within the large Evangelical community in order to keep or strengthen their public authority. Even though the diverse evangelical sectors tend to construct an image of unity and cohesion, their public discourse and practice reflect diverse *representations of legitimacy* through "new forms of social organizations, new leaders, [as well as] new ways to express their hopes..." (Stoll, 1990: 331).

At the political level, we can observe that "the traditional negotiating capacity of Protestant leaders and their skill at transforming their religious clientele into a political clientele" (Bastian, 1993: 51) propel them to create new interactions and negotiations into the corridors of power. At social and cultural levels, they construct a leadership model based on less rigid religious discourse, opening a relationship culture, a dialogue of goodwill, and debate on public secularized issues.

However, this landscape does not necessarily reveal a process of de-institutionalization of the religious field, but instead a kind of re-institutionalization, since the emergent Evangelical groups and networks are building new institutional structures that contrast with the hierarchical model of traditional institutions:

> In the Peruvian case, this new movement has a more Episcopal style, more charismatized. They express Evangelical re-institutionalization, the change in Evangelical institutionalization, because even though they do not claim the name of *evangélico*, but of Christian communities, they are building a new project in contrast the ecclesiastical old model. They want to be different than the traditional Evangelical. Their model is characterized by non-rigid moral norms (Bernardo Campos, personal interview, May 2, 2009).

Social and Cultural Interactions in the Secular Public Sphere

Strategically, one may notice that many of the groups linked to the Charismatic and neo-Pentecostal sectors have developed diverse tactics and strategies to set up close relationships and sustainable interactions with influential social and political agents. These strategies are based on the idea that interaction with *public legitimators* is the best way to be recognized in the public sphere, and to have a legitimated and influential presence in the public sphere and the political arena. Many of these organizations actively participate as members or interlocutors within *secular* organizations and movements. Even though many of the principles of these civil society-based organizations contrast with the moral assumptions of Evangelical groups, the Evangelicals do not consider this as a problem because their strategic aim is to gain public and political power, to be recognized, and to play a visible role as legitimate claim-makers on social problems.

However, their discourse and practice demonstrate that these contemporary Evangelical leaders are not necessarily interested in building a movement for civic engagement; rather they are working to establish a recognizable political voice and power in the wider public sphere to influence public policy from their conservative *religious agenda*.

This is particularly relevant because many groups that in the past focused their political engagement on institutional politics, are now moving toward other civil society-based spaces in the public sphere. This reallocation is producing new scenarios where Evangelical leaders begin to see themselves as citizens and as social actors with their own voice,[10] and to set up strategic relationships with nonbelievers. Even though many conservative Evangelical groups, especially neo-Pentecostals and Charismatics, continue to adhere to messianic and millenarian doctrine, it is important to notice that many conservative Evangelical groups are moving from their relatively isolationist traditions into the frontier of public and diverse political engagement.

This new scenario allows us to observe, for instance, that "the concern of Protestant morality is shifting from pietistic preoccupation with private morality .... to public morality" (Tusalem, 2009: 884).

However, it is important to note that many conservative groups are constructing their public engagement from the perspective of *redemptive discourse* which means, on the one hand, that the main way to change society is based on the individual conversion as a point of departure. On the other hand, the presence of born again Christians is one of the sine qua non conditions for producing changes in the nation.

This contrasts with groups that employ a transformative approach which includes not only institutional empowerment in the public arena but also civic engagement practices, and proclaims the need for changing social structures.

It is important to observe in this case that although the emergence of religious publics implies that "religion takes part in the ongoing process of contestation, discursive legitimation, and redrawing of the boundaries" (Casanova, 1994: 66), it does not necessarily imply that religion has abandoned its place in the private sphere. Rather, I have observed a dialectical process of interaction between the two. Many moral issues that Evangelical groups place in the public sphere are raised from collective discussion in the private and domestic religious spheres. In this way, the private religious field is one of the key mediating spaces that influence many political decisions and public actions in which Evangelicals collectively participate.

New Forms of Evangelical Mediatization[11]

The history of Latin American Protestantism has been marked by the use of local media to convey the Evangelical message. Usually, local churches and interdenominational ministries used the media—such as radio, magazines, and bulletins—to reinforce the spiritual life of their members. Nevertheless, in the 1980s, the televangelism phenomenon produced a noticeable change with regard to the Evangelical media strategy.

In this process, especially notable has been the influence of the US electronic church[12] movement offering serious competition to local churches in Latin America. Smith (2001) coordinated a study of the impact of US religious broadcasting on Central America's active Christians. He and his colleges found that 70 percent of the sample found the teachings of televangelist Jimmy Swaggart to be more useful in their daily lives than those received in their local parish. They characterized the benefits of such programs as "spiritual blessing," "consolation," "healing," and "blessing for family life" (Smith, 2001: 7).

Along with televangelists Jimmy Swaggart and Pat Robertson, Spanish language preachers Luis Palau[13] and Hermano Pablo[14] created a media evangelization style characterized by a message designed for *converting the unbelievers* and for reinforcing the identity of the Evangelical Movement. These programs also represented both the conservative and messianic view of Evangelicalism. Such televangelists—Hoover argues—feel that they are recovering authentic religious faith and community (Hoover, 1988: 208).

Latin American investigators (Assman, 1987; Gogin, 1997; Pérez, 1997; Smith, 2001) agree with Stewart Hoover that these televangelistic programs provided "symbols, codes, and leaders that speak to the crisis of modernity and thereby revitalize fundamentalist values" (Hoover, 1988: 216).

However, as Smith observes, the dominance of the US media evangelists was short-lived.

A combination of the personal and legal problems suffered by Jimmy Swaggart and Jim Bakker in 1987 and 1988, the collapse of the Berlin Wall in 1989, and innovations in the marketing of symbolic goods developed by the Brazilian media evangelists in the 90's led to the end of the US monopoly on electronic religion in Latin America (2001: 5).

In this context, US Evangelical media organizations helped to setup Evangelical TV and radio stations in many Latin American countries. Trinity Broadcasting Network has been a key player in these initiatives. In this sense, the 1990s saw the emergence not only of national and local Evangelical media production and media entrepreneurs, but also of Latino *media Evangelists*. Churches moved from program production or an occasional appearance in the media to the commercial appropriation of mass media which implied setting up and running their own communication enterprises, entering into direct competition with commercial media, and becoming creators of mass cultural identity (Pérez, 1997; Smith, 2001).

In many countries, Evangelical radio played an important role in strengthening the ties among Evangelical denominations. For instance, *Radio del Pacífico*, an Evangelical medium, founded in Peru, in 1963, by US missionaries, established a close cooperation with American ministries, such as Christian Broadcasting Network, Focus on the Family, *Hermano Pablo* Ministries, Campus Crusade for Christ, etc. In the last decade, *Radio del Pacífico* has become an influential institution among Peru's Evangelical denominations and interdenominational organizations.

Mostly Evangelical TV and radio in Latin America has not strayed substantially from their instrumental view of the media or from their traditional theological commitments. Thus, "[P]roducers of evangelistic messages for the electronic media came to conceive of religious conversion in reductionistic, individualistic terms as demanded by the principles of marketing" (Smith, 2001: 6).

Today, there are more than 30 radio stations that have adopted the theological and communicational perspective of *Radio del Pacífico*. Even though many Evangelical leaders assume that these media enterprises reinforce the public presence of Evangelicals, some studies (Gogin, 1997; Pérez, 1997) have showed that their real impact and influence is relegated to the Evangelical community.

In the past, Evangelical radio stations played an important legitimizing role. Pastors of churches, leaders of interdenominational organizations, and lay leaders considered these radio stations as spaces not only for evangelization, but also to strengthen Evangelical community life.

Today, we can observe that Charismatic and neo-Pentecostal media have changed their strategy in two important ways. First, contemporary media preachers are "simplifying the message, eliminating doctrine and reducing the message to a commercial transaction of symbolic goods" (Smith & Campos, 2005: 62).

Second, in many places, the *Evangelical media* still fulfills the key functions of strengthening the spiritual life of believers. Now, there is an added emphasis: They also help to create a sense of community and interdenominational cooperation.

However, the public emergence of Evangelical groups and movements is creating new forms of mediatization in which traditional *evangelical media* are being reshaped and replaced. Many Evangelical leaders consider that traditional Evangelical broadcast media are not strategic resources for acquiring a more effective presence and legitimacy in society. In the past, most of them assumed that evangelical radio, for instance, was the effective *public window* to a greater presence in society. Now, they consider that their own media are insufficient for building effective influence in the public sphere.

Media as Spaces for Reinforcing Boundaries

This new mediatization process reflects that evangelical groups are conceiving of media less in terms of an *indoctrination tool,* and more as a space from which it is possible to build socialization webs beyond the church. In this sense, the use of the media is not restricted to the production of *Evangelical programs* or diffusion of evangelistic media products. Rather, they are producing public events designed to catch the eye of the secular media, as well as cultivating social networks through the internet. Many groups maintain an active presence on social networks, such as Facebook and Twitter.

Jorge Márquez, leader of the Evangelical State Servants Network, has created a site on Facebook, and has a Yahoo-groups list called AEQUUS about news and reflections on Evangelicals and civic participation. Six thousand leaders receive news, reflections, and interviews through his mailing list which is connected to his blog and Facebook site. Márquez and his team use this media platform not only to convey their views as Evangelicals on social debates and political events, but also to legitimize the faces and voices of the Evangelical sector that they represent.

What is interesting to observe is that these organizations produce information not only related to Evangelical events, but also about diverse secular social activities. This strategy reveals that their goal is not only to get an influential presence within non-Evangelical spaces and population, but also to dialogue with the secular voices as well as help to their seekers to interpret current events from the Evangelical view.

In this case, as Horsfield (1997) observes, media acquire a central hermeneutic dimension of culture to which all other social institutions have to adapt themselves. This process constitutes a kind of re-mediatization of Evangelical religiosity that

> impels churches not only to compete—even over their 'own' symbols, functions, services and heritage—, but moreover, the media, as the central hermeneutic dimension of culture, function as a matrix for values and meaning and as a lens or framework through which we see and experience any other social collective. (De Feijter, 2006: 94)

Another aspect in this topic is related to the discursive negotiations that the interaction between religious authority and media authority produce. Evangelical groups that are interacting within secular media spaces are in permanent confrontation between their points-of-view and the nonreligious perceptions of social problems, political struggles, and moral debates. In this case, we can observe "that media not only have taken over the function of ritual and sacred symbolism, shaped by the process of mediation, but also define social and personal ethical issues, in a discourse churches cannot control" (ibid., 97). This new scenario, as De Feijter warns, compels religious groups to compete over their own *core business*, with media determining its position in the web of culture (ibid.).

Media as Sources for Legitimating Public Authority

Many of the Evangelical leaders who are actively boosting social efforts in the public realm perceive the *secular media* as fundamental sources of legitimacy. As we have mentioned, in the past, most of them assumed that their *inner* legitimacy, based on the support of their local churches or the Evangelical media, was sufficient for them to properly fulfill their role in society. Nowadays, they agree that one of the key aspects of their strategy for public empowerment is the construction of close relationships with opinion leaders legitimated by the media.

In this sense, it is important to observe, on the one hand, that Evangelical groups are more embedded in media institutions and their cultural commodities (Hoover, 1997). On the other hand, they are aware that the secular media become a privileged mediating space to construct public symbols of authority (De Feijter, 2006).

Many of the Evangelical leaders see the secular media as a direct challenge to their authority because, on the one hand, they make boundaries between a sacred culture inside the faith and a profane culture outside increasingly relevant (Hoover, 2008: 13). On the other hand, they are aware that the existence of the media in the public sphere validates authority and relevance; in contrast, "the absence of church in the public realm of the media diminishes people's perception of the relevance of faith to their everyday existence" (Horsfield, 1997: 179).

In this sense, a challenge being faced by churches is:

> to rethink the public relevance and applicability of their ideology in a situation in which almost every function that the church used to serve is now alternatively available as an often more attractive consumer commodity, in which they can no longer control how they are represented or how their symbols are used. (ibid.)

Another important aspect is that global media platforms have made it possible for many Evangelical groups to construct active relationships with similar transnational and global movements. For instance, they are participating more fluently in global advocacy campaigns fostered by international Evangelical ministries. Such experiences constitute a kind of de-territorialized religious practice. But these groups are also experiencing an intense process of re-territorialization because, at the same time, they are embedded in local and national cultural and political processes.

Mediatized globalization has created not only new media and communication strategies, but also new discourse characterized by the construction of linkages with globalized networks which are used as important capital to gain authority both among believers and secular organizations.

In this case, globalization has not constituted a threat to the identity of these groups. Instead, they have gained advantage because globalization has reinforced an important aspect of the traditional Evangelical mentality: to be part of the wider community of believers. In this way, global platforms are providing cultural resources for the construction of this imagined and decentralized religious community.

In light of the fact that Peruvian Evangelical groups are deploying efforts to leave behind material and symbolic marginality, local and transnational media play a key role by creating a new space in which religious actors can reimagine their presence and develop new interactions, as well as produce new discourse beyond the local and domestic religious spheres.

Hence, the public representation of contemporary Peruvian Evangelicals constitutes mainly a mediatized practice. In this sense, media spaces and media culture are shaping the logic, discourse, and practice of public engagement-based Evangelical movements and organizations. I have found evidence that shows that these groups are not only using media technology to gain more visibility and to communicate their religious values, but also have developed strategies to appropriate media culture to interact more fluently in the secularized public sphere.

In this sense, the Peruvian case reveals that, on the one hand, the public emergence of Latin American Evangelical groups—linked to the mega church networks—is increasingly embedded into the public sphere. In this process, media institutions and platforms are playing a significant role.

On the other hand, this mediatized public engagement is creating a less hierarchized form of religious power and authority. It also confirms that the rapid emergence of contemporary Evangelical groups is re-signifying the authority and legitimacy of traditional ecclesiastical institutions.

Finally, such mediatized public engagement confirms what several scholars in this field (Hjarvard, 2008; Hoover, 2009; Livingstone, 2009; Martin-Barbero, 1988) have long affirmed: that mediated religion is constructing not only new forms and logics of religious ritualization, but also a new form for understanding and assuming religious authority as well as a sense of institutional belonging and representation. Clearly, contemporary Charismatic and neo-Pentecostal groups are building their public strategy of evangelization, and social and political influence taking into account the logic of contemporary media culture.

In summary, contemporary Evangelical groups, especially Charismatics and neo-Pentecostals, derive their legitimacy from factors, such as their capacity to engage in mediated discourse, their relationship with and closeness to political power and opinion leaders, the construction of a secularized image, their insertion into the larger religious marketplace, and their elaboration of a moral discourse linked to the construction of political power by the articulation of public claims about social problems.

Notes

1. The analyses and reflections in this chapter are part of the findings of the study led by the author on the public participation of Evangelical groups—mainly Charismatic and neo-Pentecostals sector—in Perú. In this sense, we have observed the practices, as well as collected the perceptions of the main leaders of the following organizations: Union Nacional de Iglesias Cristianas Evangélicas del Perú (Union of Peruvian Evangelical Christian Churches), Confraternidad Peruana de Pastores Evangélicos (Peruvian Fraternity of Evangelical Pastors), Ministerio de Acción de Gracias (Thanksgiving Ministry), Red de Funcionarios y Servidores Públicos Evangélicos (Evangelical Public Workers and Servants Networks). These organizations represent the main churches and ministries linked to the mega churches platform in Perú.
2. In the Peruvian context, it is mainly Charismatic and neo-Pentecostal congregations that are adopting the key characteristics of mega churches. This is the case of congregations, such as Iglesia Camino de Vida (Path of Life Church), Centro Evangelistico Rios de Agua Viva (Evangelistic Center *Rivers of Living Water*), and Iglesia Tabernaculo de Fe (Faith Tabernacle Church). The common characteristics of these congregations are: They want to portray what they do as more vital than other traditional congregations; they are connected to the larger fraternity of global Charismatic and neo-Pentecostal organizations; their missiological practice is based on a conservative theological approach; most of them are including the *apostolic model* in their ecclesiastical structure; they are embracing modern architectural forms and a contemporary worship format; even though the main pastor is the central figure in the life of the congregation, they encourage lay leaders to be part of the pastoral team; they intentionally present themselves as non-bureaucratic, non-hierarchical, and non-traditional entity; they build a kind of congregation open to engaging social and cultural dynamics beyond the inner life of the church.
3. With regard to the Peruvian case, according to the Public Opinion Institute of Catholic University of Perú, the population of believers is 91 percent, the percentage of non-

believers is of 4.23 percent, and the percentage of indifferent is 4.72 percent. Among the believers, 79.2 percent are Catholics (less than the report of 2007 Census), 12.8 percent are Evangelicals or Pentecostals (slightly similar to the 2007 Census), 3.7 percent are Adventists, Jehovah Witness, Mormons, or Israelites of the New Universal Pact, and other 3.19 percent are people who consider themselves as believers with no religion. According to the last national census, the total population in Perú is 28,220,764 inhabitants, and according to the 2007 national census, 16,960,443 citizens profess Catholic religion, which is 81.3 percent of the population. The second important is the Evangelical religion which reached 2,606,648 people, that is, 12.5 percent of the population. The 3.3 percent (679,807 people) profess other religions and the 2.9 percent (608,770 people) do not have any religion.

4. Levine explains why contemporary Latin American religiosity reflects not only pluralism but also plurality:

> A Plurality of churches, social movements identified with religion, and voices claim the moral authority to speak in the name of religion; pluralism is increasingly evident in civil society and in lower barriers to entry into public spaces. Just as religious plurality and pluralism transform social and political life, putting more actors, voices, and options into play, so too the consolidation and expansion of democratic politics, the reduction of barriers to organization and access, and the gradual elaboration of practical rules of the game for a plural civil society have a visible impact of the daily life of religion and change the way religious institutions situate themselves in society and politics (2009: 407–408)

5. Contemporary studies reveal that Afro-Brazilian spiritist religions, New Ageism, Buddhism, and indigenous Creole faiths are also on the rise in many parts of the continent. The Incas, Mayas, Aztecas still maintain their own various ancestral folk beliefs and practices (Smith & Joshua, 1999: 1). In the same way, Martin (1990) has noted other varying religious expressions, such as South Asian immigrants who have come to Trinidad, Guyana, and Surinam, bringing forms of Islam and Hinduism with them. The same is true of Japanese immigrants settled in Perú and Brazil (ibid., p. 55). Parker (1996, 2009) analyzes the emergence of the new syncretisms, which aggregate traditional and historical forms. He observes that the new religious map is characterized by "[m]ultiple affiliations, interactions among religions, the neo-magic (hermetic and magico-ritual mysticism), all the Pentecostals (Catholic or Evangelical), ethnic shamanism and variety popular religions as well as new spiritualities" (2009: 167).

6. Reconstructionists emphasize, on the one hand, that the Biblical command to Adam to dominate the earth applies today to Christians:

> The Biblical law or covenant is that it constitutes a plan for dominion under God .... The purpose of God in requiring Adam to exercise dominion over the earth remains His continuing covenant word: man, created in God's image and commanded to subdue the earth an exercise dominion and regeneration. The law is therefore the law for Christian man and Christian society. (Pottenger, 2007:77)

7. It corresponds to the interpretation of the Bible reference at Deuteronomy 28:13: "The LORD will make you the head, not the tail. If you pay attention to the commands of the LORD your God that I give you this day and carefully follow them, you will always be at the top, never at the bottom."

8. It is important to observe that it is the same discourse that American movements, such as Moral Majority Coalition and Christian Coalition of America supported many of

their political actions. Toulouse (2006) writes: "The mission of the Christian Coalition is simple," said Pat Robertson. It is to mobilize Christians – one precinct at a time, one community at a time – until once again we are the head and not the tail, and at the top rather than the bottom of our political system" (ibid., p. 80).

9. *Evangelical Te-Deum* constitutes an Evangelical version of the traditional Catholic service as part of the Peruvian Independence Day celebration.

10. The construction of this new public face is relevant because in the past many of these Evangelical organizations and church groups were seen as easily manipulated groups in favor of political interests and supporters of the political status quo. Bastian (1993) has observed that in the past, Evangelical leaders have been able to establish themselves in certain Latin American countries "as a political clientele of the authoritarian regimes in the traditional sense of corporatist mediator" (ibid., p. 50). He mentions two remarkable cases: The 1990 election of Alberto Fujimori in Peru supported by the majority of Evangelical denominations, and Jorge Serrano, the first democratically-elected Protestant Latin American President, in Guatemala, in January 1991.

11. The theoretical approach to religious mediatization assumes both media and religion as fields of social and cultural construction (De Feijer, 2006; Hoover, 2006; White, 1997). From this view, on the one hand, media constitute a "locus where cultural identities are created, communities are configured, and social actors are constituted" (De Feijer, 2006: 88). On the other hand, the media constitute "a kind of mirror of the culture, or even a cultural forum through which important relations in the culture is aired, articulated and negotiated" (Hoover, 2006: 10).

12. In his influential 1988 book on mass media religion, *The Social Sources of Electronic Church,* Hoover examines the social impact of the American electronic church. He argues that this religious phenomenon revealed that "Evangelical and Fundamentalist organizations were among the first to see the power of broadcasting as a proselytizing tool" (p. 49).

13. Luis Palau is an Argentinean Evangelist founder of the Luis Palau Association. He is best known for his worldwide Evangelistic festivals and his radio program, Luis Palau Responde (Luis Palau answers). His festivals combine popular music, action sports, family-friendly entertainment, and his evangelistic sermon.

14. Paul Finkenbinder (Hermano Pablo) is the director of the *Hermano Pablo Ministries,* a radio and TV broadcast ministry. His well-known radio and TV program Un Mensaje a la Consciencia (A Message to the Conscience) "is seen, heard, or read throughout 30 countries over 20,000 times per week and is in over 80 periodicals. Paul Finkenbinder (Hermano Pablo) began broadcasting in 1962. Paul is the board chairman, and he travels extensively across Latin America conducting seminars, conferences, and evangelistic crusades." Retrieved from http://www.ministrywatch.com/profile/hermano-pablo-ministries.aspx on October 14, 2009.

Bibliography

Amat y León, Oscar. 2004. "Carisma y Política: Motivaciones para la Acción Política en el Perú contemporáneo." In Dorothea Ortmann (ed.), *Anuario de Ciencias de la Religión: La Religión en el Perú de Hoy.* San Marcos: Fondo Editorial de la Universidad Nacional Mayor de San Marcos.

Asen, Robert. 2000. "Seeking the 'Counter' in Counterpublics," *Communication Theory*, 10(4): 424–446.
Assman, Hugo. 1987. *La Iglesia Electrónica y su impacto América Latina*. San José, Costa Rica: Editora DEI.
Barbero, Martin. 1997. "Mass Media as a Site of Resacralization of Contemporary Cultures." In Stewart M. Hoover & Knut Lundby (eds), *Rethinking Media, Religion, and Culture*. Thousand Oaks, CA: SAGE .
Bastian, Jean Pierre. 1993. "The Metamorphosis of Latin American Protestant Groups: A Socio-historical Perspective," *Latin American Research Review*, 28(2): 33–61.
———.1998. "The New Religious Map in Latin America: Causes and Social Effects," *Cross Current*, 48(3): 330–346.
———. 2001. "A Metamorphosis of Latin American Protestant Groups: A Sociological Perspective." *Mexico, Latin American Research Review*. 28(2): 33–62.
Berger, Peter. 1967. *The Sacred Canopy: Elements of a Sociological Theory of Religion*. Garden City, NY: Doubleday.
Campos, Bernardo & Oscar Amat y León. 2007. *Poder para Reinar: Modos y Motivaciones de Participación Política en la Vida Nacional*. Lima: IPER.
Cornwall, Marie. 1987. "The Social Bases of Religion: A Study of Factors Influencing Religious Belief and Commitment," *Review of Religious Research*, 29(1), 44–56.
Casanova, Jose. 1994. *Public Religion in the Modern World*. Chicago: The University of Chicago Press.
De Feijter, Ineke. 2006. *The Art of Dialogue: Religion, Communication and Global Media Culture*. Berlin: Lit Verlag.
Freston, Paul. 2001. *Evangelicals and Politics in Asia, Africa and Latin America*. Cambridge, UK: Cambridge University Press.
———. 2007. "Latin America: The 'Other Christendom,' Pluralism and Globalization." In P. Beyer & L. Beaman (eds), *Religion, Globalization, and Culture* (pp. 577–599). Netherlands: Koninklijke Brill NV.
———. 2008. *Evangelical Christianity and Democracy in Latin America*.Oxford: Oxford University Press.
Gogin, Gina. 1997. *Presencia Religiosa de las Radios Religiosas en Lima*. Lima: Fondo Editorial de la Universidad de Lima.
Hagopian, Frances. 2009. *Religious Pluralism, Democracy, and the Catholic Church in Latin America*. Indiana: University of Notre Dame Press.
Hoover, Stewart M. 1997. "Media and the Construction of the Religious Public Sphere." In Stewart M. Hoover & Knut Lundby (eds), *Rethinking Media, Religion and Culture*. Thousand Oaks, California: SAGE Publications.
———. 1988. *Mass Media Religion: The Social Sources of the Electronic Church*. Beverley Hills, CA: SAGE.
———. 2006. *Religion in the Media Age*. London: Routledge.
———. 2008. *Media and Religion: A White Paper for the CMRC*. Boulder, Colorado: University of Colorado.
———. 2009. "Transformations: The Case of Religious Cultures." In Knut Lundby (ed), *Mediatization: Concept, Changes, and Consequences* (pp. 123–138). London: Peter Lang.
Horsfield, Peter. 1997. "Changes in Religion in Periods of Media Convergence." In S.M. Stewart M. Hoover & Knut Lundby (eds), *Rethinking Media, Religion and Culture* (pp. 167–184). Thousand Oaks, California: SAGE.
Hjarvard, Stig. 2008. "The Mediatization of Religion: A Theory of the Media as Agents of Religious Change," *Northern Lights*, 6(1): 9–26.

Jasper, James M. 1997. *The Art of Moral Protest: Culture, Biography, and Creativity in Social Movements*. Chicago: University of Chicago.
Levine, Daniel H. 2006. "Religión y Política en América Latina. La Nueva Cara Pública de la Religión." *Sociedad y Religión* (Buenos Aires), 18(26/27): 7–29.
———. 2009. "Pluralism as Challenge and Opportunity." In Frances Hagopian (ed.), *Religious Pluralism, Democracy, and the Catholic Church in Latin America* (pp. 405–428). Indiana: University of Notre Dame Press.
Levine, Daniel H. and David Stoll. 1995. "Religious Change, Empowerment, and Power: Bridging the Gap in Latin America," *Journal of Iberian Latin American Studies*, I(1, 2): 1–33.
Lindsay, D. Michael. 2007. *Faith in the Halls of Power: How Evangelicals Joined the American Elite*. New York: Oxford University Press.
Livingstone, Sonia. 2009. "On the Mediation of Everything," *Journal of Communication*, 59(1): 1–18.
Lopez, D. 2008. "Evangelicals and Politics in Fujimori's Peru." In P. Freston (ed.), *Evangelical Christianity and Democracy in Latin America*. Oxford: Oxford University Press.
Martin, David. 1990. *Tongues of Fire: The Explosion of Protestantism in Latin America*. Massachusetts: Basil Blackwell Ltd.
Martín-Barbero, J. 1988. *Procesos de comunicación y matrices de cultura: Itinerario para salir de una razón dualista*. México: Gustavo Gili.
Meyer, Birgit & Annelies Moors. 2006. *Religion, Media and the Public Sphere*. Indiana: Indiana University Press.
Miller, Daniel R. 1994. *Coming of Age: Protestantism in Contemporary Latin America*. Maryland: University Press of America.
Palti, J. 2001. "Recent Studies on the Emergence of a Public Sphere in Latin America," *Latin American Research Review*, 36(2): 255–266.
Parker, Cristián. 1996. *Popular Religion and Modernization in Latin America: A Different Logic*. New York: Orbis Books.
———. 2009. "Education and Increasing Religious Pluralism in Latin America." In Frances Hagopian (ed.), *Religious Pluralism, Democracy, and the Catholic Church in Latin America* (p. 31). Indiana: University of Notre Dame Press.
Pérez-Guadalupe & Jose Luis. 2007. "Ecumenismo, Sectas y Nuevos Movimientos Religiosos." *El Comercio*, Lima. April 23.
Pérez, Rolando. 1996. "La cultura de los medios en la ritualidad evangélica." *Signos de Vida*. Consejo Latinoamericano de Iglesias, CLAI. 2.
———. 1997. "La iglesia y su misión en la opinión pública," en *Iglesias, medios y estrategias de evangelización*. Buenos Aires: Asociación Mundial para la Comunicación Cristiana-América Latina.
Pottenger, John R. 2007. *Reaping the Whirlwind: Liberal Democracy and the Religious Axis*. Washington: Georgetown University Press.
Romero, Catalina. 2009. "Religion and Public Spaces: Catholicism and Civil Society in Peru." In Frances Hagopian (ed.), *Religious Pluralism, Democracy, and the Catholic Church in Latin America* (pp. 364–404). Indiana: University of Notre Dame Press.
Smith, C. & Joshua Prokopy. 1999. *Latin American Religion in Motion*. New York: Routledge.
Smith, Dennis A. 2001. "Religion and Electronic Media in Latin America." Paper presented at the Latin American Studies Association. Washington, D.C. September 6–8.
———. 2006. "Los teleapóstoles guatemaltecos: Apuntes históricos y propuestas para la investigación". Paper presented at the meeting of the Latin American Studies Association. San Juan, Puerto Rico.
Smith, Dennis & Leonildo Campos. 2005. "Christianity and Television in Guatemala and Brazil: The Pentecostal Experience," *Studies in World Christianity*, 11(1): 49–64.

Stoll, David. 1990. *Is Latin American Turning Protestant?: The Politics of Evangelical Growth*. Los Angeles: University of California Press.

Toulouse, Mark G. 2006. *God in Public: Four Ways American Christianity and Public Life Relate*. Louisville: Westminster John Knox Press.

Tusalem, Rollin F. 2009. "The Role of Protestantism in Democratic Consolidation among Transition States," *Comparative Political Studies*, 42(7): 882.

White, Robert. 1997. "Religion and Media in the Construction of Culture." In Stewart M. Hoover & Knut Lundby (eds), *Rethinking Media, Religion, and Culture*. Thousand Oaks, CA: SAGE.

Wynarczyk, Hilario. 2006. "Partidos Políticos Evangélicos Conservadores Bíblicos en Argentina," *Civitas-Revista de Ciencias Sociales*, 6(July–December): 2.

———. 2009. *Ciudadanos de dos mundos*. Buenos Aires: Editorial de la Universidad de San Martín.

The Southern Factor: Prospects and Challenges

Jonathan D. James

In just 100 years, Christianity has become established as a non-Western faith in the South. The preceding chapters in the book have alluded to the fact that this demographic shift, which I term the *Southern factor*, can be understood as both a product and an agent of globalization. The processes of the global world have brought the Pentecostal and Charismatic strands of Christianity, described as a faith *made to travel* (Dempster et al., 1999) to the South. In the same vein, globalization is aiding the flow of Southern Christianity to the rest of the world.

In this concluding chapter, I will give a brief summary of Southern Christianity and its mega churches, highlight a few salient features and prospects pertaining to the faith, and identify the key challenges facing Christianity in the South.

Africa is poised to become the leading Christian continent in the South, with Latin America and Asia following close behind. The Pew research findings note that Christianity has *grown enormously* in sub-Saharan Africa, as the Christian population has climbed from a mere nine percent in 1910 to a staggering 63 percent in 2010 (Guzman, 2011). The sheer sizes of churches there with large congregations, one with a seating capacity of 50,000 (see Chapters 2 and 3), point us to a new center for Christianity.

The situation in Latin America is quite unprecedented because Evangelical Christianity is gaining spiritual ground and swiftly moving into mainstream politics: More than 20 political parties have been founded by Evangelical Protestant mega church pastors, thus imitating the actions of the dominant Catholic denomination in the continent (Freston, 2001).

Asia is a vast and diverse continent and although Christianity is gaining ground, it is still lagging behind compared to the other continents in the South. Our study does not deal with China due to the lack of research personnel to do a thorough study of the Church scene there. Nevertheless, there are mega churches in China and with a population of 67 million Christians, future studies will no doubt focus on this nation (Guzman, 2011). The crucial question pertaining to China is: Which faith will fill the vacuum left by Marxism and be the majority faith? (Guinness, 2008).

The situation in the Philippines is rather different because it is home to the largest Christian population in Asia, with a ranking of the fifth largest Christian nation in the world (Guzman, 2011). South Korea hosts the world's largest church and has redefined the concept of mega churches: In that country, a mega church is one with 10,000 or more attendees, whereas 2,000 is the bench mark for the USA and the North (see Sebastian Kim's study in Chapter 4).

The growth of Christianity in India is small compared to other nations in the South. With a Christian population of 31.9 million in India (ibid.), American missiologists underplay the impact of the faith here, stating that India is the "largest non-Christian country that is at all open to the gospel" (Winter & Fraser, 1992: 198–210). I will address this phenomenon of lower growth in India, but first I need to provide background information.

The church scene in India needs to be understood in the light of some deep-seated historical and cultural issues. Early Christian missionaries in India (with the notable exception of Nobili, Ziegenbalg, and Carey)[1] ignored the ingrained aspects of caste and community, thereby promoting *extraction evangelism* (conversion, which involves extracting Hindus from their community into isolated camps of Christian churches). Therefore, to become a Christian in India virtually meant becoming an *outcaste*.

In the 1930s, the *rethinking group* of Madras proposed a new model for Christian mission in India. Chenchiah, one of the main members of this alternative group, argued that Christian conversion and church membership should not be classed together (Chenchiah, 1938). He saw conversion as a change of life, without the church insisting on the convert's identification with the *Western* church. In the 1960s, Indian theologians, such as M.M. Thomas introduced the notion of *Christ-centered secular fellowship* in contradistinction to the Western church (Thomas, 1972). It is important to understand that Thomas' call for a *secular fellowship* did not imply making the Gospel secular. *Secular* for him meant *truly religious without being communal* (ibid., 74). This call, if taken seriously, would result in the formation of a Christian community within Hindu society; Christians would no longer be treated as outcastes, and they would bridge the gap with Hindus. His call eventually led to the creation of what is known as *Christian Ashrams* or Indianized churches, such as *Christu Bhakt* (disciple of Christ) movements. However, these groups are still few in number and never emerged as a viable movement in India because indigenization was not encouraged in any real sense. It seems likely that if this method of missions had been seriously explored and initiated, the shape and form of contemporary Christianity in India would be radically different today.

Missions in India developed since the colonizers left with what I term *post-colonial churches* (James, 2010). These are basically Western denominational entities that were introduced during colonization, with all the trappings of Western structure, clergy, liturgy, etc. Denominations, such as Lutheran, Anglican, Presbyterian, and Methodist, grew when large sums of money were invested from abroad to build elaborate churches, each according to their own tradition (see Chapter 7 where Sudhakar Reddy describes mainline churches as part of the Church Union). Most Christians today are part of these *mainline* churches. It is apparent that some of these churches may have lost their reason for being because in many mainline churches, there are numerous litigation cases being heard in courts of law over the issue of property. (In Indian law, all land and property belonging to a church is deemed to belong to the Bishop of the denomination.) Today, many well-meaning Christian groups from abroad are still investing funds, personnel, and Western strategies in India without understanding the nation's real missiological and cultural issues.[2]

To sum up, there are four types of churches in India:

1. Post-colonial (mainline) churches that are organized in a Western manner in accordance with traditional and ritualistic denominational styles of worship and liturgy.
2. Indigenous groups and churches in various shapes and forms.
3. Pentecostal and Charismatic entities that are generally upbeat, using aggressive methods and American strategies of evangelism and Hillsong-style worship. These churches tend to attract people of all castes and classes. Most of the mega churches in India would fall under this category, although there are also some non-Charismatic mega churches in India, such as the Dimapur Ao Baptist Church with more than 6,000 attendees in the mother church and another 9,000 attending their 12 *satellite churches* in Dimapur, Northeast India.[3]

4. Single-ethnic group churches, such as the Syrian Mar Thoma (followers of St. Thomas) churches. This church is only attended by Malayalam-speaking people from the state of Kerala, and has branches all over India and the world where this ethnic group is found. The various ethnic community churches of the *Ao, Lotha, and Garo* tribes in Northeast India also come under this category.

Winter and Fraser (1992) believe there is potential for explosive Christian growth in India, especially if a truly indigenous Indian church is developed among the Brahmanical Hindu community: "Some estimates indicate that about 100 million Hindus would become Christians tomorrow if someone would take the necessary pains to establish a believing fellowship within their own social grouping" (1992: 198).

This is a reference to approximately 400–600 million traditional Hindu Indians who are averse to Western approaches and strategies. These Hindus will not drink the Gospel from a *Western cup*.[4] Christian scholars are in agreement that vital indigenous movements "bubble up from below... they do not come as foreign imports" (Dyrness, 2011: para 28). Judging by the increased awareness and recent calls for indigenization in India by scholars, such as Bharati (2004), there is every possibility that there will be a revival of the Brahmanical form of Christianity in the coming years.[5]

Understanding Southern Christianity

Before I consider the features of Southern Christianity, I will give an overview of what underpins contemporary Northern theology. Often the Northern Church is incapable of hearing its Southern counterpart because of the different values that stem from each other's worldview.

The Northern Church's theology is shaped in part by the high priority given to individualism and the *liberal self*, where "the individual exists prior to and apart from society so that the primary locus of religion is the individual" (Dyrness, 2011: para11). In the South, community and relationships are *pre-existent, involuntary, and constitutive* (Dyrness, 2011; Goizueta, 2008). Dickson describes this reality in the African context:

> It is commonplace that the sense of community is strong in Africa. A society is in equilibrium when its customs are maintained, its goals attained and the

spirit powers given regular and adequate recognition. Members of society are expected to live and act in such a way as to promote society's well-being; to do otherwise is to court disaster, not only for the actor but also for society as a whole. (1984: 63)

Furthermore, the post-Enlightenment lens from which the Christians in the North view the world precludes or downplays the world of spirits, demons, and the whole exercise of exorcism. However, the Southern worldview does not separate the material, physical world from the supernatural world of God, angels, and spirits. In the name of orthodoxy, many traditional mainline churches of the North tend to marginalize the non-rational aspects of religious experience: "So far from keeping the non-rational element in religion alive in the heart of religious experience, orthodox Christianity manifestly failed to recognise its value and by this failure gave to the idea of God a one-sidedly, intellectualistic and rationalistic interpretation" (Otto, 1923: 3).

Kalu (2008: 16) concurs with this view, saying that church leaders in the North are in "bondage to the tyranny of [the] modern world view and secular social science models...ignoring the miraculous and experiential dimensions [of Christianity]" and placing their faith on science, technology, and rational thought instead.

There is a materialistic and economic aspect to the North–South church discussions, as pointed out by Jesudas Athyal in Chapter 1 of this book. The growing economic disparity between the North and the South means that the North sets the standard of what is deemed successful, and often progress is measured largely in economic terms according to the standard of living of the Northern countries. These economic and material indicators have also inadvertently filtered into the thinking and practice of the Southern churches (as seen in the examples given in the preceding chapters on mega churches), and so it seems that the Southern church has fallen prey to the same economic and power pitfalls of the North.

Christianity is well and truly a multicultural world religion; it has found a home in a multiplicity of cultures, idioms, and languages. Our study of Southern Christianity is restricted to a study of representative mega churches in the South. These churches have combined the global aspects of the Charismatic and Pentecostal strands of Christianity with their own local cultural values. In the main, the chapters in the book reveal that Christians in the South, at least in the mega churches, are renegotiating their faith in the following ways.

Rereading the Text

The world portrayed in the Bible, an agricultural world, resembles many of the countries of the South which have agrarian economies. When Christians in the South read the Old Testament text, which contains narratives of prophetic pronouncements of plagues and famine, they can identify with these experiences because the South is no stranger to natural disasters, such as floods, famine, and plagues. And so the biblical text comes alive with richness and relevance unknown to believers living in the industrialized, technologically-savvy nations of the North. This rereading of the Bible with fresh eyes (without the hermeneutical principles of the Northern Church) brings with it a multiplicity of new and intriguing interpretations. For example, Lamin Sanneh cites the example of an African convert who experienced this perspective: "... We thought it [the Bible] was a thing to be spoken to, but now we know it has a tongue. It speaks and will speak to the whole world" (Sanneh, 2011: 101–102). In 1984, African preacher–prophet Mensah Otabil preached an extraordinary sermon using as his text, 1 Samuel 13: 16–22, an Old Testament passage referring to how the Israelites were under Philistine bondage and forced to use foreign blacksmiths. Otabil preached:

> ... I get amused when we talk of breaking the yoke of colonialism and still use the blacksmith called the IMF or World Bank to sharpen our tools... We see the sons and daughters of Africa roaming the streets of Europe and crying for crumbs from the master's table... In our generation let us develop blacksmiths, people who will sharpen us, set us ablaze.... right here in our land. (cited in Gifford, 1998: 88)

Recapturing Christianity's Spirituality

Belief in spirits and witchcraft are commonplace in many countries in the South (Asamoah- Gyadu, 2009). However, many of the traditional mission churches marginalized and underemphasized the supernatural. In Africa, these strong beliefs have resulted in the formulation of a theology called *witchdemonology*, which is a synthesis of both African traditional religion and Christianity. Even though, as I will point out later, that this rather simplistic understanding of how people can succeed in life is fraught with problems, it represents an opportunity for African Christians to practice Christianity within the framework of African primal religiosity. It also takes the culture of the people seriously, by dealing with Africans' beliefs and fears in their new faith through a synthesis of both old and new systems. Meyer describes this example of African Christianity: "in contrast to the mission-church, Christianity ...[it]... offers the possibility of approaching in the safe context of deliverance what people seek to leave behind but still disturbs them" (1994: 216).

The spirituality of the South is really unique and invites more scholarship. An extraordinary phenomenon known to be practiced by Christian mystics in Latin America and the Philippines is *stigmata,* an intense concentration on Jesus' passion to such a degree that these mystics (known as *Stigmatics*) receive visions and revelations. Almost always, these Stigmatics are known to break out in bleeding in various parts of the body, just as the New Testament account describes the intense suffering of Jesus Christ at the crucifixion (New World Encyclopedia, n.d.). Even though there is some skepticism about this practice of spirituality, it illustrates the depths of the mystical nature of Southern Christianity and the fact that the Christianity experienced in the South is more than just abstract creeds and dogma.

Smith (2003: 15) recalls that during the World Cup Finals in 2002, after the victory, the Brazilian team removed their national stripes to reveal *Jesus loves you* T-shirts, while the team held hands in a time of obvious Christian worship and praise. Smith interprets this act as an "aspect of the emerging world picture which is invariably overlooked by Western commentators... the significance of non-Western Christianity."

Re-Evangelizing the North and Reaching the World

A new phenomenon has occurred in Christian missions with increasing transnational linkages originating from the South to reach the diaspora cultures, as well as the citizens of the North. Missionaries from Brazil and South Korea are now in many regions of the world; in fact Brazil is the second largest missionary-sending nation in the world (the USA is the first) with 34,000 missionaries (Johnson, 2012). It is estimated that there are 21,500 South Korean missionaries in 175 countries worldwide (Mandryk, 2010).

The chapters on Africa by Asamoah-Gyadu, Walter Ihejirika, and Godwin Okon (Chapters 2 and 3), reveal the fascinating trend of Christian missions to the North from the South, which represents a new pattern of missionary outreach. This phenomenon needs to be seen from two standpoints. First, as diaspora communities from the South fuel the fire of Christian missions in the North, they perpetuate the Northern Church as a vibrant center of Christianity. Wuthnow and Offutt (2009) report that 74 percent of Americans attend churches with immigrant populations and that the immigrants make up 8 percent of the total religious workforce in the USA.

Second, new geo-political groupings are being formed in the South because Southern agencies and churches are involved in intra-Southern partnerships and linkages, which are changing the previously dominant North–South flow of missions. Goh argues for this point with reference to the Asian scene:

> Evangelical Christianity has been making significant advances in the latter part of the twentieth century.... in a number of 'hubs' such as South Korea, Singapore, Hong Kong and the Philippines. These hubs mark the rise of a highly organized, globally networked, and socially transformative vision of Asian Christian identities that, unlike the missionary movements of the nineteenth and twentieth centuries, are largely driven by Asian organizations and agencies. (2004: para 1)

Repositioning the Church in the Public Sphere

The chapters in this book reveal that there are three basic ways through which the Southern Church is repositioning itself in the public and private spheres: By using the business model for doing church, by espousing the latest in media technologies, and by entering into the political and civil spheres through political and social activism. Jeaney Yip, in Chapter 5 uses Hillsong, in Australia, as a prime example of a branded mega church that perpetuates its own products and services in the marketplace of Christianity. Walter Ihejirika and Godwin Okon in Chapter 3 describe the high visibility of Nigerian mega churches through multimodal media expressions. Freston (2001: 308), in his analysis of the church in Latin America, suggests that the attitude to the state will determine the future of Evangelical political activism in the South. His startling claim about the concept of "the church.... at the centre of society" though presently unrealistic because of the perceived disunity amongst the Evangelical community, is not beyond the realms of possibility. In Southern mega churches, some of the *prophets* have become *king makers* because many senior pastors have the power to influence votes and legislation. This is in keeping with Kim's findings that the distinctive feature of Asian Christian mission is its approach to socio-political and religious problems (Kim, n.d.). Southern Christianity is seen to be making forays into the realms of politics, economics, nation building and also, along the way, contributing to sociological and ideological changes in the region (ibid.).

Critics of the mega church worldwide bemoan the fact that the church was intended to be a fellowship, yet both institutionalism and size have come in the way of the church's true purpose (Brunner, 1952).[6] Others argue that the focus on the church size is a reflection of the American obsession with wealth and power (Olson, 2012). Contemporary Christian scholars point out that the mega church model may not be the most effective means for the practice and promotion of the faith, highlighting that the *missional* church is more effective than the *attractional* church:

> Those with a missional perspective no longer see the church service as the primary connecting point for those outside the church. While there is nothing wrong with attracting people to participate in various meetings of the church, the missional church is more concerned about sending the people in the church out among the people of the world, rather than getting the people of the world in among the people of the church. Some have described this missional-attractional distinction as a challenge to 'go and be' as opposed to 'come and see' (Wright, 2011).

In the balance, however, scholars like Elisha (2011) have concluded that mega churches are here to stay and that they are meeting real needs by offering a wide array of ministries and services ranging from spiritual growth and religious education to youth programs, volunteer opportunities, social networking, and even career development. Furthermore, by virtue of their size, mega churches have ample resources, staff, and space to provide more meaningful participation for people of all walks of life than the average-sized church. Elisha's study concludes that the mega church is part and parcel of contemporary Christianity and culture:

> The megachurches .... have a considerable influence on the religious culture of the region, not only because they are high-profile institutions that

tend to attract powerful and influential members, but also because they are often regarded as standard-bearers for new and emerging styles of Christian spirituality in their region. (2011: 222)

Even in India, where deep-rooted problems of caste and religion have been experienced over the years, Sudhakar Reddy (Chapter 7) reveals that postmodern mega churches are attempting to create a niche for both rural and urban dwellers by adopting the ethos of folk religion.

Challenges of Southern Christianity

The Southern factor—the shift of Christianity to the South—while being a novel phenomenon is not without its challenges. In this concluding section, I will outline what I consider as some of the key challenges facing Southern Christianity.

Contestation

The global spread of Christianity has increased the contestation of the faith both within Christendom and without. The Catholic denomination is facing a serious challenge because Evangelical Protestantism, especially the brand of Charismatic Christianity, is spreading rapidly in several nations of Latin America and in the Philippines, in Asia. In other countries, in the South, the proliferation and visible presence of Christianity poses a challenge to Islam and Hinduism. There is a tendency in some of the mega churches in the South to demonize all other faiths except those of the Evangelical, Charismatic, and Pentecostal persuasion. In our increasingly pluralistic world, this can often cause unnecessary tension between Christianity and other faiths. In the light of this, Guinness (2008: 128–193) cautions the worldwide church to take the approach of civility pointing out that all faiths and no faiths should be free to engage issues from their own perspective and "what is a right for one is a right for another and a responsibility for all." He argues that even though he believes that Christianity can hold its own in the marketplace of ideas, "we are taught [from the Bible] to respect and to listen and debate each other persuasively and civilly" (ibid.).

Lingering Northern *Perceptions*

Christianity may have moved southward, but the perception that the North is still the epicenter of the faith still lingers in the minds of some people both in the Northern and Southern churches. Resources, such as libraries, study centers, finances, and worldwide initiatives for conferences and gatherings are still situated in the North. One such example is the *Lausanne* Movement which is responsible for convening worldwide conferences taking its name from a worldwide gathering of Evangelical leaders convened by Rev. Billy Graham in Lausanne, Switzerland, in 1974. The 1974 gathering led to a foundational document called the Lausanne Covenant, a coordinating body known as the Lausanne Committee for World Evangelization (LCWE), and successive conferences still referred to as *Lausanne* conferences even though held in Manila, Philippines, and Cape Town, South Africa. Whilst the key leadership in the Lausanne Movement is becoming more and more reflective of the Southern demographics of Christianity, there are still residual Northern overtones in the communications and the overall organizational culture suggesting that the distribution of power is still fundamentally in the North. [7]

Southern leaders have expressed the sentiment that Christianity's growth in the South should result in the intentional development and empowerment of Southern leaders in their own contexts, so that theological and missional consultations begin to emanate from the South with distinctive Southern perspectives.[8]

Varieties of New Teachings and Christianities

As has been mentioned, the theology of *witchdemonology* in Africa helps Christians come to terms with primal beliefs that are part and parcel of their belief system; thus, we see traditional religion and Christianity coexisting as a *coherent theology* (Onyinah, n.d.). However, there is a downside. If all problems are purported by some African church leaders to stem from witchcraft and spirits, people are relieved from acknowledging and taking responsibility for their wrongdoing, conveniently shifting the blame on someone else, who often becomes the enemy of the whole community (ibid.): For example, although during my fieldwork, males who claimed that they were practicing witchcraft outnumbered females (eight against two); victims of exorcism are often women, children (especially girls), and maids (ibid.).

Furthermore, the primitive animistic belief system keeps people in a constant state of fear, thereby preventing growth and progress, and also inviting false teachers who take advantage of people's fears:

> During my fieldwork there were many instances where people had stopped building houses in their hometowns for fear of witches... The socio-economic factor in Africa causes many people to begin prayer centers just as a means of financial support. Since it does not need any training, certificate, or formal recognition from a body of Christians to begin a prayer centre, charlatans and the unemployed who have strong personalities can easily claim spiritual encounters and begin centers with a profit motive in mind. (ibid.)

Christianity has grown in South Korea, but with that there has come a plethora of sects and cults originating from the church there. One such extreme group is the World Mission Society Church of God (WMSCG)[9] with headquarters located in Sungnam City, Kyunggi Province, near Seoul. The followers of this group believe that Jesus has already come back and they are exclusive possessors of his second coming. They also use biblical texts, such as Galatians 4: 26,[10] to teach that there is a Mother God in the divine trinity, a teaching alien to historic Evangelical Christianity.[11] Founded by Ahn Sang-hong, in 1964, who once was a member of the Seventh-Day Adventist group, the WMSCG claims to have 1.7 million members and "established 2,200 local churches in 150 countries in just half a century".[12] The church further claims: "Our church is the only true church which God has established on this earth".[13]

The Christian Council of Korea, which represents Protestant Churches in the country, has declared the Church of God heretical; however, this group is located in 150 countries worldwide and has brought confusion to many leaders in several nations in the South. Most leaders in the South do not have the courage or the theological discernment to make assessments about such groups.[14] Southern leaders feel it is up to church associations in their respective countries to take a theological stand on such groups.[15]

This raises the question: Is Southern Christianity in danger of losing its coordinates? There are evidences of incomplete theologies and at times an *increased toxicity* as new *Christianities* uncritically absorb aspects of the culture of the North and introduce novel interpretations of the Bible.

Thankfully, *self-theologizing*, that is, Southern churches critically examining their theologies in accordance with the Bible, is on the increase; and this activity may bring about more tested and sustained varieties of *Christianities* in the South. And so the challenges associated with culture and Christianity continue in the Southern churches:

> Balance is advisable... Collectively, humans in social interaction do not eliminate the taint of sin. Cultures bear the marks of fallen humanity. Cultures are not amoral or neutral in the contextualization dance. People and cultures are given to flux and flow of every wind or thought. Yet it is the Bible that tethers believers during the gales of life. Contextualization or self theologizing without the Bible can be akin to taking a walk outside a space shuttle without the life preserving tether. (Eitel, 2010: para 13)

However, rather than seeing these variations in purely negative terms, I believe it is time to recall that each Christian generation grappled with its own challenges as the faith coalesced with contemporary values and took on the culture of the day. For example, the early Christian Church wrestled with purity of the faith in the midst of differing views and permutations, and, in AD 312, the Council of Nicaea was convened to resolve such theological issues. Therefore, there is the likelihood that the Southern Church will congregate to wrestle with some of the new Christianities and announce new creeds in the process. As Southern Christianity grapples with poverty, sickness, and oppression, their theologies and spiritualities will no doubt take new forms widely different from the Northern appropriations of Christianity. Furthermore, it seems likely that Southern Evangelicalism will become more introspective of its weaknesses and eventually play a leading role in *opposing market-driven globalization* and smoothening out existing ethnic differences (Freston, 2001: 315).

Conclusion

The noted historian Panikkar (1953) predicted that as Europe's supremacy fades away, so would Christianity's influence in Asia. However, this book refutes that prediction as Christianity has indeed grown in Asia and throughout the Southern Hemisphere. We are intrigued by this phenomenon—which is becoming the norm-setting faith of the future, and we welcome the opportunity to explore its new vistas of inquiry. Yet, there is a sobering side to our study. In this early foray, we have detected that Southern Christianity has perhaps been hasty in its adoption of the cultural and commercial aspects of the North and its churches there. It has unashamedly borrowed the terms and references of popular culture. It has become institutionalized and embraced the *here and now*. In doing so, arguably, it has overlooked the words of Christ: "My Kingdom is not of this world" (John 18:36). As Southern Christianity adopts the values and aspirations of the North, such as capitalism, and its economic indicators of success, and prosperity, this begs the question: Where is the fragility and the vulnerability of the faith (see the introduction) which Walls (2005) so eloquently describes as being characteristic of Christianity?

Furthermore, and in keeping with Walls' (2005) description of Christianity as iterative, with its ebb and flow over time and nations, another set of important questions emerge: Where will the new centers of Christianity be located when Southern Christianity reaches its ebb? Who then will be the new recipients of the life-giving germ of the gospel?

Hopefully, these questions will be taken up by future scholars as they research the next phase of this global, moving faith.

Notes

1. Robert de Nobili was an Italian Jesuit priest, who worked in South India from 1605 onward. Bartholomew Ziegenbalg, a German Lutheran missionary, who came to India in 1706, was responsible for the translation of the first Tamil Bible. William Carey was an English Baptist missionary who arrived in Kolkata, in 1793.
2. Harper's (2000) bold book, *In the Shadow of the Mahatma*, draws attention to how the Western church has not been sensitive to India's cultural thought patterns and norms resulting in dialectic tensions and even counter-productive ministries.
3. I visited the Dimapur Ao Baptist Church on April 20, 2013. Nagaland is a Christianized state (close to 90 percent) in Northeast India with the first missionary arriving there in 1894. The Baptists brought the Gospel to the tribal, animistic people and as a result, there are many strong and large churches (predominantly Baptist) there today.
4. This phrase is attributed to Sadhu Sundar Singh, a well-known Sikh who became an avid follower of Christ in India.
5. Indian leaders are increasing their calls for greater indigenization. Also, books, such as: *Living Water and Indian Bowl* by Bharati (2004); and *Communicating Christ among Indian Peoples* by David (2008) are influencing the thinking and practice of Indian Christianity.

6. Brunner's thesis is that the current church and the concept of *ecclesia* are not the same thing. He argues that the current church has become an institution rather than ecclesia, a *communion of persons*.
7. These comments were discussed with the author during visits with Evangelical leaders in Singapore; Kathmandu, Nepal; Hyderabad, India; and Yangon, Myanmar between the years 2011 and 2013.
8. These sentiments were discussed with the same leaders mentioned in note no. 7.
9. It must be pointed out that there are countless Korean groups which represent historic Biblical Christianity as well. I have deliberately chosen an extreme group as my example of the new *Christianities* in the South.
10. Galatians 4:26 is the text used by this group: *"But the Jerusalem that is above is free, and she is our mother."*
11. See http://zionusa.org/. Retrieved on March 30, 2013.
12. Ibid.
13. Ibid.
14. This was the consensus of five key church and Christian organizational leaders I spoke to in Nepal, India, and the Philippines in various visits from November 2012 to April 2013. See "World Mission Society Church of God." Retrieved from http://www.refworld.org/cgi-bin/texis/vtx/rwmain?docid=42df611d20 on April 22, 2013.
15. The five church leaders I spoke to when I visited Nepal, India, and the Philippines felt that the Evangelical Alliance of each nation, which is often affiliated with the World Evangelical Alliance (WEA), should be given the task of taking a theological stand on all cultic and sectarian group.

Bibliography

Asamoah-Gyadu, J.K. 2009. "The Promise is for You and Your Children: Pentecostal Spirituality, Mission and Discipleship in Africa," paper presented at West Africa Consultation of Edinburgh, Ghana, March 23–24.
Bharati, S. 2004. *Living Water and Indian Bowl*. Pasadena: William Carey Library.
Brunner, E. 1952. *The Misunderstanding of the Church*. Cambridge: The Lutterworth Press.
Chenchiah, P. 1938. "The Church and the Indian Christian." In D.M. Devasahyam and A.N. Sunarisanam (eds), *Rethinking Mission* (pp. 80–99). Madras: Hogarth Press.
David, G. 2008. *Communicating Christ among Indian Peoples*. Mumbai: GLS Publishing.
Dempster, M., B. Klaus, & P. Douglas. 1999. *The Globalization of Pentecostalism: A Religion Made to Travel*. Carlisle: Paternoster Press.
Dickson, K. 1984. *Theology in Africa*. Maryknoll, NY: Orbis Books.
Dyrness, W.A. 2011. "I'm Not Hearing You: The Struggle to Hear from a Global Church." In Fuller Seminary, *Theology, News and Notes*. Retrieved from http://cms.fuller.edu/TNN/Issues/Fall_2011/I_m_Not_Hearing_You/ on March 3, 2013.
Elisha, O. 2011. *Moral Ambition: Mobilization and Social Outreach in Evangelical Megachurches*. Berkeley: University of California Press.
Freston, P. 2001. *Evangelicals and Politics in Asia, Africa and Latin America*. Cambridge: Cambridge University Press.
Gifford, P. 1998. *African Christianity: Its Public Role*. London: C. Hurst & Co. Publishers.

Goh, R.B.H. 2004. "Asian Christian Networks: Transnational Structures and Geopolitical Mappings," *Journal of Religion and Society*, 6(2004): 1–13.
Goizueta, R. 2008. "Liberalism." In W.A. Dyrness & V. Karkkainen (eds), *Global Theology* (pp. 485-486). Downers Grove: Inter Varsity Press.
Guinness, O. 2008. *The Case for Civility and Why Our Future Depends on It*. New York: HarperCollins.
Harper, S.B. 2000. *In the Shadow of the Mahatma: Bishop V. S. Azariah and the Travails of Christianity in British India*. Grand Rapids: Eerdmans.
Guzman, Lawrence De. 2011. "Philippines Still Top country in Asia, 5th in World." Retrieved from http://globalnation.inquirer.net/21233/philippines-still-top-christian-country-in-asia-5th-in-world on March 3, 2013.
James, J.D. 2010. *McDonaldisation, Masala McGospel, Om Economics: Televangelism in Contemporary India*. New Delhi: SAGE Publications.
Johnson, T. 2012. "Brazil Becomes Second-Largest Christian Missionary Exporter in the World." Retrieved from http://global.christianpost.com/news/brazil-becomes-second-largest-christian-missionary-exporter-in-the-world-70079/ on April 22, 2013.
Kalu, O. 2008. *Clio in a Sacred Garb: Essays on Christian Presence and African Response, 1900–2000*. Trenton, NJ: Africa World Press.
Kim, S.C.H. (n.d.). "The Identity and Mission of the Church in the Asian Contexts of Communal Conflict, Poverty and Injustice". Retrieved from http://www.2010boston.org/assets/files/Mission-AsianContext.pdf on December 8, 2012.
Mandryk, J. 2010. *Operation World*. Colorado Springs: Biblica Publishing.
Meyer, B. 1994. "Beyond Syncretism: Translation and Diabolization in the Appropriation of Protestantism in Africa." In C. Stewart and S. Rosalind (eds), *Syncretism/Anti-Syncretism: The Politics of Religious Synthesis* (p. 216). London: Routledge.
New World Encyclopedia. (n.d.). "Stigmata." Retrieved from http://www.newworldencyclopedia.org/entry/stigmata on April 2, 2013.
Olson, R. 2012. "Theological Thoughts About Mega Churches." Retrieved from http://www.patheos.com/blogs/rogereolson/2012/05/theological-thoughts-about-mega-churches/ on April 2, 2013.
Onyinah, O. (n.d.). "Deliverance as a way of Confronting Witchcraft in Modern Africa: Ghana as a Case History." In *CyberJournal for Pentecostal-Charismatic Research*. Retrieved from http://www.pctii.org/cyberj/cyberj10/onyinah.html#_ftn104 on March 3, 2013.
Otto, R. 1923. *The Idea of the Holy*. Oxford: Oxford University Press.
Panikkar, K.M. 1953. *Asia and Western Dominance*. New York: Collier Books.
Sanneh, L.O. 2011. "Post-Western Wine, Post-Christian Wineskins?" In W.R. Burrows, M.R. Gornik, & J.A. McLean (eds), *Understanding World Christianity: The Vision and Work of Andrew F. Walls* (pp. 101–102). Maryknoll, NY: Orbis Books.
Smith, D.W. 2003. *Against the Stream: Christianity and Mission in an Age of Globalization*. Leicester: IVP.
Eitel, Keith. (n.d.) Retrieved from http://www.theologicalmatters.com/index.php/2012/09/18/seeing-things-inside-out-evangelicals-and-world-christian-studies/ on April 2, 2013.
Thomas, M.M. 1972. "Baptism, the Church and Koinonia: Three letters and a Comment," *Religion and Society*, 19(1): 69–90.
Walls, A.F. 2005. *The Cross-Cultural Process in Christian History*. Maryknoll, NY: Orbis Books.

Winter, R.D. & D.A. Fraser. 1992. "World Mission Survey." In R.D. Winter & S.C. Hawthorne (eds), *Perspectives on the World Christian Movement: A Reader* (pp. 329–346). Pasadena: William Carey Library.

Wright, C. 2011. "What is Missional?". Retrieved from http://missionalchurchnetwork.com/what-is-missional/ on April 22, 2013.

Wuthnow, R & S. Offutt. 2009. "Transnational Religious Connections," *Sociology of Religion*, 69(2): 209–232.

About the Editor and Contributors

Editor

Jonathan D. James is a researcher and writer on media, religion, and culture. His research interests include cultural globalization, the social effects of new media, new religious movements, indigenization, diaspora Asians in the West, and the image industry in Asia.

With an early education in Singapore, and later trained to be a television producer in the USA, Jonathan D. James is currently an adjunct lecturer at Edith Cowan University, Perth, and well known in the Asia-Pacific region as a consultant, lecturer, and guest speaker. His articles have appeared in refereed journals in Australia, the UK, and North America, including *The Journal of Religion and Popular Culture,* and *Studies in World Christianity and Continuum: Journal of Media and Culture.*

Widely traveled in Asia, North America, and the Pacific, Jonathan D. James is the author of *McDonaldisation, Masala McGospel and Om Economics: Televangelism in Contemporary India* (SAGE, 2010) and the editor of *The Internet and the Google Age* (forthcoming, 2014).

Contributors

J. Kwabena Asamoah-Gyadu is a Baeta-Grau Professor of Contemporary African Christianity and Pentecostal/Charismatic Theology, at the Trinity Theological Seminary, Accra, Ghana. His teaching areas include non-Western Christianity, theology, and media in Africa. Kwabena has served as a visiting scholar in several institutions, including the Center for the Study of World Religions and Harvard University (2004). Kwabena is the author of *African Charismatics: Current Developments within Independent Indigenous Pentecostalism in Ghana* (2005), *Christianity, Missions and Ecumenism in Ghana* (2009), and *Strange Warmth: Wesleyan Perspectives on Renewal, Ministry and*

Discipleship (2011). He has authored numerous articles and served as a co-editor, with Frieder Ludwig, of *African Christian Presence in the West: New Immigrant Congregations and Transnational Networks in North America and Europe* (2011), and *Contemporary Pentecostal Christianity: Interpretations from an African Context* (2013).

Jesudas M. Athyal is currently a visiting researcher, at the Boston University School of Theology, in Boston, USA. He served as an associate professor of Dalit Theology and Social Analysis, at Gurukul Lutheran Theological College, Chennai, India (2003–2008). He is the associate editor of *Oxford Encyclopedia of South Asian Christianity* (2011), and also the editor of *Religion in Southeast Asia: An Encyclopedia* (forthcoming, 2015).

Leonildo S. Campos is a Religious Studies Professor, the Methodist University of São Paulo, Brazil. He has degrees in philosophy, theology, and business administration. His PhD dissertation was entitled *Theatre, Temple and Market*, based on the Brazilian mega church *Igreja Universal do Reino de Deus*. He is the author of many articles on Pentecostalism in Brazil, many of which have been translated into several languages.

Virginia Garrard-Burnett is a Professor of History and Religious Studies, the University of Texas, Austin, USA. She specializes in the religious history of Latin America with a focus on Protestantism and new religious movements, including neo-Pentecostalism. She has authored two landmark books: *Protestantism in Guatemala: Living in the New Jerusalem* (1998) and *Terror in the Land of the Holy Spirit: Guatemala under General Efraín Ríos Montt, 1982–1983* (2010). Together with Paul Freston, she edited the *Cambridge History of Religion in Latin America* (2011).

Walter C. Ihejirika is a Senior Lecturer of Communication Studies, at the Federal University of Port Harcourt, Nigeria. He is one of the leading scholars in the fields of media, religion, and culture in the African continent, and has written extensively on various themes in these fields. He was the guest editor for two journals—*African Communication Research* and *Politics and Religion*—in the special issues dealing with media and religion in Africa. His other research interests are in development communication and the application of new information and communication technologies.

Sebastian C.H. Kim is a Professor of and chairs Theology and Public Life, the Faculty of Education and Theology, York St John University, UK. He is a fellow of the Royal Asiatic Society and the author of *In Search of Identity: Debates on Religious Conversion in India* (2003), *Theology in the Public Sphere* (2011), and the co-author of *Christianity as a World Religion* (2008). He is the founding and current editor of the *International Journal of Public Theology*.

Godwin B. Okon teaches Communication, at the Rivers State University of Science and Technology, Port Harcourt, Nigeria. He has a passion for methodical investigations and sound research, as evidenced in the publication of several books and journal articles in the field of contemporary media and communications. His other research interest is media advocacy. In recognition of his strides in the knowledge industry, he was granted Nigeria's distinguished Nation Builder Award, in 2008.

Rolando Pérez is a Professor of Communication, the Pontifical Catholic University, Peru. He has a Master's in Mass Communication Research with a focus on media and religion from the University of Colorado at Boulder (USA), and a B.A. degree in Social Communication from the University of Lima. He is also a member of the power, spirituality, and religion research group of the Latin American Council of Social Sciences. His current research interests lie in the interface between media, religion, and social change in Latin America. He also coordinates a collaborative project that studies the public role of religious groups in places characterized by social conflicts—especially related to environmental issues—in Peru.

Y.A. Sudhakar Reddy obtained his PhD degree from the Indian Institute of Technology, Madras, India, in 1987, for his thesis on peasant studies. Currently, he is in the University of Hyderabad as a Professor, and the head of the Centre for Folk Culture Studies and the Centre for Social Exclusion and Inclusive Policy. He has authored more than 60 articles in various local and international journals. He is the editor of *Folklore Fellows of South Indian Languages* and serves on the editorial boards of *Folklore Journal of South Indian Folklorist* and *Indian Folklore Research Journal*. He is one of the founder trustees of the National Folklore Support Centre in Chennai, India.

Dennis A. Smith has served as a Presbyterian Church, USA, lay mission worker in Latin America, since 1977, and now lives in Buenos Aires, Argentina. Trained in communication, his research focuses on media, religion, and culture. His most recent publication was a chapter included in *Global and Local Televangelism* (Thomas & Lee, 2012). Since 2008, he has served as the president of the board of directors of the World Association for Christian Communication, an organization based in Toronto, Canada.

Katharine L. Wiegele received her PhD degree from the University of Illinois, Urbana-Champaign, USA, and is the author of numerous articles and the book—*Investing in Miracles: El Shaddai and the Transformation of Popular Catholicism in the Philippines*—for which she received the prestigious National Book Award, in the Philippines. She is currently the Adjunct Assistant Professor of Anthropology, Northern Illinois University, USA.

Jeaney Yip is a Lecturer of Marketing, at the University of Sydney, Business School, Australia. Her research involves the study of discourse, identity, and practice in organizations, and examines how business discourse shapes identity and practice in *non-business* contexts. She has published in *Advances in Consumer Research* and *Social Compass*. Well known in the Asia-Pacific region, her ongoing research intersects between marketing and organization studies, which explores how identities are constructed in various contexts, including religion, consumer culture, and higher education.

Index

Abraham, K.E., 149
Abrahamic covenant story, 59
Action Chapel International (ACI), 47
Adeboye, Enoch, 44, 53, 56, 63, 68, 71
African Christianity, 221
African churches
  Holy Spirit, doctrine of, 11, 44
  rise of mega churches, 4, 8
  women empowerment, 11
African Independent Churches (AICs), 47
Afro-Brazilian religions, 174
Akindayomi, Josiah O., 56
Akingbola, Erastus, 79
Aladura (people of prayer) movement, 47
Alay Pagmamahal, 135
American Reconstructionism, 196
America's Christian culture, decline of, 33
Anglican Church, 32, 162n5
  sexual orientation within, 33
anomie, theory of, 92
Apostles, 46
Appiah, William Egyanka, 47
Ashimolowo, Matthew, 53
Assemblies of God (AoG), 173, 176, 178–180
Athyal, Jesudas, 219
The Atlas of Global Christianity, 21
Azusa Street (Los Angeles, USA) Revival movement of 1906, 46

Bakker, Jimmy, 54
Balokole (the saved ones or the chosen ones) churches of Uganda, 47

baptism, 143
  of the Holy Spirit, 177
Bardales, Miguel, 197
Barrett, David, 29
Barriger, Robert, 197
Base Ecclesial Communities, 186
Believers Loveworld Incorporated, 63
Bergoglio, Cardinal Jorge, 21
Bethany Evangelistic Church, 91
Bible Mission Church, 155
bigness syndrome, 93
Billy Graham Crusade revivalists, 90
Boatright, Raymond, 177
born-again Christians, 72
branding a church, 114–117
consumerism and material aspirations, 117–121
Brazilian evangelicals, 175
Brazilian Protestantism, 171–174
Bro Eddie Villanueva, 11
Brown, Judith, 34
Bu, Korle, 57
Buzzplant, 9

Calvary Temple, 160
Campos, Bernardo, 183, 195
Campus Crusade for Christ, 90
Canaan Land, 56
Carnatic music, 146, 162n8
Catholic Adoration Ministries, 63
Catholic Bishops Conference of the Philippines (CBCP), 138–139
Catholic Charismatic El Shaddai group, 5
Catholic Charismatic Renewal Movement, 184–185
Catholicism, 170

Index   237

Catholic lay movement, 128
Cauracuri, David, 195–196
Chakko, Sarah, 32
Chandran, J. Russell, 37
Chao, Timothy S. K., 89–90
Charismatic Christianity, 4, 44
Charismatic movement, 149, 163n13, 176
Chelladurai, Rev Sam, 9
Chinese Christians, 36
Cho, David Yonggi, 57
Choudhury, Purushottam, 146
Christ Chosen Generation Revival Ministry, 80
Christian converts in Nigeria, 26
Christian Disneyland, 71
Christian Ethics Movement of Korea, 100
Christianity
  acceptance of homosexuality, 32
  Asian-African-Latin American forms of, 35
  contestation with other world religions, 3
  decline, 34
  expansion of, 2
  gender and sexuality, 31–33
  Jenkins' perception, 3–4
  patriarchal social structures, 31–32
  rebranding, 4
  recession of, 1–3
  Walls' perception, 1–3
Christianity in Nigeria
  appropriation and use of modern media technologies, 72–78
  controversies, 78–80
  grandeur of physical structures erected, 67–72
  mega church buildings, 67–72
  missionary vision, 68–70
  size of followership and reach of ministry, 66–67
  theological themes, 64–66
Christian *jatras* and harvest festivals, 147

Christians, 1
Christ's incarnation, 2
Chung-hee, General Park, 87
church communitarianism, 88
Church Growth International, 57
Church History Association of India (CHAI), 26
Church of God in India, 149
Church of God Mission International, 55
Church of Pentecost (CoP), Ghana, 49
Church of South India's (CSI's), 145
Church of the Army of the Cross of Christ, 47
Church Union Movement, 145
Collins, Pastor Cleiton, 179
comity, 145
Comte, Auguste, 170
Comunidade Canção Nova, 185–186
Congregação Cristã no Brasil (CCB), 176
conservative evangelical Christianity, USA, 49–51
conservative utopia, 187
Convenção Geral das Assembléias de Deus no Brasil (CGADB), 178
Cook, Robert F., 149
Covenant University, 71
Crusade, Billy Graham, 90
Cruzada Nacional de Evangelização, 177

365-day revival movement, 94
Deeper Life Bible Church, 63
de-Europeanization of American Christianity, 34
dehumanization of the workforce, 151
Duncan-Williams, Pastor, 9, 55
  TV program by, 9

Ecumenical Association of Third World Theologians (EATWOT), 37
EDSA People Power Revolution, 129

El Shaddai, 127
  Catholic affiliation, 129, 134–135, 137
  class-based cultural models, 129
  congregation, 128
  in-house publications, 135
  Mega Worship Center, 138–139
  radio and TV program, 130–134
  rallies and prayer meetings, 128–129
  religiosity, 128, 137
  ritual innovations and experiential elements, 129
  ritual space and Holy Spirit, 134–138
El Shaddai The Almighty God, 135
EMI Christian Music Group (CMG), 112
Episcopal Church, 32, 145
Estevam, 182
evangecalism
  conservative religious concerns, 196
Evangelical Churches, 191–193
evangelical churches
  conservative, USA, 49–51
  evangelical mission churches in Brazil, 171
  Gossner Evangelical Lutheran Church, 147
evangelicalism, 88–89
  evangelization campaigns in South Korea, 89–90
  evangelization strategies, 193–194
  forms of evangelical public representation, 198–201
  idea of the restoration of society, 195
  in Latin America, 191–194
  mediatization, forms of, 203–209
  North American, 59–60
  in Peru, 194–198
  public involvement, 194–195
  social and cultural interactions, 201–203

evangelical media, 205
  as sources for legitimating public authority, 207–209
  as spaces for reinforcing boundaries, 205–206
evangelical music, 174

Faith Academy Secondary School, 71
faith brands, 8, 106
Faith Tabernacle, 56, 71, 79
flexible accumulation, 151
100-fold return, 128
folk Catholicism, 174, 184
Fordism, 151
Francescon, Luis, 176

García, Alan, 200
Gifford, Paul, 44–45, 48
Global Christian Forum, 21
global Christian music industry, 111
globalization of Western culture, 28–29
The Global Project, 112
Gooty Mission, 155
Gossner Evangelical Lutheran Church, 147
Grace Bible Church, 56
Guadalupe, José Luis Pérez, 193
Guk-do, Kim, 96
Guti, Bishop Ezekiel, 48

Hackett, Rosalind, 74
Han, Kyung-chik, 89, 100
Han-heum, Ok, 96
Hee, Pastor Kong, 7, 10
Hernandes, Sonia, 182
Heward-Mills, Bishop Dag, 48, 56–58
Hills Christian Life Centre, 108
Hillsong, case study of
  appealing to consumers, 117–121
  artifacts, 109
  branding and market expansion strategies, 110
  as a brand name, 108–111
  form of self-expression, 114

form of worship, 113
issues of transparency and
   accountability, 109
marketing practices and discourses,
   107–108
mega identity, 110
music business, 111–114
presence of God, notion of, 113
storytelling, idea of, 116
use of leitourgic songs, 112–114
Hillsong Music Australia, 111
History of Christianity in India, 26
Holy Communion services, 48
Hoover, Stewart, 204
Household of Love Church, 11–12
Houston, Bobbie, 108, 110
Houston, Brian, 108
Hwal-ran, Kim, 96
Hyun-seol, Hong, 89

Ibiyeomie, David, 63, 68, 72
Ibru, Cecilia, 79
Idahosa, Archbishop Benson, 55
Iglesia Ni Christo, 5
Igreja Internacional da Graça de Deus
   (IIGD), 182
Igreja Mundial do Poder de Deus
   (IMPD), 181
Igreja Pentecostal Deus é Amor, 178
imagined communities, 153, 159
imagined community, 136
Incheon Full Gospel Church, 95
Indian Christianity, 143
   indigenization of Indian Christian
      worship, 146
Indian Pentecostal Church of God
   (IPC), 149
Instituto Brasileiro de Geografia e
   Estadística (IBGE), 172
International Central Gospel Church,
   48
International Gospel Center, 72
International Missionary Conference
   (IMC), 24

*Is Latin American turning Protestant?: The
   Politics of Evangelical Growth,* 193

Jabez story, 59
Jaebeols, 93
Jagannadham, Pulipaka, 146
Jeongdong Church, 87, 97
Jeong-hyeon, Oh, 96
Jerusalem Council, 2
Jesus is Alive ministries, 12
Jesus loves you T-shirts, 221
Jesus Miracle Crusade, 5
Jesus-witnessing movement, 94
Joshua, T. B., 63, 72, 78

Khong, Pastor Lawrence, 9
kibock sinang, 89, 94
Kim, Billy, 90
Kim, Helen, 89
Kim-ku, 87
Kingdom Heritage Nursery/Primary
   School, 71
Kingsway International Christian
   Center (KICC), 53
Korean War (1950-1953), 87
Kraemer, Hendrick, 24
Kumar, Pastor Adbhuta, 158, 160
Kumar, Satish, 158–160
Kumiyi, F., 63
Kumiyi, Williams, 68
Kwang-soon, Lee, 97
Kyung-chik, Han, 91
Kyu-sik, Kim, 87

Lagdameo, Joro Archbishop Angel,
   139
Lambeth Quadrilateral, 145
Latin American religious context,
   169–171
leitourgia songs, 112–114
Lenshina, Alice, 32
Leon, Oscar Amat y, 195
Lighthouse Chapel International
   (LCI), 48, 56–57

Living Faith Church, 63
Living Faith Church Worldwide, 71
Lord Chosen Charismatic Renewal Ministry, 63

Macapagal-Arroyo, Gloria, 139
Macedo, Edir, 180–181
Madigas, 150
Malafaia, Silas, 181–182
Márquez, 198
Márquez, Jorge, 206
Matthias Media, 111
Mbaka, Ejike, 63, 68, 71
McPherson, Aimee Semple, 177
The Mega Church: How to Make Your Church Grow, 57
mega churches, rise of, 4–5
  ability to connect with today's generation, 9–10
  in Africa, 4, 8
  Baptist-cum-Charismatic, 10
  as business houses, 8
  Charismatic, 4
  Confucianistic principles of male domination, 11
  Deeper Life Ministry, 4
  faith seekers, 154–158
  gender dynamics, 11
  globalization and, 150–154
  in India, 4
  Korean Lakewood church, 35
  leadership, 10–11
  mediatization of faith, 8–9
  New Life, 4
  in Nigeria, 4, 13
  in Philippines, 4
  Protestant, 4
  as a socio-political voice, 11–13
  use of social networks, 9
  worship style, 10
mega churches in Andhra Pradesh, 143
  architecture of, 158
  cafeteria mode of ministry, 161
  Christian folk narrative performance, 155–157
  church union, 144–146
  as communal shelters or imagined communities, 159
  converts in, 143–144
  features of, 158–161
  Holy Spirit anointing meetings, 160
  indigenization of faith, 146–150
  leadership in, 159
  oral narratives, 155–157
  preaching in, 159–160
  principles of de-difference, 151, 157
  sermons in, 160
mega churches in Brazil, 175–176
  neo-Pentecostals, 180–184
  Pentecostal, 176–180
  Roman Catholics and, 184–187
mega churches in Peru, 194–198
mega churches in South Korea
  characteristics, impact, and criticism of, 97–102
  in context of democracy in South Korea, 88
  contributions, 99–100
  evangelism and, 88–89
  Korean Protestant Church, 85
  middle-class mega churches, 98
  mixed-class mega churches, 98
  Nevius method, influence of, 86–91
  Protestant influence, 86–88
  religio-economic entrepreneurship of clergy, influence of, 93
  urban demographic changes and development of, 91–96
mega churches of African origin, 46–49
  African immigrant, 55
  African Pentecostal churches, 44
  appropriation and use of modern media technologies, 72–78

biblical and theological foundations, 58–60
building up, 56–58
Church of God Mission International, 55
congregation, 47
in context of new territories, 53–56
culture of postmodernity, 51–52
Ghanaian perspective, 44–45, 48–49
Living Faith Church Worldwide, 43, 48
as a matter of choice, 49
new paradigm churches, 44–45
as a part of developments within world Christianity, 52–53
prophetic prayers, 47
size of congregation, 54
Ugandan perspective, 47–48
Zimbabwe Assemblies of God Church, 48
megaphones, 63
Mega Word, 54
Mello, Manoel de, 177
Methodist churches, 98
Mill, John Stuart, 170
Miller, Donald E., 44, 49
Miracle Center, 55
Miranda, David Martins de, 178
missionary Christianity, 3
missionary churches, 24–25
Missionary Movement, 22
Mountain of Fire and Miracle Ministries, 63
Mozano, 47
Muoka, Lazarus, 63, 68, 80
Musama Disco Christo Church (MDCC), 47
música gospel, 174

Nacpil, Emerito, 24
Namdaemun Church, 97

Nathaniel, Gollapalli, 146
National Evangelical Council of Peru (CONEP), 198–199
Nevius, John L., 88
new paradigm churches, 44–45
New paradigm Pentecostalism, 44
new wave Pentecostalism, 63
Nigeria. *See also* Christianity in Nigeria
geographical distribution of religious groups, 62
major cities, 62
media skyline of 10 church leaders in, 74–77
mega church pastors, 63
new wave Pentecostal movement in, 63
religious demography of, 62
vibrancy and visibility of Christianity in, 63–64
vibrancy of Christianity in, 63
Nigerian broadcasting laws, 73
North American evangelicalism, 59–60
North American new paradigm churches, 50–51
Northern Church's theology, 218

Ofoegbu, Nnamdi, 80
Okotie, Senior Pastor Rev Chris, 10–12
Olukoya, Daniel, 63, 68, 71
Oritsejafor, Ayo, 63, 68
Otabil, Pastor Mensa, 48
Oyakhilome, Chris, 63, 79
Oyedepo, David O., 48, 56, 63, 68
Oyedepo's Winners' Chapel, 44

Pablo, Hermano, 203
Palau, Luis, 203
Paul, P.J. Stephen, 158, 161
Pentecostal Churches, 173
mega churches, 176–180

242   A Moving Faith

Pentecostal Fellowship of Nigeria, 78–79
Pentecostalism, 3, 22
   admonishment of Jesus, context of, 45–46
   in Africa, 56
   features of, 49–50
   as a global phenomenon, 30–31
   historical, 45–46
   in India, 31
   neo-Pentecostalism, 8
   new paradigm, 44
   in South, 29–31
The Pentecostal Mission (formerly Ceylon Pentecostal Mission), 149
Peruvian evangelical movement, 200–201
Peruvian Reconstructionist model, 196
Pew Forum on Religion and Public Life study, 27–28
Philippine Roman Catholic Church (PRCC), 128, 138
Pieris S.J., Aloysius, 37
pneumatic churches, 47
positive confession, 128
Positivism, 170
post-Fordism, 151
Prayer City, 71
Presbyterian Church, 96, 175–176
   of Rhodesia, 32
primitive accumulation, 151
Project Smile, 10
prosperity Gospel, 8
prosperity movement, 128
Protestant Churches in South Korea, 86–88, 92, 100–101
   evangelization campaigns, 89–90
   mystical nature of, 91
   political crisis and, 90
Protestantism, 170
Protestant mega churches, 4
Protestant missionary in Latin America, 170

Quiboloy, 5
The Quodesh, 57

Radio del Pacífico, 204
Redeemed Christian Church of God (RCCG), 44, 53, 56, 63, 79
Redemption Camp, 56
religious affiliation in Brazil, 174
research standpoints
   global-local continuum of Charismatic movement, 5–6
   political and spiritual economy of Charismatic (neo-Pentecostal) entities, 6–7
Rhee, Syngman, 87
Roberts, Matthew, 21
Robertson, Pat, 128, 203
Roman Catholicism, 169, 172–173, 183
Rossi, Marcelo, 186
rurbanization, 153

Saemunan Church, 97
Salvation Ministries, 63
Samavesham of Telugu Baptist Churches (STBC), 148
Sam-hwan, Kim, 96
Sanneh, Lamin, 25
Santiago, Valdemiro, 181
Santos, Adalto, 179
seeker sensitivity, 9
Seon-do, Kim, 96
Service of Thanksgiving for Peru, 200
sexual abuse by clergy, 33
Sharon Fellowship, 149
Simonton, Rev Ashbel Green, 171
simulated intimacy, 113
Sircar, B. C., 147
Soares, Romildo Ribeiro, 182
social Darwinism, 92
Sono, Mosa, 56
Soria, Eliazar, 195

Southern Christianity, 12, 21–23
   aim for self-reliance in, 24–25
   association between colonialism
      and, 23–25
   challenges, 224–228
   factors influencing rise of, 28
   globalization of, 33–35
   inequality between Northern and
      Southern societies, 28
   missionary churches, role of,
      24–25
   new pattern of missionary outreach,
      221–222
   repositioning of Southern Church,
      222–224
   rereading of the Bible, 220
   spirituality, 220–221
   subaltern perspective, 25–26
   understanding of, 218–224
South Korean missionaries, 221–222
Spirit-baptism, 95
spiritual territorialization, 197
stigmata, 221
Stoll, David, 193–194
Sun, Ho Yeow, 7
Sung-kyu, Choi, 95
Sun-hui, Kwak, 96
survival-of-the-fittest theology, 101
Swaggart, Jimmy, 203
Sydney Christian Life Centre, 108
Synagogue Church of All Nations, 72
Syrian Christians of Malabar, 144

televangelism, 73, 160, 203
Temple of the Glory of God, 178
three-self method of church planting,
   88

Thumma, Scott, 171
Tilak, Narayan Vaman, 146–147
total evangelization, 89
Trinity Broadcasting Network, 204

Vega, Daniel, 195
Velarde, Brother Mike, 127–128,
   133–137
Villanueva, Eduardo, 11

Wanjiru, Bishop Margaret, 12
Warri, Ajamimogha, 72
Wellington, Pastor Jose, 178
Wellman, James, 10, 13
Western missionary paradigms, 50
Williams, Canterbury Archbishop
   Rowan, 32
Williams, Duncan, 7
Williams, Harold, 177
witchdemonology, 220
Woo-seok, Suh, 98
Word of Life Bible Church, 63
World Christian Encyclopaedia, 21

Yeondong Church, 97
Yeong-hoon, Lee, 95
Yeong-muk, Cho, 95
Yip, Jeaney, 8
Yoido Full Gospel Church (YFGC),
   94–95
Yonggi, Cho, 94–95
Young Men's Christian Association
   (YMCA), 89
Youngnak Church, 91, 97–98

Zimbabwe Assemblies of God
   Church, 48

HIS